REPEAT
OFFENDER

*'Sin City's' Most Prolific Criminal
and the Cop Who Caught Him*

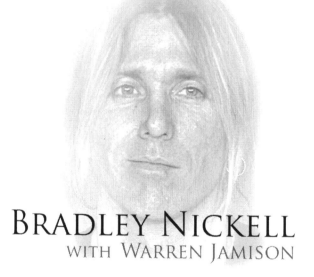

BRADLEY NICKELL
WITH WARREN JAMISON

WILDBLUE
PRESS

WildBluePress.com

REPEAT OFFENDER published by:
WILDBLUE PRESS
1153 Bergen Pkwy Ste I #114
Evergreen, Colorado 80439

WILDBLUE PRESS is registered at the U.S. Patent and Trademark Offices.

978-1-942266-09-9   Trade Paperback ISBN
978-1-942266-10-5   eBook ISBN

Interior Formatting/Book Cover Design by Elijah Toten
www.totencreative.com

Art Director Carla Torrisi Jackson

Editor Tom Panholzer
tpanholzer@yahoo.com

Some names have been changed to protect the privacy of some individuals discussed in this book.

REPEAT OFFENDER

'Sin City's' Most Prolific Criminal
and the Cop Who Caught Him

BRADLEY NICKELL

PREFACE

*E*very one of us has the capacity to do wrong. But, as a society, most of us control our baser instincts. Unfortunately, not everyone heeds this societal contract. They take what they want, when they want it. Repeatedly. They become predators.

Studies of human behavior have shown that 80 percent of the productivity in virtually every field is generated by only 20 percent of its practitioners. Whether the action is insurance policies sold, books published, or practically anything else, some ratio close to 80/20 applies.

Similar studies conducted by criminologists, major universities, and the U.S. Department of Justice show this ratio also pertains to crime; about 80 percent of all crime is committed by 20 percent of the criminals. These top-tier, repeat offenders are classified as habitual criminals.

We are their prey.

In many police departments across the United States, dealing with this special breed of criminal is the specific purpose of their Repeat Offender Programs. Detectives assigned to these teams specialize in identifying, locating, and catching habitual criminals committing new crimes. Oftentimes, covert surveillance enables this to happen while the crimes are in-progress.

I've been a detective in the Repeat Offender Program in Las Vegas for the past fifteen years. This has given me a clear understanding of how a small group of repeat criminals must be treated differently than other offenders. This is not some Orwellian ideology, or the manifestation of a cruel desire to punish offenders severely. The purpose is simple: to protect society from predators we know will strike again and again. It's something the U.S. Supreme Court has consistently recognized, most recently, in 2003, when upholding the three-strikes laws in California. The court noted: "It reflects a rational legislative judgment, entitled to deference, that offenders who have committed serious or violent felonies and who continue to commit felonies *must* be incapacitated."

There is a small amount of offensive language in *Repeat Offender*, found in quoted dialogue between characters. It's not there to be trivial; after much deliberation, I left those words in the book, so the reader could have a greater understanding of who the characters are intellectually. The dialogue in the book was crafted from transcript excerpts and conversations I actually participated in or listened to.

Repeat Offender is a true story. The names and descriptions of some of the characters have been changed to guard their identities.

1
///

IN DANGER

Just as courage is the danger of life, so is fear its safeguard.

—LEONARDO DA VINCI

*E*arly one evening, I left the Detective Bureau and soon noticed the same compact car had been in my mirror for a few blocks. A silver colored Toyota, beat-up looking with no front license plate, driven by two Hispanic-looking men. I wasn't sure if they were following me, but I didn't want to take a chance. My nerves were shot. I'd been dreading this exact thing for weeks.

A quick turn down a side street didn't lose them. Maybe if I stopped, they'd pass, but that would've made me an easy drive-by target and I was outnumbered.

I hastily formed my plan. If they continued to follow, I'd phone for patrol units to pull them over as I led them around aimlessly. A call over the police radio might tip them off, though, if they had a scanner.

I hoped a quick jaunt on the freeway might lose them, but they were still there, just a few cars behind, in the lane to my right. The rush-hour traffic slowed. Something ahead was bringing traffic to a complete stop. If these guys were assassins, this might be their best chance—pull up next to me and unload everything they have. The tactic is used south of the border more often than people in the United States know, and they're usually armed to the teeth.

I was ready. One hand on my pistol in my lap and a pump-action 12-gauge shotgun lying across the seat next to me. The car drew up on my right, and I waited for the smallest of signs. The pistol rested between my legs as I jacked a round into the shotgun's chamber. I could feel my pulse beating in my neck.

The driver rolled his window down and threw out a spent cigarette. His chiseled face, backed with dark, lifeless eyes, reminded me of a shark. I pointed the shotgun directly at him, just out of view below the door frame. Safety off. Finger on the trigger.

Each of the five rounds in the shotgun had nine, .33-caliber projectiles inside, just waiting to tear through the door panel and eliminate the threat.

He had no idea what a bad decision he was about to make. Time seemed to stand still.

Neither the driver nor the passenger had even glanced at me. Traffic started to flow again and the moment was over. I relaxed my grip on the shotgun and holstered my pistol. Before I could reflect, I was on the next freeway exit, contemplating another path home.

My heart raced. I had mixed thoughts: thankful it turned out to be nothing, and disturbed that Daimon had gotten inside my head.

Police work is rarely as you see on TV. Real investigations don't begin and end in an hour. Some take months, or years, to complete. And heart-racing, adrenaline-filled moments are sometimes scarce in the endless days of the work grind. But every now and then, maybe once in a career for some cops, a case comes along that could've been conceived by a Hollywood screenwriter.

Weeks before, Chief Deputy District Attorney Sandy DiGiacomo had called; her tone urgent. "Brad, detectives just told me someone has put a hit out on me."

My heart began to thud heavily. A contract killing is nothing to take lightly, especially for a prosecutor who has made a lot of daunting enemies.

"They asked me where my kids are, and said I might want to get them from school." Her voice shook. "And you'll never guess who the bad guy is."

"No way," I said, knowing exactly what she meant.

"Yep . . . Daimon Monroe."

Sandy and I had been working an investigation involving Daimon, a thief who had probably committed more crimes than anyone I've ever known. Clearly, things had just taken a turn for the worse.

"You do whatever they say," I said, picturing Daimon. At first blush, he seemed harmless, small in stature, dressed like a rock star from the 80s, walking with a tough swagger to counterbalance his effeminate appearance. But he was a vain and dangerously clever man with dead eyes. I had a sick feeling in my stomach. "I'll see if I can find out more and give you a call."

Chief Deputy District Attorney Sandra Allred-DiGiacomo

For More *Repeat Offender* Photos
http://wildbluepress.com/ropg

Daimon Monroe

Detective Bradley Nickell

Daimon had been in jail for months waiting to be tried on several cases, but he still had access to the phone, mail, and a network of friends on the outside. I was the lead detective in his criminal affairs. Sandy was prosecuting him as a habitual criminal, which meant if he were convicted, he potentially faced a life sentence.

As a detective in the Las Vegas Repeat Offender Program, or ROP team, I know a court case against one thief doesn't seem particularly noteworthy. Not until someone realizes the criminal is repeatedly committing crimes, do people start to see the effect one criminal has on a vast amount of innocent people. And Daimon was the most devious, calculating, prolific thief Nevada had ever seen, stealing millions of dollars of material goods, destroying livelihoods, threatening lives, and harming those who stumbled into his path.

Knowing what I did about Daimon, Sandy could be in real danger. I began checking the recorded inmate phones from Daimon's housing unit hoping to find him, or another prisoner, talking about anything that might indicate whether the threat was real or simply jailhouse talk. The inmates know the phones are recorded, and yet many still talk about their criminal activities. Most of them are smart enough to at least use coded language, but some don't bother.

Each phone call lasted around ten minutes and then the line is automatically disconnected. Depending on how many inmates are in a particular housing unit, there can be anywhere from a few dozen to a few hundred phone calls per unit, per day. Sorting through the calls to find a particular inmate's activity was like finding needles in a haystack. And listening to the calls takes time, as you have to remain alert and mentally invested in each conversation or important information can slip by unnoticed.

After hours of searching and listening, one series of phone calls caught my attention.

An inmate named Johnny had called a man named Rich. Johnny had a thick, Hispanic accent and spoke in rough street-language, but Rich sounded more formal, refined, probably educated.

"Hey, listen," Johnny said. "There's a hit out on a D.A. here, named DiGiacomo. I leaked it to some dummy, and he leaked it downstairs, thinking it was gonna get him somewhere. The guy trying to get this done is Diamond Holt or something like that."

One of Daimon's alias last names is Hoyt. Johnny must've seen some paperwork. Diamond Holt...Daimon Hoyt.

In another phone call, Johnny sounded panicked and began to whisper, so he couldn't be heard by other inmates. "Things have changed since we last spoke, man. He still wants the hit on the D.A., but now he's talking about some detective, and a Judge Leavitt, too."

Johnny sounded like he'd gotten into something he wanted no part of. He didn't want to snitch, but he couldn't sit by and let the hits go down. So he leaked it, knowing the guy would pass the tip to the cops.

Johnny said Daimon was trying to find someone to do the hits for $10,000 each. He also said Daimon might've made a connection with the Aryan Warriors prison gang, and they might've farmed it out to the Sureños gang in Southern California.

This wasn't just jailhouse talk. This was for real.

"He says his number one is this detective named Nickell."

"I'm gonna have somebody come see you," Rich said.

I stopped the tape and replayed it. *"His number one is this detective named Nickell."* Leaning back in my chair, I clasped my hands behind my head and exhaled. This was a first. As a cop, I've had people threaten me in highly charged, emotional moments, but nobody had ever hatched a real plot to kill me. I was just a cop, doing my job. Daimon was making it personal. I'd worked hard to put the Monroe investigation to rest, but things were far from over. <>

2

/////

A DAWNING
CRIMINAL

*Why would we look to the past in order to prepare
for the future? Because there is nowhere else to look.*

—JAMES BURKE

*D*aimon's adult interactions with law enforcement began
fifteen years before his case reached my desk.

In October of 1991, the owner of a high-tech sound
equipment business in Las Vegas reported a break in. Oddly,
among the items stolen was a pair of two-way radios he used
with his employees at his store. He had other shop radios
still operating on the same frequency, so when suddenly
he began hearing conversations at night between strangers,
he suspected the burglars were now using the radios while
committing other burglaries.

The Las Vegas police borrowed one of the radios to

monitor the traffic.

A couple of quiet nights passed, and then the suspicious radio traffic resumed. The first names Daimon, Bobby, and Chris were casually used over the radio. Daimon was careless enough one night to announce the license plate number for his own pickup truck. From that, the police were able to identify him and figure out where he lived.

After a couple weeks of off-and-on surveillance, officers identified Robert Holmes and Christopher Clayland as Daimon's associates. Finally, one night, the hard work panned out. Undercover officers watched Daimon and Chris break into a business.

When they were arrested, their apartments were searched and found to be loaded with stolen property from multiple commercial burglaries. The find included artwork, expensive sound equipment, video equipment, televisions, musical instruments, fish tanks, computers, and various other items. Officers also located a storage unit Daimon rented filled with expensive stolen property.

Daimon's girlfriend at the time, Regina Aurelia, as well as Robert Holmes, were also implicated in the crimes and arrested.

The next day, an officer went to the jail to speak with Daimon. He had never been in real trouble before. Daimon confessed to numerous commercial burglaries, providing planning and execution details. He described how, in one burglary, he used socks over his hands because he forgot gloves and didn't want to leave fingerprints. In another burglary, Daimon said he came in from the roof, took expensive sound equipment, and fled through the back door. In several burglaries, he used a screwdriver to jimmy the front door of the business and, once, he used bolt cutters to cut open a semi-trailer behind a K-Mart to steal bedding and boxes of toilet paper.

In the early 1990s, society was still in its infancy of the digital age. The officer didn't have a device with him to record Daimon's confession, but he planned to return the next day. Daimon claimed he would continue to cooperate.

When the officer interviewed Regina, she also said she would cooperate, in order to "get this whole thing over with so I can move on with my life." She confessed her guilt, acknowledged the stolen property in her possession, and said she was aware Daimon had been committing burglaries. The officer said he'd return the following day to record her statement as well.

When the officer returned, Daimon unexpectedly stopped cooperating. He said his attorney told him to say he made up the earlier statements because he was scared. "You won't be able to prove the charges," he said as he laughed. Daimon said he would tell the judge the officer violated his rights and beat him up to make him confess. "It's funny that I told you about all that stuff and you can't prove it because you didn't record me telling you." Daimon refused to say anything else.

The officer contacted Regina again. She'd also spoken with Daimon's attorney. She declined to cooperate further, though she did say she wouldn't recant her earlier confession.

Daimon was found guilty by a jury on eight counts of burglary and seven counts of grand larceny. He was sentenced to twelve years in prison. After the verdicts, he pled guilty to burglary and possession of stolen property in another case and was sentenced to concurrent time with the twelve-year sentence.

Regina also pled guilty to burglary and was sentenced to ten years in prison. Her sentence was suspended, and she was placed on probation for five years. Chris Clayland pled guilty to two counts of burglary and was sentenced to eight years in prison. Robert Holmes pled guilty to one count of attempted burglary. He was sentenced to two years in prison, which was suspended. He was placed on probation for four years.

Daimon served a little over three of the twelve years and was paroled to the streets in 1995. By that time, Regina had her probation transferred to California, and she was out of Daimon's life for good.

Late at night, on August 14, 1995, a citizen saw two men smash a Las Vegas recording studio window and leave—probably testing to see if the business had a burglar alarm. The men returned about thirty minutes later and were seen prying the front door open. The citizen called the police, and officers were dispatched. Arriving officers found two men walking in the parking lot. The officers ordered the men over to their car, but instead, they took off running.

One of the men was caught in the parking lot and identified as Engelbert Clifford. He went by "Engel" for short. The other man—Daimon Monroe—was caught by a K-9 unit nearby. He tried to confuse the police with a fake ID and the name Devon Matthews, but the cops didn't believe him.

Engel said he met Daimon in a bar, where he was promised easy money if he'd be a lookout. They'd come to the recording studio to break in and steal sound equipment, according to Engel.

A couple of days later, the court released Daimon from jail with an appearance date. When he didn't show up for court, a bench warrant was issued. Detectives began looking for him and, before long, found a girlfriend and an address.

June 13, 1996—surveillance began at the girlfriend's address. That very day, Daimon and a pregnant looking, blonde, teenage girl, about sixteen years old, arrived in a pick-up truck. To get a better look, a detective drove past the house. Daimon quickly backed out of the driveway and followed the detective down the street.

When other detectives tried to pull him over, Daimon rammed an undercover police car just as the detective stepped from the vehicle. The impact moved the police car several feet. Luckily, the detective was unharmed. Daimon almost ran over another detective then fled in the truck. The detectives began pursuit.

Daimon took the police on a car chase at breakneck speeds, blowing through stop signs and traffic signals for almost twenty miles on the streets of Las Vegas. He got on the freeway briefly and then tried to exit. On the exit ramp, he lost control. The truck rolled twice, spilling its contents across the road.

The police called an ambulance and when the paramedics had Daimon inside, he asked them to retrieve a black bag that had been thrown from the wreck. Inside the bag, detectives found a semi-automatic pistol. After his release from the hospital, Daimon was booked on his warrant and new charges of felony evading and felon possessing a firearm. He eventually pled guilty to evading and possession, and the burglary of the recording studio was dismissed as part of negotiations. Daimon received a twelve-year, prison sentence consecutive to the time left on his parole. He was now a nineteen-time convicted felon.

Engel had no prior felony convictions. He pled guilty to conspiracy to commit burglary and received nine months in the county jail, which was suspended. He was put on probation.

Daimon discharged from prison at the end of December, 2000. Five days later, and well past midnight, an officer spotted him acting suspiciously in a commercial area. Daimon gave the officer different names, trying to conceal his identity, but the officer figured out who he was from police records. Only then did Daimon tell the officer he'd just gotten out of prison. Daimon went to jail for providing false information and failure to register as a convicted felon, two misdemeanors that resulted in a few days in jail.

On March 17, 2003, at almost one in the morning, a citizen called the police to report two suspicious men outside a motorcycle dealership. The men were seen peering through a window and ducking behind the building. Police officers arrived and quickly found the men wearing dark clothing and gloves, briskly walking away from the building. The officers stopped the men who were found carrying flashlights in their pockets. These men were Daimon and Engel; both gave fake names.

Daimon and Engel said they were looking for cardboard boxes because Engel was planning to move. When asked how they got there, both said they rode the city bus.

One officer asked, "How are you guys going to get a bunch of boxes on the bus when you head back home?"

Daimon became belligerent and told Engel, "Don't tell them anything, don't say a thing."

The cops found Daimon's Chrysler minivan about two-hundred yards away. Inside the van were pry bars, screwdrivers, another flashlight, a Slim Jim, and an array of other tools.

Daimon was arrested for possession of burglary tools, failing to register as an ex-felon, and providing false information to the police. He was eventually sentenced to a short jail sentence and community service. Engel was arrested on outstanding bench warrants.

July 18, 2003—Daimon was stopped with a man named Bryan Fergason after midnight in an alley behind a strip mall. There had been a rash of burglaries in the area, but the officer found no cause to arrest them. He made a record of the contact and documented Bryan as an associate of Daimon's.

A mere thirteen days later, on July 31, 2003, at 1:15 a.m., Daimon and Bryan Fergason were driving around in Daimon's minivan. A citizen reported them as involved in suspicious activity, and the information was broadcast over the police radio. After spotting the minivan, an officer pulled them over. The officer believed they were casing for burglaries, as he found pry bars, two-way radios, gloves, and flashlights in the van. After a short time, the officer let them go without charges, believing he couldn't prove the tools were to be used for committing burglaries.

That was the last time Daimon would have such a simple run-in with the cops. <>

3

////

IN AND OUT

Enter, stranger, but take heed of what awaits the sin of greed, for those who take, but do not earn, must pay dearly in their turn. So if you see beneath our floors a treasure that was never yours, thief, you have been warned, beware of finding more than treasure there.

—J.K. ROWLING

September 24, 2006, at 1:14 a.m. a Las Vegas burglar alarm company received a break-in alarm from an upscale store, the Anku Crystal Palace. The store carried expensive artwork and decorations made from crystal, jade, teak, and other valuable materials. Much of the store's hand-crafted inventory was imported from Asia.

The alarm company guard arrived and found the business locked and secure. But the alarm system had recorded activation of the front door sensor and the interior infrared motion-sensors. Several minutes afterward, the rear door sensor was tripped. The guard followed procedure and contacted the shop owner, George Chen.

Mr. Chen responded to his business and, once inside, it was obvious someone had been in the store. Two large wooden sculptures were missing, each valued at several thousand dollars. Also missing were several handmade bracelets and other items of significant value. At the rear of the store, a heavy metal bar used to secure the back door from the inside had been removed and was lying on the floor.

But there was no evidence of forced entry. Mr. Chen had locked the doors when he closed the store and the doors were locked when the guard responded to the scene. No glass was broken; no holes in the roof or walls; no entry from a ventilation shaft. Did someone have a key? Mr. Chen and his wife were the only people who possessed one. Whoever did this seemed to know what they were looking for and was selective in what they took. Many valuable items were left behind.

At 2:10 a.m., the guard advised his dispatcher of the burglary and the police were notified. Patrol Officers MacDonald and Salisbury were dispatched to the call. The officers were only a few miles away and, since it was a "cold" burglary, it wasn't considered an emergency. There was no need to use their cruiser's siren.

Five minutes later, at 2:15 a.m., Kelly Akima, a bartender working only five miles from the Anku Crystal Palace called the police. One of her customers had just witnessed the dentist's office next door being burglarized. At about the same time, the same burglar alarm company received a break-in alarm from the dentist's office. The alarm reported front door activation, interior motion-sensor activation, and then rear door activation.

Officers MacDonald and Salisbury were right around the

corner from the dentist's office and were diverted to the in-progress call. They continued with their siren off, so their approach wouldn't be announced. But they drove quickly— easy to do at that time of night with no traffic on the road.

At 2:18 a.m., the officers arrived at the dentist's office and saw a white, 1997 Plymouth Grand Voyager van with dark tinted windows driving out of the parking lot. The officers stopped the van and approached with caution. The driver was Daimon Monroe and the passenger was Bryan Fergason. The nature of the contact was dangerous, so the officers had the men step out of the van where the officers could see and control the men's movements.

It didn't take long for the officers to recognize their stop was a good one. They soon learned of Daimon's and Bryan's criminal histories and that Bryan was on probation for an attempted burglary conviction.

Bryan was a bigger fella, about six-one and 220 pounds. He wore his long blond hair in a ponytail, which made him look street-tough. He came across in conversation like he was slow, but he wasn't. The officers were keenly aware of how nervous both men were and how Daimon took the lead in answering questions.

With the aid of a flashlight, Officer Salisbury was able to see into the van through the windows and through a door left open. Several items in the van fueled a hunch about his initial destination, the crystal shop burglary.

The dentist's office was checked and found locked and secure. One of the owners responded and checked inside. He found nothing missing or disturbed. The officers felt they couldn't prove anyone had been inside the dentist's office. The eyewitness who saw two men do the break in was somehow overlooked.

Another officer had been sent to the Anku Crystal Palace to handle the investigation there. Officer Salisbury called him and obtained a detailed description of the items missing from Mr. Chen's store. Clearly, the items in the van were the stolen items from the crystal store. Mr. Chen reported to where the van was stopped and recovered the stolen items.

Bryan Fergason

Daimon and Bryan were arrested for possessing stolen property and for the burglary at the crystal shop. No charges were filed for the burglary at the dentist's office.

When they were arrested, Daimon and Bryan were both wearing dark, hooded sweatshirts. Burglars often wear them to hinder being identified by witnesses or on surveillance video. Two pairs of cotton gloves were found in the van. A bunch of keys on a key ring were also found.

A bag of tools in the van were impounded as burglary tools. There were bolt cutters, pry bars, and screwdrivers. Not the sort of tools a soccer dad would keep in his van, although definitely the sort of burglary tools a nineteen-time, convicted felon and his crime partner would have in their vehicle at two in the morning, especially while leaving the scene of a reported burglary.

Daimon and Bryan were booked at the Clark County Detention Center (CCDC) in downtown Las Vegas. A probation hold was placed on Bryan, which denied him the ability to bail out until he could be brought before the judge who originally put him on probation.

Daimon's girlfriend, Tammy Tremaine was at home in bed when the phone rang.

"They pulled me over," Daimon said, "and we had that thing in the car. No big deal. Just burglary tools. They got a burg, but it ain't no big deal. No one got us in there. They didn't even charge us with that, anyway. Everything's fine. Do not stress, okay?"

"All right. Am I gonna be able to bail you out today?" Tammy said.

"Yeah, you should. Listen, I'm really sorry. I'll take a month off or whatever, okay?"

"Yeah, well."

"We was comin' back to the car and this black dude said, 'Hey, they're calling the police on you.' So we got in the car and pushed out—we didn't even do nothing there—and we got in the car and pushed out and they pulled us over. And there was like these stupid things in the car that they said were stolen and a little China guy came and got 'em and . . .

Do you understand what I'm sayin'?"

"Yeah. Right now, I'm, uh, so, what name?" Tammy said. "I think it's under either Daimon Monroe or Daimon Hoyt. I'm not givin' up Devon. I'm not doing it. You understand right? . . . I gave 'em fuckin', you know, bad information, you know what I mean?"

"Yeah."

"Okay, they're calling for me now. I have to go. I'll call you later, okay?"

"All right," Tammy said.

"I love you."

"I love you, bye."

A few hours later, the phone rang at Engelbert Clifford's house and he picked it up. A recording said, "This is a call from an inmate at the Clark County Detention Center. To accept this call, press one . . ." Engel accepted the call.

After explaining what happened, Daimon assured Engel that he wasn't worried about getting caught. "I could hear them sayin', 'We don't even know how they got in,' so, I'm not really worried about it. Well, of course I'm worried about it, but goin' to prison? No," Daimon said.

"Well, that's good news, man."

"I'll go get a good lawyer and we'll get rid of it. Hopefully, you know? And there was a lot of tools in the car, too," Daimon said.

"You had all your good shit?"

"Yep, but it's no big deal."

A couple of hours later, Tammy had Daimon bailed out of jail. They went to the tow yard and got the van out of impound. When they got home, the phone rang. Bryan was calling from the jail.

"Made it, huh?" Bryan said.

"Yeah. Look dude, look man, just remain calm.

Everything's cool. Your bills are paid. You're not gonna have a problem. You didn't do anything; I didn't do anything. It's all crazy, dude. We didn't do anything," Daimon said.

"I know. Well, fuck."

"Here's the thing: yeah, I had some sledge hammers in my car and I had some other things, like so fucking what? Those are legal. I had those bent things from when I had my fucking car keys locked out. The property in the car I found behind a garbage can, dude. I don't know if I interrupted a burg, I don't know."

"Yeah, I know. Fuck," Bryan said.

"So you have nothing to worry about. Now that's easier for me to say, 'cause I'm home now."

"Yeah, no shit."

"But other than the tools, their case is sorry, dude."

"Yeah, I know," Bryan said.

"Try to think like this: What you think about, you bring about. So think positive, you know?"

The call ran out of time and Bryan called back a little while later.

Daimon said, "Yeah, Bobby just left. I'm goin' through the same thing you are. Kinda like an emotional up and down tryin' to figure this out."

"What's going on?" Bryan said.

"Look, this is what I'm gonna say: I was out and about drivin' and I usually go get pallets. When I was goin' to the garbage can, by this back door there was, like, it was completely, everything was down. There was these two wooden things and some other stuff all scattered around, so I threw them in my car. And right after that my buddy was waitin' by the bus stop. I picked him up. We drive down the street. I gotta take a piss. I go piss and some dude calls the cops on us, and the next thing you know, they say I stole the stuff. That's it. Period."

"Yeah," Bryan said.

"But Bobby said what he thinks is gonna save us is that we didn't, there's no damage on the door. And they haven't figured out Matthew." <>

4

////

THE MATTHEW ENIGMA

It is the dim haze of mystery that adds enchantment to pursuit.

—ANTOINE DE RIVAROL

*T*wo days later, I was assigned Daimon and Bryan's case. I was in my seventh year as a detective in a covert unit called the Repeat Offender Program, or ROP. Criminals know it as "Rope," and they know when ROP is on their case, they're in a heap of trouble. I specialized in investigating career criminals.

The patrolmen didn't put together what had happened at the dentist's office. So, I knew the defense strategy would be to challenge the car stop and the search of the van to undermine the crystal shop charges. The crux of the case was that no one knew how Daimon and Bryan got into the businesses without leaving evidence of the entry.

My unit specializes in surveillance on hard-to-follow crooks, so right away, I wanted to find out where Daimon was to get eyes on him. The impound sheet for Daimon's minivan listed Tammy Tremaine as the owner and provided a home address and a phone number. With a little research, I learned Tammy was about ten years younger than Daimon, and had once worked at a child daycare facility. No criminal history. Nothing indicated if or how she knew Daimon—at the time, I thought perhaps the van was stolen from her.

I placed a call to the phone number and a young woman's voice answered.

"Is this Tammy?"

"Yes."

"This is Detective Nickell with Metro."

"Yes?"

Trying to play it safe, I said, "The other night when your van was impounded, was it stolen? Did those guys have permission to have it?"

"No, it wasn't stolen."

"I'm looking at this situation, and it seems like you're a typical soccer mom. You've never been in any kind of trouble as far as I can tell, and I can't figure out why a nineteen-time convicted felon had your van."

"Um, he has an attorney and I don't think I should be talking to you."

I gave Tammy my phone number and said if she ever wanted to talk, she could call any time. She hung up quickly, and I was suddenly worried that I'd blown it. She wasn't some innocent soccer mom in all of this. Daimon would probably be spooked by the call, but fortunately, I didn't say anything about ROP. Still, I'd probably have to let him cool off before we surveilled him.

Mad at myself for jumping too early, I turned to the

recorded jail calls. I hoped Daimon or Bryan had used the phones and said something valuable—most criminals don't think anyone will take the time to listen to the recordings. Early on in the calls, it was clear Daimon was smart, and he had a lot to hide. He often used coded language, but fortunately, he usually had to repeat things in simpler terms for Bryan to understand. When I listened to the call where Daimon made up the pallet story, I knew it would be good material to help prove his guilt. And then I heard that cryptic line, "They haven't figured out Matthew."

"Matthew?" I thought. "Who was Matthew? Did someone get away?"

I dug through page after page of old reports checking for someone named Matthew associated with Daimon or Bryan. Nothing.

But what did he mean, "figured out Matthew?" A strange way to put it.

I continued listening to the calls.

In another call, Daimon said, "Look, they didn't see us do anything. The guy that said he seen us in there, there's nothing even there. They didn't charge you for that so that's nothing. Conspiracy? Conspiracy to what? That's gone bye-bye. The burglary tools I was worried about 'cause of Matthew and stuff, but what's that used for? So that's gone bye-bye, those are work tools for a car. None of those places were pried into; they can't prove none of that. So that's gone bye-bye. The possession of stolen property, that's the biggest thing. But it can be pled down to a misdemeanor possession, I'm telling you. It's not like they caught you with Matthew running out of a building."

Suddenly, I didn't think Matthew was a person at all. Matthew was a *something*. But what?

I drove to the evidence vault, hoping something in impound would jump out at me. Once there, I cut open the sealed evidence bag and laid the tools and keys out on a table. Instantly, one tool stood out from the others. It had been at one time, a regular eighteen-inch screwdriver like you can buy from any hardware store, although someone had put great effort into transforming it. The shaft of the screwdriver was ground thin, down to only about an eighth of an inch. Halfway down, the shaft bent at a 90 degree angle. Someone had used a blow torch to heat it cherry red, so it would bend. When it cooled, it left a scorched metal look.

As I picked the tool up, I thought, "Matthew." But how did it work? What made Matthew so special to make it Daimon's favorite tool? And why call it Matthew?

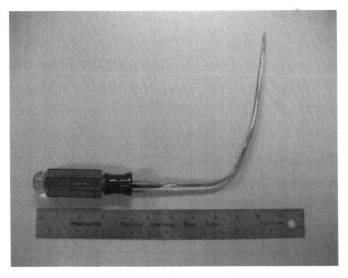

The "Matthew" Tool

I took the keys and tools to the Anku Crystal Palace and introduced myself to Mr. Chen. George Chen was in his 30s. He had been raised in China and had immigrated with his family to the United States in search of the American Dream. He was polite, articulate, and calm.

I examined the store's front doors, which were double-doors of steel framed glass construction. One of the doors locked to the door jamb with a pin; the second door was secured to the first with a dead-bolt when closed. A thumb-turn mechanism on the inside of one door locked and unlocked the door from the inside.

I saw no evidence of tampering or damage to the lock. I tried each of Daimon's keys in the lock. None of them worked.

I went to the back door and discovered it was spring-loaded and locked itself when someone exited. Nothing about the door was remarkable, but I knew it wasn't the point of entry from the alarm company logs.

I returned to the front of the business and locked the front doors. I took Matthew out of the evidence bag and stood there looking at the door. I had an idea, but it couldn't be so simple, right?

I slipped the shaft of the tool through the tiny space in between the doors. Matthew fit between the doors with such ease that I knew it was altered precisely for that purpose. I was able to make contact with the thumb-turn mechanism and started turning it. From start to finish, I was able to unlock the door in less than a minute. Someone experienced with the tool undoubtedly could unlock the door quicker than I did. Matthew didn't leave a mark on the door or the thumb-turn mechanism. I repeated the process and took step-by-step photos to document how Matthew unlocked the doors.

I thanked Mr. Chen for allowing me to interrupt his day and left for the dentist office a few miles away. I was pretty sure of what I'd find.

Walking up to the business, I could see that the doors and lock mechanisms were the same types as the ones at the crystal shop. I met with the co-owner, Sam Hopkins, and the dentist, Dr. Adams. They were normal, polite, and happy to help.

I retrieved Matthew, using it in the same way to unlock the doors. I checked the back door and sure enough, it would close and lock itself after someone exited.

It made perfect sense now. Daimon or Bryan probably operated as a lookout while the other used Matthew to unlock the door. Entering the business, they tripped the silent, door alarm. The first order was to lock the door behind them, making sure there would be no unwelcome visitors like a security guard or a cop.

They probably operated quickly, knowing the alarm company was alerted—grab what they were there to get and leave out the back door, knowing it would lock on its own. Hustle to the getaway van and on down the road. If an alarm company guard or the cops did show up, they might not realize an actual burglary occurred.

The only problem was someone saw them go into the dentist's office. They must've gotten spooked and took off out the back door before taking anything.

I thanked Mr. Hopkins and Dr. Adams for their help and headed next door to the bar. I was hoping the bartender who had called the police that night was working.

Inside the bar, I asked the bartender if Kelly Akima was there.

"You're lookin' at her," she said.

Her suspicious look from behind her flowing brown hair turned into a smile when I showed her my badge. She put down her towel and asked another bartender to cover for her.

We went outside and Ms. Akima lit a cigarette. She said one of her regulars, named "Kenneth," had come into the bar in a panic. He said some guys wearing dark colored, hooded sweatshirts had broken into the dentist's office. Ms. Akima called the police while her cook, Michael Mims, went outside.

Ms. Akima only knew Kenneth by his first name. "But he'll probably be in sometime tonight after midnight."

I gave Ms. Akima my business card and asked her to have Kenneth call. She then introduced me to her cook, Michael Mims.

Mr. Mims said he ran outside to see what was going on. "I saw two guys wearing hoodies come from behind the dentist's office in a hurry. I hollered at them that the police were coming. They jumped into a white van, drove out of the parking lot and got pulled over by the cops, right down the street over there." Mr. Mims said he couldn't see the men's faces because of the hooded sweatshirts.

Before I left the bar, I advised Ms. Akima and Mr. Mims to watch for subpoenas. They'd probably be called to court.

Kenneth Engle called the next day and said he was the customer at the bar. I thought about his last name sounding the same as the nickname for Daimon's buddy, Engel. A funny coincidence.

I met with Mr. Engle and secured his statement. The most interesting part was when he said the guys went through the door so quickly, he thought maybe they had a key. He said he didn't think he could identify them if he saw them again. "It was just too dark that night, and they had their hoodies on covering their faces."

The sequence of events was clear and the dentist office burglary, although circumstantial, could be proven. Daimon was also charged with this crime and my job was to make sure he wouldn't get off so easy this time. <>

5
/////

CRIMINAL
MINDS

*We are like chameleons, we take our hue and the
color of our moral character, from those who are
around us.*

—JOHN LOCKE

A few days passed and I returned to the room where we
monitored the jail phone calls. There was no foot traffic,
no windows, dim lighting, and nothing on the dull, gray
cinderblock walls. It became like a dungeon as I sat chained
to the computer by a headphone cable.

Bryan continued calling Daimon several times a day.
The calls quickly revealed they didn't think getting caught
was a big deal. They knew there would be some trouble from
it, probably more for Bryan since he was on probation, but
they weren't worried about going to prison. Daimon thought

the cops wouldn't be able to make the case stick.

They spoke vaguely a few times about burglaries they'd done, yet even more about burglaries they were still planning. In one call, Daimon provoked Bryan, saying, "God, I just feel so bad about when I go out and get stuff and you're not around."

"Yeah? Fuck off." Bryan said.

"I already know where I'm going when we go out next time."

"Oh, you think so, huh?" Bryan said belligerently.

"Yeah, I was finding two or three spots me and you can just run through real quick," Daimon said. "But now, I'm going to go do it."

Daimon laughed and taunted Bryan and then softened. "I want you out, too, because I can't go out and do shit. And you know, I don't think they're going to figure out Matthew."

"I don't think so."

"Yeah, those guys are just throwing it in there for evidence. Gonna bag it up in evidence and that's it. So yeah, I think we're cool on that. I'm gonna have to make a couple more of them though, but that's cool."

Daimon said he was hiring Bryan an attorney to help get him out of jail. Near the end of the call, Bryan asked how much money it would cost.

"Does it matter? Do you want to get out? I'm so pissed off. I'm losing money. I don't care, but you know what? Think about this: we found five, we found five . . ." The ten minutes on the call was up and the line disconnected.

The next day, Daimon and Bryan were talking again about getting Bryan an attorney. Daimon said, "I just think, you know, we don't ever have this problem. We might go out another five years and not have a problem and have it again, you just don't know. And if it costs us four or five thousand every five years, you know what? I can live with it."

Later in the call, Daimon said, "You know what? The more I think about it, the more I think they thought we were just little guys. They didn't think we were anything big."

Bryan agreed.

Daimon said, "I'm making a new Matthew. Down the line you don't think it will cause us a fit, right?"

"I don't think so," Bryan said.

In the next call, Daimon said, "It sucks so bad. I want you out every day. Like last night I went out. I told you, right?"

"No."

"I just wanted to get out and see if I still had the nuts to do anything, you know? I went and seen Old Sony, to see what he was doing. Aw, fucking awesome. But it's not the same without you. It's really not. Do you want me to just go lay my neck down for a minute?"

"Well, I don't know; don't go all crazy," Bryan said.

Daimon antagonized Bryan and said, "I'm going to do *everything* we planned now."

"What? Yeah, fuck off," Bryan said.

"I'm going to go pressure wash all the spots. Especially that one I told you had four you know, and had one." The call ran out of time and disconnected.

The next day, Bryan was taken to court for a probation hearing, although it ended up being continued. While there, he overheard a prosecutor mention something to the judge about his new case being handled by ROP. When that word is mentioned in court, all of the defendants pay attention.

Bryan was taken back to the jail where he quickly called Daimon. He told Daimon the prosecutor had said something about ROP.

"God, you just gave me the shivers," Daimon said. "My stomach just knotted up."

"Yeah? Who you tellin'?"

Daimon settled down and said, "This is what I'm thinking, 'kay? They've put our folders in front of ROP now, and I think we have to be careful they're not following you." He said "you," obviously referring to himself since he was the one out of jail.

"Yeah, no doubt," Bryan said.

"Listen man; I can't even go outside right now because they're watching this house."

"Are you sure?"

"No. But this is the deal, this is what I think happened because I remember when the cops pulled us over and they were talking and one said, 'Has anybody notified ROP on these guys?' I remember them saying that. And let me explain something else to you: I've read some stuff on them. As soon as you get out, they're waiting and they follow. So, you really gotta do some maneuvering 'cause I'm not even gonna take you to your Budget Suites, you know what I mean? Uh, you gotta get a game plan when you're getting released. You can't just stand outside and get picked up. What we're gonna have to do is . . ."

Bryan interrupted. "Yeah, I know, I know, I know."

Daimon tried to make it sound as though Bryan was living at Budget Suites, a heavily crime ridden, weekly motel chain. However, I'd already found the apartment where Bryan was really living.

The call ran out of time and Bryan called Daimon right back.

"Okay," Daimon said. "Here's my question: do I drive over and check your spot or not because these ROP guys could be around?"

Daimon had been taking care of Bryan's apartment while he was in jail.

"Naaa, I don't know, dude," Bryan said. "Have you noticed anybody?"

"Well, I just figured out last night. I had someone check on the name Nickell. He's the guy that called Tammy. And what it seemed like to me is he was trying to find out why she knew us, you know? It didn't make sense, and I finally found out the reason he wanted to know is 'cause he needs somewhere to follow. He doesn't know where to go. And uh, this is the only place I could think of him following. So, I just want to be quite careful."

In another call, Daimon said, "We gotta get you out. I've been taking boxes to your house so you can move too, you know."

"Have you?" Bryan said.

"Yeah, that way you can just move when you get home. But I don't like the fact that we got this heat. ROP is heat, brother. And we really gotta be careful, 'cause they're probably listening."

"Yeah, I'm sure they are."

Daimon said, "I wonder if the reason they called the ROP guys is they know they don't have much of a case on this and they know you're gonna be able to hang out for a while. And they're like, 'You know what, you gotta get some meat on this.' 'Cause the story I was reading is, they have eleven of them."

"Eleven what?"

"Eleven officers. They work on the day and the night. Five in the day, six at night. The five day guys find out where you are and target you, and the six night guys follow you around. They went through stories where they said they actually had helicopters going above the guys watching what they were doing."

"Oh, great," Bryan said as he sighed.

"So, I'm talking about, just chill, man."

"Yeah, well, fuck," Bryan said worriedly.

"We don't do nothing, anyways. I'm just saying, I mean

you can't even go digging in the trash cans no more. I mean, we're done with that."

"Yep."

"But they can only do it for so long," Daimon said.

"Yeah I know. They can only do it for I think, like, what? Six weeks, dude."

"No, not even that. Way too long. Yeah, maybe six weeks. I don't even know if that long."

"I heard it was like six weeks," Bryan said. "And if nothing happens they gotta say, forget it."

"Well, that's a lot of money to be put into you," Daimon said.

"Well, let them come and watch us do nothing, dude."

I'd never heard two criminals talk like this on the phones before. A mixture of brazenness and nonchalance, but the inflection in their voices made it clear when something was meant to be disinformation in case the cops were listening.

In the Michael Mann film *Heat,* Robert DeNiro portrayed the leader of a group of highly skilled and experienced thieves. When I listened to this conversation between Daimon and Bryan about ROP, I was hearing DeNiro's character speak.

Daimon struck me as that same breed of criminal—he knew his stuff. He spoke about our tactics, how many detectives we had in our unit, how much time we could invest in a case and on surveillance. Not everything he said was accurate, but he was in the ball park.

How did he know this stuff?

Maybe Daimon was right, maybe the police did think they were just little guys—but not anymore. I had a feeling this would be the biggest case I'd ever seen. Still, I never guessed it would bring a serious threat on my life. <>

6

/////

BOBBY

There are no secrets that time does not reveal.

—JEAN RACINE

The phone calls were piling up between Daimon and Bryan so heavily I started working between fifteen- and eighteen-hour shifts to catch up. Daimon spoke about "Bobby" so often I knew he had to be important. But all I had was a first name and a hunch. Could this Bobby be Robert Holmes from fifteen years before?

In one of the phone calls with Bryan, Daimon said Bobby had been arrested, and he saw Bobby's car in the police impound when he got Tammy's van out. This was my chance to check my hunch.

Sure enough, Robert Holmes was locked up in CCDC. Detectives in another unit had arrested him involving thefts committed at the Wynn Resort on The Strip. A VIP host at the Wynn stole about $30,000 in slot tickets from a high-roller.

The high-roller had gambled away so much he didn't even know the money was missing. The VIP host gave Bobby the tickets to cash at the casino cage.

Bobby had the cash and was long gone when the tickets were discovered missing. The tickets were tracked back to the cage where Bobby used his driver's license to cash them. Casino reps called the police. Bobby was lucky it wasn't about fifty years ago when the mob ran the casinos—the cops never would've been called, and he probably would've ended up taking a dirt nap.

The detectives on the Wynn case served a search warrant at Bobby's house. When they were inside, they noticed a lot of high-end commercial sound equipment and expensive sports memorabilia. Some of the stuff had been reported stolen and Bobby was arrested. A Corvette he owned was impounded at the same impound yard that Tammy's van had been at. Hunch confirmed.

I found a couple of phone calls in the system that Bobby made from the jail to Daimon. They spoke about Bobby's charges and Daimon tried to reassure him. Daimon said, "To prove possession, they're gonna have to prove it was someone else's shit, okay? Who in the world is going to come to court four years later, three years later even if they're saying it was theirs, dude? They're saying half that stuff was five and six years old. Do you think someone's going to take their time and still be mad after five years? You gotta be kidding me."

"Right," Bobby said. "It don't make sense, man."

The next day, Bobby made bail, and the jail called prior to his release. I and a few detectives from the ROP unit set up surveillance around the jail. We were hoping to develop a line of intel on Bobby that would come into play with Daimon. I might come across someone who could infiltrate their group and snitch. Or maybe I could catch Bobby in a petty crime and turn him against Daimon to save his own skin.

When Bobby came out of the release doors, he was by himself. Bobby's an African-American man with light eyes. He shaves his head bald, dresses a little flashy and likes to wear gold. He sported two earrings in his left ear. Bobby has a big smile and really white teeth.

Robert "Bobby" Holmes

It was already dark outside, which made it easy to stay unnoticed, even in the midst of the flash of the casino marquees. I carried an empty beer bottle to help blend in with the Vegas tourists.

Most inmates being released have arranged to be picked up unless they're homeless or riding a bus. But Bobby started walking toward the casinos a few blocks away—walking with purpose, like he knew right where he was headed. I was on foot, following from across the street.

After a few blocks, Bobby walked into the Horseshoe Casino, to a back area where only employees are allowed. I already knew he worked there as a busboy, so no big deal. We stuck around for a little while to make sure he didn't leave right away and then called it a night.

A few days later, I found a call where Bryan and Daimon were talking about Bobby. Daimon said, "Bobby's gonna come around today, and we're going to go for a drive. He's gonna go see if he wants to buy anything, and he's gonna get the car. He's gonna see if Diana knows anybody."

Daimon's tone clued me in that he was talking about something important. Go for a drive? Get what car? And who was Diana?

Bobby had several automobiles registered to him, including the Corvette, a newer Ford Excursion, and a big twenty-seven-foot cargo truck. He also owned three houses in Las Vegas, which seemed strange for a busboy. And I learned Bobby married a woman named Diana in 2001. She was working as a cocktail waitress at another Las Vegas casino.

With Bobby and Diana working in low-level positions at casinos, how were they able to afford three homes and expensive cars, including a Corvette? And what was this crew doing with a cargo truck? <>

7
///

NOT SO ORDINARY

A family is a place where principles are hammered and honed on the anvil of everyday living.
—CHARLES R. SWINDOLL

The next day, Daimon answered the phone for Bryan's call and said, "Carlos is here. Can you call back in five minutes?"

"Fuck, you might as well finish the call. I might not get the phone again."

Daimon put Bryan on hold and spoke to a man in the background. He had a distinct Hispanic accent.

Daimon said, "Do you want some chips? Get into that cupboard right there and get some chips."

"No, ees okay. I'm good," the man said.

Daimon came back on the line and spoke about an

attorney he hired for Bryan. Then he added, "I'm not taking no felony on this case. I'm getting a good attorney and I'm gonna get a misdemeanor."

Bryan said, "Yeah, me too. I can't take a felony with my probation."

"Oh and your attorney, she said don't be talking on these phones because they're recording and listening to everything," Daimon added.

"Oh, I'm sure they are."

A young boy's voice spoke up in the background. "I wanna change it, Daddy. I wanna change it."

Daimon said, "You want to change the channel?"

A young girl said, "I can change it for him, Dad."

"Okay, change it for him. He wants you to change it," Daimon said.

Another young girl spoke in the background. "Dad, I want something to eat."

"Hold on, baby," Daimon said.

Daimon continued telling Bryan about the attorney, and said he thought she was pretty good. He wanted her to get Bryan out of jail.

After a few minutes, Daimon told the kids, "Go make sure your room is clean and get your jammies on."

Daimon finished his conversation with Bryan and they hung up.

In another call, Tammy answered the phone and said, "Uh, he's not home right now. He should be home soon, but I can't stay on the line 'cause I have to get to work."

Bryan said, "What time does school start?"

"In a little while."

"Do you like it?"

"Well, I'm just a substitute teacher, but I actually have my own class right now, since the teacher is out."

"Oh, really? That's cool."

"Yeah, I might have this class for the whole year. I like working at this elementary because it's not far from the house."

"All right. Well, I'll call back in a little while when Dinkie's home."

There was much more to Daimon and Tammy than I first thought. One of the girls sounded like she was around ten or eleven and the other had to be a few years younger. The little boy sounded like he might even still be in diapers. I realized Tammy must've been the young pregnant girl that got out of Daimon's pick-up ten years earlier, when he took the police on a car chase. And now she was a schoolteacher? I also wondered why Daimon's nickname was Dinkie.

With Daimon spooked, my investigation was going to take time. To better understand the people involved, I drove by Daimon and Tammy's house in my undercover car. I wanted to get a feel for the house and the neighborhood. I also wanted to see if other vehicles were at the house; if so, I could run their plates.

The house was in an upper-middle class area, west of The Strip by a few miles. A sleepy neighborhood of single-family homes, teeming with retirees. There was a Toyota Avalon in the driveway registered to Tammy. I quickly noticed iron security bars on the front door and the windows, which made the house stand out from the others on the street. I also spotted several surveillance cameras mounted underneath the eaves of the roof.

I left the area for a moment and returned from the other direction. As I approached, I saw through the side gate a black Ford Explorer was parked in the backyard. I saw the license plate and knew it belonged to Bryan.

As I passed the house, someone came outside, into the front yard. Out of the corner of my eye, I could tell it was Daimon. When people first see him with his long, bleached-blond hair, they sometimes think he's a girl, or gay—but he's not. He was about five-six and skinny. He's vain and obsessive about his appearance to a fault. He likes the 1980s rock bands, or "hair bands" as many used to call them. I've been told he's actually quite an accomplished musician.

Daimon looked at my car for a moment as I passed by. I acted like I wasn't paying attention to him and I think it worked. I calmly drove out of the neighborhood.

A mile or so from the house, I turned into the parking lot of the elementary school where Tammy taught. The van Daimon had been arrested in was parked out front. I'd have no trouble recognizing Daimon's vehicles now. I hoped it would lead to good intel for surveillance at some point.

As I drove back to my office, I pondered the situation. Living in a somewhat affluent neighborhood with a schoolteacher and kids made Daimon appear like a normal, average guy living in the suburbs. But there was much more to him. If you lightly scratched the surface, a criminal appeared. The jail calls made that evident.

It would be no surprise if Daimon had returned to crime almost immediately after his release from prison in 2000. During those six years, he drew the attention of the police a couple of times, although not strongly enough to launch a ROP investigation. This is more easily understood when you know ROP has identified well over fourteen hundred career criminals in Las Vegas—and that's just the ones we know about in a city of a million and a half people. Still, this information shouldn't be shocking, considering this kind of bad guy is present in every decent sized community. Career criminals are in your community, too. One might even live on your street. You just don't recognize him yet. <>

8

/////

TAKE A SWIM

He who does not fear death cares not for threats.
—PIERRE CORNEILLE

The next day, it was back to the phone room.

"What are you doing?" Bryan said.

Daimon said, "Just trying to debate everything. Trying to figure out when we get back on track and stuff. Is it cool to go back to pressure washing? You know what I mean? I mean, that shouldn't cause us no fits, right?"

"No, just chill out a little bit. Fuck, I don't know."

"What about the one thing I was telling you about?"

"What?"

"Where we postponed it for three weeks."

"What about it?" Bryan said.

"That one should be okay, right?"

"Yeah."

Daimon changed the subject. "I don't think the little

China guy is going to show up."

"You don't think so?"

"No, because he got everything back. Why would he even show up for court? You haven't done anything. I'm thinking about it, 'cause if he don't show up, all the charges get dismissed. How they gonna have a case if he don't go?" Daimon said.

"He doesn't know anything anyways. He just heard somebody's got his shit in the back of a car."

Daimon said, "What's funny is I went and hung out with Bobby—fuck dude, he says, 'Ten, fucking, bye.' "

Bryan didn't understand. "What?"

"He said, 'For ten, bye.' And I said, 'Naaa, not right now, dude.' "

Bryan still didn't understand. "What?"

Daimon said impatiently, "He said for ten G's, people could, you know, go swimming for a little bit."

"Huh? . . . Oh!" Bryan said as he nervously chuckled.

"You know, I said, 'Naaa, we don't need to do that,' ya know?" Daimon said unconvincingly.

"Maybe he won't even come to court," Bryan said.

"That's what I'm hoping. I can tell you this: probably for a little less, we could definitely have what you was gonna do to GQ done, but bad, you know what I mean?"

"Yeah, I think I do, but . . ."

"Right now, let's just get you out," Daimon said. "And then postpone it forever."

I listened to the conversation several times to make sure I heard it right. Each time I reheard it, my concern grew stronger. This changed my entire perspective on Daimon and of what he might be capable.

I found another call where Daimon told Bryan that Bobby went to the crystal shop. "He went there to kind of feel him out and see what kind of guy he is," Daimon said.

He also wondered aloud if Mr. Chen might be someone that could be bought off.

Even though fear might make him an uncooperative victim, I had to speak with George Chen. I wouldn't be able to live with myself if something happened and I hadn't warned him. Plus, I needed to know if Bobby indeed did go by the shop. But I had to do this face-to-face. This wasn't something to do over the phone.

As I walked into the store, Mr. Chen and his wife greeted me from behind the counter.

"Detective, how are you doing?" Mr. Chen said.

"I'm doing great. Nice to see you again, George," I said.

"Would you like something to drink, water perhaps?" Mrs. Chen said.

"No, thank you. I'm fine. I came to speak to you about the investigation. I've been listening to phone calls made between some of the people involved in the case."

"That sounds interesting. Do you need something from me?" Mr. Chen said.

"Have you ever seen this man in your store?" I said, handing him a mug shot of Bobby.

Mr. Chen studied the picture. "I don't remember seeing him. But I have many customers. Sometimes people come into the store when I'm not here or when I'm busy with someone else. I don't get to talk to everyone," Mr. Chen said. "What's this about?"

"Well, I came because I need to tell you that I listened to the bad guys in your case talking about possibly harming you or trying to buy you off so you won't come to court."

Mr. Chen's face was calm, but he didn't know how to respond. Mrs. Chen tried to act like she didn't hear what I said and scurried off to a back room.

"So, what are you saying, detective? Are we in danger?"

"I don't know. It sounded like they were half-joking about

BRADLEY NICKELL

the idea of spending $10,000 to 'make you go swimming.' And they also talked about having someone come out here to your shop to feel you out and see if you might accept money for not coming to court. It could be real or they might be exaggerating. You know, like jailhouse talk."

"I see. That's a little scary. Is there something we should do?"

"I know some of these people are no strangers to prison and the criminal life. Would they really resort to doing something like this? I don't know. But I do think you should take some precautions."

I gave Mr. Chen some ideas about security at work and at home. I suggested he discuss these things with his wife. Mr. Chen asked to let him know if I heard anything more about the scare.

"Okay. Well, I'm going to leave you with my cell number. I want you to call me anytime, day or night, if you need something. But if there's an emergency, call 9-1-1, because they'll be able to help you quicker than I can. And remember the things I suggested about your security," I said.

As I left the store, I wondered if Mr. Chen would come to court. The first hearing where he'd be needed was coming in a few days. I'd be bothered if he didn't show up, but I wouldn't blame him, either. He was a normal, average guy trying to raise a family and operate a business. And then Daimon and Bryan crawled into his life and turned it upside down. <>

9

///////

THE SIGNS

Civilized society is perpetually menaced with disintegration through this primary hostility of men towards another.

—SIGMUND FREUD

When I walked into her office, Sandy looked up and smiled. The D.A. was in her thirties and about five-ten with long, straight hair. She's naturally a brunette, but colors her hair blush-blonde to "hide the gray better," she says. A smart dresser, Sandy's always well-turned out in stylish clothes that look great on her slender form. Her smile lights up a room, and you can hear her laugh down the hall.

Sandy and I had known each other for only a few weeks, although she'd been prosecuting criminals in Vegas for about seven years. She'd earned the prized assignment of prosecuting ROP cases because she was a zealous and hard-nosed prosecutor. Sandy's a driven person—Type A personality all the way. Daimon's case was her first as a ROP D.A.

I went over the developments in the case and how I figured out the Matthew tool. Sandy was relieved, as she expected problems in obtaining a conviction before this new information came to light. There had been too many unanswered questions for the case to go to trial. Now she was confident she could have Daimon sentenced as a habitual criminal if he was convicted.

I told Sandy about the jail recordings and the talk about having George Chen go swimming. Sandy looked up from her notepad, "Get me a copy of that recording. I'm going to need that for the next court hearing."

Before I left, I mentioned I might soon have enough information to get a search warrant for Daimon's house. "They're talking loosely about burglaries they've done and burglaries they were planning. He's got to have some stolen stuff in his house. When I think I have enough to get a warrant, I'll give you a call," I said.

"All right. Let me know what you come up with. Oh, and don't forget a copy of that take a swim jail call," Sandy said as I walked out the door.

Back at my office, like coins from a broken slot machine, the jail calls kept coming. Bryan called the house and Tammy answered the phone. Daimon was out, so she made a three-way call to his cell.

Daimon said, "At the end of this month we're moving you, bro. We just got to get Bobby so we can use his car. You know what I mean?"

"Well, I don't care, if Tammy can rent me one, too," Bryan said.

"Bro, we don't have to. I'm telling you, Bobby's got a huge one. That way it's not on a timer. You can use it all day, you know what I mean?"

"Yeah, if he'll let us use it."

"I already asked him," Daimon said.

The following day, Bryan called and Daimon said, "I went out for, I don't know, an hour last night. I had to get out and get some air to clear my head."

"Yeah, anything happening?"

"I went to Rancho, the area you love, and walked through and I'm gonna wait until you get out. But Engel's loving it, dude."

"Oh yeah, I bet he is. I bet you he's calling every day, wanting to go hang out," Bryan said.

Bryan didn't like Engel much. Engel was Daimon's partner before Bryan came along and now he was competition. They even had a fight once about it. Now Engel was in the clear to saddle up while Bryan was stuck in jail. Engel's a thick, tough looking, Hispanic man. He shaves his head, wears a thin fu-manchu and has thin chops for sideburns all the way down to his chin. An old four-inch scar on the back of his head shows he was probably no stranger to violence.

In the next call a couple days later, Daimon said, "I'm already evacuating the bottom part right now. I have to bro, 'cause I can't wait 'till the last of the month and you say to get rid of everything."

"Yeah, just put it all in a box, dude," Bryan said.

"Everything, top and bottom, right?"

"Yeah."

"Okay, I'm just going to do bottom tonight and I'll do the top later."

Bryan's apartment was an upstairs unit and he had a garage on the ground level.

Daimon said, "Let me tell you something, bro. Right now I'm making sure I'm losing them. I'm making sure I've got nobody on my tail. Engel's with me now, and he's gonna help me. And he said, not a problem on anything."

"Yeah?" Bryan said with an uneasy tone.

"Everything's okay," Daimon said.

"Well, tell him good looking out. Give him . . ."

Daimon quickly interrupted, saying in tune with Beethoven's 5th, "*La-La-La-La, shut-the-fuck-up.* Already taken care of."

"Okay. Yeah, well, tell him good looking out though," Bryan said with a defeated tone.

"He's a good guy. I already gave him a hundred bucks for doing it, all right? So don't even worry about it," Daimon said.

"Oh, okay, okay."

In another call, Tammy connected Bryan to Daimon's cell.

Daimon said, "I won't be able to get the truck into your spot because it's twenty-seven feet."

Tammy was still on the phone and said, "It's like twice the size of a UPS truck."

Daimon said, "Engel, is this the size truck you and Bryan used to drive at that spot?"

A man's voice said something.

Daimon said, "Yeah, it's the same size, he said."

After an awkward silence, Daimon said, "You suck!"

"Why?" Bryan said.

"Because you're fucking gone and I gotta go faster because of you."

"Yeah, whatever," Bryan said.

Daimon was trying to make Bryan not feel so bad about Engel hanging around.

"But, the December thing, you can't go there for a while," Daimon said.

"The what?" Bryan said.

"The December thing, that's in *December*."

"What are you talking about?"

"That thing I was asked to do in December, dude," Daimon said. "Don't go nowhere by that for a second."

"No, I know, yeah, yeah, yeah," Bryan said.

"And what we're gonna do when we hook up on the weekends is you're gonna drive somewhere. 'Cause hopefully they don't know where you are, and then you'll . . ."

Bryan interrupted. "I was thinking about meeting you at, like, a gas station or something, bro."

"No, even better than that," Daimon said. "You're gonna go to the Horseshoe and park your car. And then I'll drive up there and we'll get in my car and we'll go out. We can always come in a little early and if they're on you, you'll know it."

"Yeah, I know we're gonna have to figure something out like that. I don't know."

"It's all good, though, but we have to live our lives, dude. I mean, we're cool right now and we're getting stuff put away and we're fine," Daimon said.

A phone call from the next day was a little hard to follow. When Daimon answered the phone, Bryan said, "Hey, where the fuck you been, dude?"

Daimon said, "Well, just kinda follow me, okay? Um, remember the signs we used to hang?"

"Yeah."

"I made more of them with all theirs, identifying who they are."

"You mean what we were thinking about before?" Bryan said.

"Well, here's what I did: since they wanna play, I wanna go ahead and play back and give their names. You follow me?"

"What are you talking about now?" Bryan sounded confused.

"You know, the dude who called Tammy, tryin' to get in her pants."

"Yeah?"

"Well, my partner gave me a call. I asked him if he'd do me a favor and just find out if he had all of his friend's names too. I went ahead and did the signs. And if you walked outside right now, you'd see 'em everywhere."

"What?—No way." Bryan said.

"Yep. Little pieces of paper with him and his friends on there."

"Oh what, the guy's name?"

"Sshhh!" Daimon cut Bryan off.

Bryan didn't hush. "Name and number and all?"

"Everything. They wanna play and I just sat out there and put up about a hundred, maybe a little more or so. Yeah, they wanna play? We can play."

"But there's nobody lookin' at you, right?" Bryan said.

"Yeah," Daimon said.

"They are?"

"No."

The conversation didn't make sense. Still, I knew it was important. Daimon was too excited for it not to be important. It didn't take long to figure out what was going on. Later that day, Sandy forwarded an email from another D.A. in her office, Brian Kocher.

D.A. Kocher walked out of the courthouse and was waiting to cross the street to his office. He noticed a flashy looking, letter-sized poster stuck to a light pole at the curb. The paper read, "WARNING! FELONS: Repeat Offender Detectives are following you, waiting to set you up or catch you committing a crime. Watch your back!" A cartoon image of a person wearing handcuffs and a list of names was on the paper. My name was there. Another ROP detective's name was there. All of the other people on the list had been in ROP in the past.

D.A. Kocher looked down the street and saw several more of the signs on light poles. When he returned to his office, he sent Sandy the email, knowing she worked closely with the ROP detectives.

I drove downtown and sure enough, I found about twenty more of these signs stuck to light poles around the courthouse and the jail. I removed all I could find and headed back to my office. I saved one of the signs in my case file and gave a copy of it to another detective. He put it up on the wall by his desk. Good for laughs, but also as a reminder about what goes on in the minds of the criminals we deal with regularly.

Could Daimon think something so feeble—or even something more formidable—would intimidate the cops into letting up on him? He must've considered this might intensify our efforts in bringing his criminal behavior into the light. Still, my biggest question was where did he get the names? I'm sure he got mine from Tammy. Most of the names he had used proved his intel was stale, but he was close. Was someone in the department helping him? <>

10

////////

AN ORDINARY BIRD

Every man, in his own opinion, forms an exception to the ordinary rules of morality.

—WILLIAM HAZLITT

A few days passed, and I was busy catching up on the jail phone calls from over the weekend. The relationship between Daimon and Bryan became simple to understand. Daimon was the undersized know-it-all who always had an answer for everything. He was bossy, pesky, couldn't stand silence, and thought he was invincible. Bryan was definitely the follower in the relationship, and Daimon used it to his advantage.

In one phone call, Daimon spoke about how he thought he was being followed. He was at a store with his son and kept seeing some guy he thought was watching him. He said he made sure he wasn't being followed when he left.

"Oh, and I checked on my signs. Guess what? They're all down. Tom and John better stop playing around, dude. This mother-fucker ain't the ordinary bird," Daimon said.

"Yeah, no shit," Bryan said.

Daimon said he put up a new sign where jurors at the court take their smoke breaks. He said the message on the sign was about how the police are corrupt and shouldn't be trusted.

Daimon wasn't the ordinary bird. He seemed to enjoy antagonizing the police. Most criminals want to avoid the police and go unnoticed. Many of these multiple-time felons are heavy drug abusers. It makes them easier to catch since their perception is dulled. Daimon boasted about how he'd never used drugs or alcohol. He wanted to stay sharp. And he wanted Bryan to stop using drugs so he could stay sharp, too.

When most people drive around or walk to the store, they don't pay much attention to what's going on around them. Daimon was not like that. He had trained his mind to act as though the police were always nearby. Most people would say he was paranoid, but it's not paranoia. It's something that looks like paranoia and can probably turn into clinical paranoia, although it was the engine that had kept Daimon from getting caught for so long. I bet he could tell many stories where he almost got busted, but his criminal instincts got him out of it.

Criminals like this develop skills in counter-surveillance. The objective of surveillance, of course, is to follow the target without the target knowing you're there. When a bad guy jumps in his car and drives around, doing u-turns, changing speeds from fast to slow, and stopping in unexpected places, it's hard for surveillance officers to avoid discovery. The bad guy might jump on the freeway, take the first off ramp, and get right back on the freeway again. If a car follows him, or he sees the same car more than a couple of times, he'll surely know you're there. This is what we call "tail-checking."

A quick cure for a tail-checking bad guy is aerial surveillance by helicopter or airplane, or electronic tracking equipment. I won't describe the different types of equipment or provide technical information here. This isn't a how-to-be-a-better-bad-guy manual. But I will say using tracking equipment bears two risks: being discovered when applying the tracker to the target, and the tracker being discovered when it's already deployed. The second risk is worse than the first, as chances are high that a piece of expensive hardware will be destroyed.

One time, a bad guy discovered our tracker and moved it to a car from California. The tourist drove back home on our days off and, upon returning to work, the signal from the tracker didn't bring good news. We contacted our counterparts with the LAPD who retrieved the equipment and shipped it back to us. We found the bad guy again a few days later and arrested him on some warrants.

When it comes to surveillance and trying to be invisible, the fact is, even the best surveillance team in the world, using the best equipment, isn't capable of following someone skilled in counter-surveillance for long if he's spooked. The thing on our side is, if he thinks you're a cop, he never knows for sure unless you tell him. So you engage in a psychological battle, playing on his doubts.

One crook I worked was highly skilled at counter-surveillance and did his homework. From staking out our office, he knew what most of our undercover cars looked like. We switched our cars with old, beat up jalopies that didn't look at all like police cars. I was driving a thrashed Jeep Cherokee and put my bicycle from home in the back to give extra mobility.

One night at about two in the morning, this bad guy and his girlfriend went into a bar and stayed so long that I decided to go in and see if he was still there. He might've slipped out a back door and left in a friend's car. These guys are always trying to ditch the cops, even when we're not there.

I parked the Jeep nearby and rode my bike to the bar, parking it inside by a newspaper machine. The only person I saw was the bartender. Still, I could tell the bad guy was right around the corner, barely out of view. After a moment, he and his girlfriend stood up to leave. I ducked into the restroom and quietly let the rest of the team know he was coming out. After they left, I rode back to the Jeep and caught up with the surveillance team a short distance away.

A couple of hours later, the bad guy drove into a neighborhood and was somewhere in a row of cul-de-sacs. We wanted to know the exact house he was at so we could check on it after he left. Maybe he broke into the place, or if it was a friend's house, license plates would generate good intel.

I hopped on my bike and rode into the neighborhood. Trash night. I was unshaven, dressed pretty scummy and my hair was almost to my shoulders. I had a heavy flannel shirt on that made the look work. I stopped at a few houses on the street and dug through their trashcans at the curb. Grocery sacks hung from my handlebars with little knick-knacks in there to make it look good. As I approached the cul-de-sacs, the bad guy came out driving in his car. He stopped at the curb right next to me and rolled his window down.

"Hey, wasn't that bike parked over at the bar a little while ago?" he said.

I knew better than to freak out or give myself up. "What are you talking about?"

"Yeah, I saw that bike over at the bar on Craig Road, didn't I?"

"I don't know what you're talking about, dude. You got any crystal on you?" I said. I played the role the best I could.

I worked on the doubt in his mind even though it might only be a molecule. After a couple of moments, he drove off. My heart was pounding.

Daimon is this same kind of bad guy. Smart, courageous, and relentless. <>

11

////////

A STASH

If you want to keep a secret, you must also hide it from yourself.

—GEORGE ORWELL

I'd compiled a lot of information from the jail phones in hopes of a judge granting a search warrant for Daimon's house. My sergeant suggested doing surveillance on Daimon. However, I voiced my concern that it was a bad idea. Daimon was knowledgeable and way too spooked. My sergeant also thought it might be a good idea to put a tracker on Daimon's van. I thought the risk of him finding and destroying it was too great. I'd previously heard Daimon tell Bryan that he installed a remote engine starter on his van. Daimon was no novice with do-it-yourself car mechanics and probably stuck his head under his cars from time to time.

Despite my warnings, my sergeant had a couple of detectives start looking at Daimon. They were supposed to sit on the house and see who was coming and going. They might come across a wanted person or someone they could motivate to work as a snitch. Not a bad approach, usually, but still too risky to go anywhere near Daimon.

One of the detectives found a spot down the street from Daimon's house where he could park and go unnoticed. Only a matter of seconds passed after he was situated before Daimon came outside. He walked to the curb, looked down the street, and went back in the house.

A few seconds later, Daimon came out with Tammy. They jumped in Tammy's car and drove toward the detective. The detective drove out of the neighborhood. Daimon followed him. The detective continued driving, trying to blend in with the daytime traffic, but Daimon wouldn't go away—he followed the detective's every turn.

The term we use for what Daimon did is "mad-dogging." Daimon mad-dogged the detective for several miles and finally turned off. The surveillance was terminated. It's a safe bet that Daimon wrote down the description and license plate of the detective's car.

The next day at work, I heard about what happened. It bothered me. I thought we knew better. My sergeant thought he invented police work and didn't trust my instincts, even though he was new in the unit and I'd been doing this for years—something that irked me to no end. I figured things with Daimon would only get more difficult, and the last thing I needed was a boss who made my job harder.

Daimon's proclivity for confrontation and antagonistic behavior was an eerie reminder of the situation in 1996, when he rammed a detective's car and took the police on a car chase. How many of Daimon's neighbors and their visitors had been mad-dogged over the years? It provides peace of mind, though, when I think I've been burned on surveillance. Even when I'm at home, all cozy in my bed asleep, these bad guys think I'm there, watching. They always think I'm there.

The Las Vegas ROP unit is one of the most competent surveillance teams in the country. Highly skilled detectives with many years of experience are doing surveillance every day. We have an excellent inventory of equipment, including night vision, listening devices, tracking equipment, encrypted communications equipment, and props to help a detective blend in.

By design, we don't look like cops. Often times when a cop comes into a room, even in civilian clothes, people know he's a cop. It's how they carry themselves, their body language, and how they speak. Detectives in the ROP unit, on the other hand, have learned how to walk into a room and not look or act like cops.

But to physically surveil Daimon, especially when he was spooked, was risking more than it could reward. My investigation was going strong, and it was only a matter of time, if we were careful. He was sealing his own fate on the phones.

Back on the jail phones, Daimon told Bryan he thought the cops were watching his house. He said he was pretty sure he'd chased a cop off the day before. "But what we gotta be careful of is—we don't do nothing—but what I'm saying is, we can't even go dig in the trash cans no more. 'Cause I think it's a misdemeanor and I don't want to get arrested for that."

"Yeah, just chill out, dude," Bryan said.

"When is your storage due? Oh!—Why did I say that!" Daimon's voice shrunk. "I know it's in your mom's spot, it don't make no difference, but when is that?"

Daimon tried to cover-up what he just leaked: Bryan had

a storage unit. Game changer.

Bryan sighed. "Uh, December," he said. He sounded exasperated because Daimon revealed the storage unit.

"Oh, that's okay then. That's the one in Laughlin, I don't want to drive out there anyway," Daimon said.

"No, I just send it in when I need to."

Laughlin, Nevada, is about an hour and a half south of Las Vegas on the Arizona border at the Colorado River. This was a weak attempt at disinformation. But I didn't expect this to be a repeat of 1991, when Daimon and his friends had storage units to hoard their stolen stuff. I only needed to know where the storage unit was and find out if maybe Daimon or Tammy had one, too.

I retrieved the Las Vegas business directory and started calling storage unit businesses, one-by-one, to see if I could find storage units rented to Daimon, Tammy, Bryan, Bobby, or Engel. Some of the businesses were cooperative over the phone, some weren't. I couldn't blame them; there was no way for them to know for sure I was a cop. I resolved to visit them in person.

The first storage unit business was a bust. At the second one, I showed the manager a picture of Daimon. He said, "Hey, that's the guy who comes in every other month and pays on that one girl's unit." Additional checking showed Tammy had rented a storage unit there since 2001.

I asked the manager to keep the whole thing confidential, and he said he was happy to help. That didn't end the search, though, as this storage unit was rented to Tammy. Daimon and Bryan had talked about Bryan having one. I continued checking but didn't have any luck. It's next to impossible to find every storage unit business in a city as big as Vegas.

Later that day, I drove by Daimon's house on my way home. As I came onto Daimon's street, I saw a big, white cargo truck parked in front of the house. This had to be

Bobby's truck I'd heard so much about. I got the plate. Sure enough, it was.

I contacted the sergeant of our surveillance team and gave him the details. He said the team couldn't drop what they were doing, although if they got a chance to make it to Daimon's, they'd get on it. I thought it shouldn't be too hard to surveil Daimon if he was driving this big, cumbersome truck. It's pretty hard to do tail-checks and counter-surveillance in something so big and slow, and hard to turn.

Later, several detectives set up in the neighborhood. After a short time, they saw Daimon come out of the house and drive off in Bobby's truck. There were enough detectives covering the area that nobody had to move for Daimon's position to be under almost constant surveillance. Daimon wasn't leaving the neighborhood without someone spotting him. He made a few feeble attempts at checking his tail, but with the size of the truck, it was useless.

Daimon drove to a storage unit business about a mile from his house. He went in the gates and around a corner, out of view. A detective climbed on top of a building and, with binoculars, watched Daimon unloading stuff from the truck into a storage unit. There were large items of furniture and a lot of boxes. Tammy and the kids showed up in her car and helped.

The surveillance team briefed me the next day on what they'd seen. I figured there might be other storage units, but my leads were exhausted. Maybe they rented other storage units under fake names. Daimon had a history of using fake names.

As we were wrapping up the meeting, my sergeant said he wanted us to put a tracker on Daimon's van. I repeated my concerns about Daimon finding it, but they were brushed aside. Seeing I had no choice but to go along, I said, "Well, if we're going to get a tracker on the van, the ideal place to do it would be at the school."

We went to the school and found the van in the parking lot. It only took a moment to get the tracker deployed. Nobody noticed us. As I drove away, I tried to convince myself maybe Daimon had cooled down. Maybe he wouldn't find it. <>

12

///////////

PREPARATIONS

*Of all the hardships a person had to face, none was
more punishing than the simple act of waiting.*
—KHALED HOSSEINI

A few days went by and the surveillance team was busy
with other matters, so they hadn't had a chance to watch
Daimon. Nothing useful was coming from the tracker. It was
mostly showing at the house or at the school. No nighttime
movement at all. Maybe Daimon had decided to shut things
down for a while.

At home, Daimon answered the phone. "This is a call
from an inmate at the Clark County Detention Center. To
accept this call, press one . . ."

After accepting the call, Daimon said he was still moving
stuff out of Bryan's apartment. "I took McNealy out and the
little thing behind the pillow and you're drawer full of things.
And just listen, all your Gs, I took them all out of there."

"What now?" Bryan said.

"Yeah, I took them all out of there. I put them in the unit for now."

Daimon was worried Bryan's probation officer might show up at his apartment. "So I went over there and saw that everything's pretty normal. Ts are fine, I think all that's fine but let's get all the little things out. The little thing out. You understand what I mean?" Daimon said.

"So you took all the pictures out?"

"All the McNealys. I didn't take Mr. Scales because I'd break him and you'd kill me. But don't worry; they're all put up in a nice little spot."

"You took the one stuff out of the dresser?"

"Yeah. That's where most of all that was. I dug through your closet to make sure there's no bottles there. Um, the little thing behind the pillow I put away. All your Gs are gone."

"What Gs? What are you talking about?"

"Four strings, six strings," Daimon said.

"Oh yeah, yeah, yeah, yeah."

"Just anything I thought they might steal from you, you know? I didn't want nobody stealing from you. Now is there anything on the outside I have to worry about, or you cool?"

"What do you mean?" Bryan said.

"Any on the *outside*, anything outside you got locked up?"

"No, uh-uh."

"So if they went in there, no big deal at all?"

"Well, nothing really, dude. It's all just stuff."

A call from a couple days later revealed Daimon was done moving Bryan's stuff.

Bryan said, "Did you get all the stuff out of the washing machine?"

"Yeah."

Daimon hollered, "Hey Tammy, you already got the stuff out of the washing machine and dryer, right?"

"Yeah, I got it," Tammy said.

"Yeah, it's all out, bro. Everything's gone. I rented a ten-by-twenty that's full. The other one with all the McNealys is full, and I might have to rent another smaller one for the rest."

A *Google* search didn't give hint of what a McNealy might be. If they had mentioned more specifics about some of the property, it might've helped me figure out from which business it was stolen. Then I could've worked backwards to connect the dots. Nevertheless, it was obvious they were hiding and moving stolen property. If I was able to search Daimon's house, I'd at least find his stash of burglary tools and a new Matthew. I was also confident stolen property would be there.

I stayed late to finish my search warrant affidavits. I requested authorization to search Daimon's house, both storage units, Bryan's apartment, and Bobby's cargo truck. When I finished, I emailed the documents to Sandy for her review.

Past midnight, I was tired and packing up to head home. I figured I'd get a response from Sandy in the morning. As I began to leave, Sandy's reply hit my inbox. She said everything looked good. Surprised, I called her desk. "What are you doing working so late?" I asked.

"Same as you, working on the Daimon Monroe case."

Strange that Sandy and I were miles apart, relentlessly working on the same case long after quitting hours, yet unaware of what the other was doing.

The next morning, bright and early, I called Sandy and asked if she could locate a judge to review the warrants. After a few minutes, she called back, saying District Court Judge Stewart Bell and his secretary were expecting me.

Judge Bell had a strong and dignified reputation. He was elected District Attorney of Clark County in the 1990s and prior to, had been a criminal defense attorney for around thirty years. I'd never testified in his court or had him review a search warrant before now. I wondered if he'd be tough on me. With his years of experience, I knew he'd be no slouch.

In chambers, Judge Bell asked about the case. He reviewed the affidavits and swore me in. After signing the warrants, he asked when they would be served. I said we had planning to do first, although the search would be within ten days, as the law required. He wished me well, and I thanked him for his time. When I arrived back at my office, I informed my superiors the warrants were signed.

Department policy required the S.W.A.T. team to serve the warrant at Daimon's house. The fortifications, video cameras, Daimon's history with firearms and violence toward the police made it mandatory. S.W.A.T. would develop a tactical plan, serve the warrant, and when the premise was secure, hand it over to my team.

It was Friday; the decision was made to serve the warrants early Monday morning. S.W.A.T. would gather their own intel on Daimon's house over the weekend. They usually drive by, take photographs as they pass and try to get a look into the backyard to get advance notice of what to expect. They become familiar with blue prints and floor plans of their targets, so they know how many rooms they're dealing with and identify potential hiding spots and danger zones.

Arrangements were made for other detectives to hit the storage units and Bryan's apartment simultaneously while S.W.A.T. was hitting Daimon's house. This would prevent anyone from destroying or removing evidence elsewhere while we were at Daimon's.

I went back to my dungeon, the phone room, for one last

check on phone calls. I needed to know if anything might throw a hitch into the plan for Monday. Daimon had been talking about traveling to California. If he was gone when we served the warrants, it could change our plan significantly. Only one call had anything interesting, though it didn't provide reason to think Monday's plan should be changed.

Daimon said, "Wait till you get out, though, bro. We're gonna have a Big Montana, play pool until we feel comfortable again, and then do our thing, man. Everything's cool."

Bryan laughed.

"What I'd really like to do is hang my signs again. But I gotta be careful that Tom and John aren't around because they'll probably want to kick my ass," Daimon said.

"You better watch out . . ."

Daimon interrupted. "Oh, I spoke to my buddy today, the cop. He says they let the inmates out of lock-down at certain times, then they watch them and figure out who's using the phones. That makes it easier for them to listen to the recordings."

Daimon didn't hint as to who this supposed cop friend might be. Perhaps the same person who helped him gather names for his signs. It bothered me until I realized a lot of people were aware of at least some of our tactics. I was giving him too much credit. If he was so smart, he wouldn't have been be talking on recorded jail phones at all.

But Daimon's tenacity was incredible. Most people in his situation would give up crime, at least for a while, until things were smooth again. It was like having my alter-ego, right there in front of me—persistent, relentless, driven, and unstoppable. I respected him for that. I just wished he could've turned it for good.

When my day ended, it felt good. Probably the first time I'd exhaled in weeks. Nearly two straight months of eighteen-hour shifts dealing with the jail phone calls and follow-up had worn me down. Still, I was optimistic about what we would find on Monday.

I went to the evidence room and put together a small kit. I grabbed a dozen grocery bag-sized evidence bags, a handful of evidence envelopes, some evidence tags, and evidence seals. I figured if we needed more we could get it later.

As I drove home, I hoped everything would go easy when S.W.A.T. did their thing. The kids and Tammy would probably be there. I was certain Daimon wouldn't be expecting S.W.A.T. to come over for coffee. <>

13

////////

ALADDIN'S CAVE

Fame is a vapor, popularity an accident, and riches take wings. Only one thing endures and that is character.

—HORACE GREELEY

Monday morning, November 6, 2006—I was off to work early; show time was set for 5:00 a.m. As I drove to the side of town where Daimon lived, I gazed at the skyline of the Las Vegas Strip before sunrise. The brilliance of the neon lights is an amazing sight, even from a distance. I imagined how many people stayed up all night down there, spilling their dollars out in hopes of striking it rich. I'm a Christian man and gave up even recreational gambling a long time ago. I often think of how many lives gambling addictions have destroyed.

The ROP team met with S.W.A.T. in a parking lot not far from Daimon's house. S.W.A.T. arrived in two of the big black BearCat armored personnel carriers in which they travel and use to carry their special equipment. The S.W.A.T. officers reviewed their assignments and made sure everything was in order. They briefed their tactical plan, approach, inner-perimeter security around the house, who would take out the video cameras, and who would breach the fortifications at the front door.

The ROP detectives were responsible for outer-perimeter security in the neighborhood surrounding the house. We'd be watching for anyone fleeing on foot or trying to go to the house.

The S.W.A.T. Commander asked for Daimon's phone number. His plan was to call the house after the front door was breached. He might be able to coax Daimon out rather than storm inside and surprise him. There wasn't a huge urgency to prevent the destruction of evidence—we weren't looking for drugs that could be flushed down a toilet. With the home's video cameras disabled and the front door breached, S.W.A.T. could wait Daimon out or make a tactical entry and clear the house. The S.W.A.T. Commander would make the decision on the fly, depending on Daimon's response.

We left the parking lot en masse and headed toward Daimon's house. S.W.A.T. was in the lead and I brought up the rear. The caravan had to be an awesome sight for early risers driving to work. The loud tires on the BearCats hummed through the streets.

I parked my car around the corner from Daimon's house and put on my yellow "raid jacket" that clearly identified me as police. One of the BearCats was parked in front of Daimon's neighbor's house. The other BearCat blocked Daimon's driveway, so nobody could unexpectedly drive out of the garage. The S.W.A.T. team, dressed in green fatigues, deployed around the house.

I could barely hear the noise when the video cameras were

raked down from the eaves. At the same time, a S.W.A.T. officer hooked the BearCat's winch cable to the house's iron-barred security door. The winch tightened the line and jerked the door open. After attempts to call the house went unanswered, the S.W.A.T. Commander got on a loudspeaker and ordered everyone in the house to come out.

After a couple of minutes, a S.W.A.T. officer in full gear with ballistic helmet and armor was swiftly moving toward me, holding Daimon by the arm. His wrists were secured behind his back with plastic flex-cuffs. He was completely nude. I ran over and took control of him. He had a smug look on his face. Not an embarrassed look, but kind of like a smile. He seemed to think it was funny that he was stark naked in the middle of the street. I grabbed a yellow foam emergency blanket from a BearCat and wrapped him in it.

The S.W.A.T. officers swept the house; soon, Tammy was brought over to me. She looked dazed, still in her pajamas, wiping the sleep from her eyes. She was a pretty blonde in her mid-twenties, of average height, and Rubenesque from the hips down. She had a rather innocent face and bright eyes.

I noticed Daimon had a small scrape on one of his wrists, caused by the rigid plastic flex-cuffs. The scrape was slowly oozing blood. I removed the flex cuffs and put more comfortable, soft, nylon restraints on his wrists. Sometimes showing a little respect goes a long way toward getting someone to cooperate.

When S.W.A.T. gave the all clear, Tammy was taken back to the house to mind the kids. I told Daimon I had a search warrant for his house.

Daimon said, "What are you searching for?"

"The warrant says I can search for stolen property and burglary tools."

"You're not going to find anything stolen in my house."

"Why don't you come back with me to the house and show me everything that's stolen and help us get it back to the rightful owners?" I said. "If you do that, I can tell the prosecutor how you were cooperative, and it might help you in the long run."

"I don't know what you're talking about. There's nothing stolen in my house," Daimon said, with that smug look on his face again.

The chill in the air and the inadequate foam blanket gave me an opportunity to show a little more respect, so I let Daimon sit in my car with the heater on. After a brief period, I left him with another detective and walked down the street to the house.

As I walked up the sidewalk, other members of the ROP team were already there. One detective came out of the house, shook his head, and said, "Amazing," as we passed. I went inside, stood in the entryway for a moment and couldn't believe what I saw. Nearly every inch of wall space was covered by some kind of extravagant decoration, lavish artwork or expensive home electronic component. The place was set up better than most palaces.

I walked through the house and saw the same in every room. There were several huge LCD screens, plasma TV's, artwork that appeared to be original pieces, expensive furniture, home electronics of every kind, and collectible items everywhere. There were several computers in different rooms in the house, an enormous quantity of autographed sports memorabilia like pictures, jerseys, helmets, footballs, and baseballs. The names on them were amazing—Elway, Manning, Rice, Montana, Ali, Jordan, Byrd—and there were dozens of them. Many had certificates of authenticity. It was like being in the Hall of Fame for every major sport.

Autographed movie star memorabilia from Roy Rogers, Sammy Davis Jr., DeNiro, Pacino, Schwarzenegger, and many more were on display. Nearly two dozen expensive electric guitars, acoustic guitars, and bass guitars were found, many of them autographed by world famous musicians. A room on the first floor appeared to have been converted into a sound production room. The value of the top-quality professional sound equipment in this room would run into the hundreds of thousands of dollars.

A large quantity of prized old foreign and domestic coins were found. In the kids' rooms upstairs, there were computers, expensive décor, and several original cartoon cells from The Jetsons, Raggedy Ann, Pinocchio, and the Pink Panther. Cartoon cells are the actual drawings for each frame of the original animated movies. They're one of a kind and bring top-dollar at auctions.

We had our hands full, although seeing this meant nothing unless we could prove some of these objects were stolen.

I went back to my car and spoke with Daimon. I told him this would be his last chance to come clean. "Come back to the house and help. It will surely be better for you in the end," I said.

Daimon said in a scoffing tone, "Not happenin', bro. Nothing's stolen."

Detectives wanted Tammy's Toyota and the van out of the way, but they had to be searched first. Daimon's stash of burglary tools was found in the trunk of the Toyota. I took a look and saw a flashlight, gloves, large screwdrivers, and two more Matthews. I knew Daimon would go to jail at least for the burglary tools.

Had Daimon started capering in the Toyota instead of the van? The tracker on the van showed no strange activity at night. What made him switch cars?

Detectives searching the house found a gold mine of the same kind of stuff in the attic above the garage. This included numerous expensive pieces of original artwork, musical instruments, autographed memorabilia from several U.S. Presidents, along with more of the same from famous names in sports and entertainment.

The garage had several large restaurant-style stainless steel freezers packed full of lobster, expensive meats, and huge cuts of beef for roasting. A $2,000 commercial meat slicer was found in the house and an operational restaurant-style soda fountain was found in the garage. Unfortunately, many of the electronics and other items had their serial numbers ground off.

Before long, a detective had a lead on some stolen property. The warrant service at Bryan's place had finished up and his apartment and garage were found virtually empty. However, something found on the floor of Bryan's garage was important. A single business card for a woman named "Annie Lee" remained. This information was relayed back to detectives at Daimon's house.

A detective checking out the garage's attic heard about the business card and discovered the name "Annie Lee" inscribed on several of the original oil paintings. A check through police records identified Annie Lee as the owner of an art gallery in town that had been burglarized, with thirty-three original oil paintings stolen. She was contacted and asked to come to the scene.

Daimon Monroe's Garage

Autographed Collectibles

While Annie Lee was on her way, I went back to Daimon and took him a pair of sweat pants. I said, "We found your burglary tools in the trunk of the Toyota, and we're beginning to find things we think are stolen in the house."

"The tools in the Toyota are for working on cars and there's nothing stolen in the house," Daimon said. "Am I under arrest?"

"Yes."

"For what?" he demanded.

"Right now, you're under arrest for possession of burglary tools."

Daimon said in a contemptuous tone, "Oh, by the way, I found your tracker."

"What?"

With a proud look, Daimon said, "Yeah, I found your tracker on my van and I sent pictures of it to my attorney."

So what, I thought. It's perfectly legal for us to use tracking equipment and (at that time) it didn't even require court approval. If Daimon was as smart as he thought, he would've known that. But now I knew why he switched vehicles.

I was irritated my boss hadn't listened to my warnings. We didn't accomplish anything by putting the equipment at risk and, sure enough, he found it. Still, I didn't want to give Daimon the satisfaction of knowing he busted us. I remembered the best rule to follow in such circumstances: they don't know for sure unless you tell them.

I said, "I don't know anything about a tracker."

"Yeah, well somebody put a tracker on my van and my attorney is gonna get them in trouble."

"Is Bobby being followed?" I said.

"Why would Bobby be followed?"

"With all the money he's been stealing from the casinos, I bet the Feds are watching him. Maybe the Feds put a tracker on you to try and get to him."

As I walked away, I swear I could hear the gears turning in Daimon's head. He didn't know what to believe now. Before this, he didn't even know I knew about Bobby. <>

14
///////////

THE HOARD

Gluttony is an emotional escape, a sign something is
eating us.

—PETER DE VRIES

*B*ack in the house, I briefly separated Tammy from the
kids.

"We're starting to find stuff in the house that's stolen," I
said. "Do you have any family in town?"

"No, my closest family is my mom, and she's in Kansas,"
Tammy said.

"Well, it would probably be smart for you to save yourself
for the sake of your kids. They'll have to go to Child Haven
if you and Daimon both go to jail for possession of stolen
property."

Child Haven is a government-run emergency shelter for
kids.

"If you cooperate, I won't arrest you today and you can

make your own arrangements for the kids."

Tammy was clearly scared. Who wouldn't be? But I wasn't worried about her being scared. I was disgusted that a schoolteacher with young kids of her own could be loyal to a guy who obviously had no regard for society's rules. There was no way the kids didn't know what their dad had been doing. I thought about the warped sense of right and wrong these parents were implanting into their children. Yet, at the same time, I saw something in Tammy's face that seemed like she was begging for help. Something just below the surface that wanted to break free. But after a moment, Tammy made her choice: she wanted to talk to an attorney before saying anything.

I gave her my business card and asked her to call if she changed her mind. Tammy was placed under arrest.

I told my sergeant Daimon had found the tracker and claimed he took pictures of it. He was surprised and, although I didn't say it, I had an "I told you so" attitude. Later, we checked the van and found the tracker, untouched.

I said, "Good thing he didn't destroy it." The tracker was removed and put away.

My sergeant found a digital camera in the house containing pictures of the tracker. The camera was the kind that used a mini-disc. The mini-disc was confiscated—no need for Daimon to pass pictures of our equipment around to his friends.

Annie Lee arrived and identified the oil paintings as being the ones taken from her art gallery. They were valued at around $16,000 each. There were six Annie Lee paintings found at the house. The paintings were photographed and released back to her.

Another detective checked on the freezers in the garage. Some of them were identified by serial number as having been stolen from a commercial appliance sales company. A representative of the business was on his way with a truck to collect them.

I asked Tammy what she wanted done with the food in the freezers. I couldn't suggest donating it to a homeless shelter or giving it to a friend. I didn't want anyone to think I forced her to give the food away.

Tammy said, "Just leave it out, I guess."

So that's what we did. We filled boxes in the middle of the garage and left them—probably a few thousand dollars in perishable food.

Daimon was taken to the jail and placed on phone restriction until six that evening. Jail personnel were also instructed to keep him separate from inmates who did have phone privileges. We didn't want him calling someone and having them dispose of evidence in some location we didn't know about yet.

Transportation was arranged for the kids to go to Child Haven, while Tammy was taken to the jail for booking. She was put on the same phone restrictions as Daimon. By this time, I realized the pitiful evidence kit I'd put together last night wasn't enough. Not even close.

Bryan's Explorer was overflowing with property similar to the stuff being found in the house, although much of it had a medieval-style, like swords and paintings of knights. Paperwork in the truck revealed the location of Bryan's storage unit—a welcome break and an interesting twist.

ROP Detective Schoening started working on a search warrant for the newly discovered storage unit while I hustled down to the jail. I wanted to talk with Bryan, and needed to do it before he found out what was going on. I hoped to catch him off-guard rather than give him time to plan what to say. At the jail, I arranged to have Bryan brought to a private room. He was agitated and red-faced as I introduced myself.

"Just listen for a second, before you say anything. I want

what I say to be clear. I'm here to talk to you about search warrants being served at your apartment, Daimon's house, and some storage units, and we've started finding stolen property. I don't need you to give a confession to make my case. But if you want to say anything on your own behalf, to tell your side of the story, this will be your one and only chance." I read Bryan his rights and paused. He didn't say anything. He just kind of puffed as he breathed.

"Do you want to speak with me?" I said.

"I think I want to talk to my attorney," Bryan said.

"That's fine."

Bryan was placed on phone restriction. I headed back to the house. A lot more work needed to be done.

On the way, I called Sandy and told her what was happening. "You should come out and see for yourself," I said. "We've never seen anything like it."

I arrived at the house, and Sandy wasn't far behind. She did a quick walk-through, and then stayed outside, out of the way. By now, a couple dozen detectives were at the house, helping sift through the hoard.

Two Jacuzzis were on the back patio. One was found to have been stolen from a local spa company; workers showed up with a truck to haul it away. One hundred and eighty-six bottles of miscellaneous spa chemicals were tied to another spa company burglary. Forty large boxes of expensive chocolates stolen from See's Candies were found.

Crime Scene Analyst Vince Roberts was at the house taking photos. He'd worked a burglary at Milton-Homer Fine Furniture months before where over $100,000 in goods were stolen. He thought a lot of the furniture might be from that burglary. This was highly expensive furniture you can't buy just anywhere. A Milton-Homer rep came to the house and quickly identified dozens of pieces of furniture, accessories, wall decorations, and other items as belonging to the store.

Logistical problems grew with how much stolen property was being found. The question came up about the remaining contents of the house. We had a pretty good idea that most, if not all, of the extravagant property in the house was stolen.

Sandy provided a legal opinion: if a piece of property had a serial number, or the serial number was visibly removed, it was to be impounded. Items that appeared rare or unique were also to be impounded. Further follow-up would be done to locate the true owners. If none could be found, the property could be released back to Daimon or Tammy, if the courts deemed it appropriate.

The spectacle was the top news story on a couple of local TV stations. They had satellite trucks on the street and cameras set up on the sidewalk in front of the house. We were able to put the news to good use, since reporters were broadcasting as we brought property outside to be cataloged in the driveway and front yard. We had the news reporters ask the public to call the police if they saw anything in the video that might belong to them. The TV coverage helped us reunite victims with their property.

The evidence vault sent a cargo truck with a crew of evidence technicians. When the truck was full and the documentation complete for that load, they took it to the evidence vault and unloaded. I don't remember how many trips they made that day, but there were many. The police department had to rent an additional warehouse just for this case.

The service of the search warrants at the first two storage units was ongoing. A judge signed the warrant for the third storage unit and that search was underway. The same types of property found at the house were discovered in the storage units, including a large quantity of autographed memorabilia from famous musicians like The Rolling Stones, The Beatles, Bob Dylan, and Aerosmith. There was a stolen hyperbaric chamber, the kind used at wellness spas to help increase tissue oxygenation.

A number of autographed gold and platinum records from numerous world-famous musicians were photographed and impounded. Also in the collection: an autographed, framed and matted photo of five U.S. Presidents together in the Oval Office; an authentic, handwritten letter with doodling from Jim Morrison; a shadow box containing a large, authenticated piece of debris retrieved from the remains of the Titanic; and five more Annie Lee paintings. One extravagant and rare piece after another in an astounding collection only a billionaire could afford.

Could you imagine if the rent on one of Daimon's storage units went unpaid and ended up on the popular reality cable-TV show, *Storage Wars*? The auction winner would have the find of his life.

Storage Unit

Storage Unit

Continuing the search at Daimon's house, ROP Detective King checked the kitchen drawers. When he saw a pair of oven mitts, he could tell something was hidden inside. He thought he might find a piece of stolen property or a burglary tool. Maybe a stolen watch or stolen rare coins. Instead, he found almost $14,000, mostly in one-hundred dollar bills.

Tammy's pay stub from the school district was found in the kitchen. It showed she had made a little over $2,000 so far that year, up to the middle of October. It was her first year teaching and the school year was only a couple of months old. I knew Daimon didn't have any legitimate employment, so it seemed we had a pretty strong case to show these monies were proceeds from selling stolen property. All of the cash monies were impounded for seizure.

Numerous sheets and rolls of postage stamps were found, indicating Daimon had broken into a post office or a mail box store. A large assortment of rare, collectible stamps was also found.

Detective King found an electronic stun-gun device in a kitchen drawer and accidentally zapped himself with it. I wondered what Daimon might use it for. Daimon didn't do robberies. Still, it's against Nevada law for a felon to have a stun-gun, so it was impounded.

A fake ID in the name "Ashton Devon Monroe," with Daimon's picture on it, was found in a purse in the kitchen. A rental agreement for another storage unit rented to "Ashton Monroe" was discovered. Another search warrant would have to be written and served, but since it was already past business hours, it would have to wait until the next day.

Police reports from the crystal shop and dentist office burglaries were found in the house, although that was nothing out of the ordinary. Daimon must've gotten them from his attorney as part of the discovery materials from the D.A. However, the phone numbers and home addresses for Mr. Chen and other witnesses weren't redacted—Daimon and his friends now knew where they lived.

A total of about thirty detectives spent somewhere in the area of six-hundred-man hours recovering nearly two hundred pieces of known stolen property that day and into the wee hours of the next morning. We impounded more than seventeen hundred other items for follow-up.

Not everything from the house was impounded. With some things we would never be able to link to the rightful owners. Items lacking serial numbers or identifying marks, or items that weren't of such unique design and construction that research would likely not reveal their source, such as clothes, bedding, family pictures, generic-type furniture, and usual things people own, were left behind.

I was proud of the work that dozens of investigative personnel had done and the enormous amount of effort put forth. There were several hundred years of police experience among us there that day, and nobody had ever seen anything like this. <>

15

///////

THE LITTLE
THING

*Our fatigue is often caused not by work, but by worry,
frustration and resentment.*

—DALE CARNEGIE

"Is this Bobby?"

"Yeah, yeah."

"Um, uh, I have a message for you from Dinkie."

"Okay."

"Dinkie says to clear out all the cell phone uh . . . what'd
he say? He said clear out the cell phone things."

"Okay," Bobby said. The call ended.

Several hours later, Daimon was off phone restriction
and called Bobby. He was more guarded than usual in how
he spoke. "Do you know what's going on?"

"Yeah, it's on the news," Bobby said.

Daimon's voice picked up. "It was on the news?"

Daimon seemed infatuated with the fact that something he'd done was on TV. He asked what the news was saying and Bobby told him about it.

"Do you know what they said? You know the thing I found? They said it was from the Feds, for you," Daimon said.

"From the Feds for me? Man, you believe that?"

"Nope," Daimon said. "Hey, that spot's got to be cleaned, dude."

"I know, but I can't do it right now. You can't do nothin' right now."

"But, they already know, you understand?"

"How do they know?"

"I think they found the paperwork on it. Didn't some dude call you already?"

"What?"

"Some dude said he called you for me," Daimon said.

"Yeah, yeah, yeah, I already knew. I already knew what you was talking about. But yeah dude, ain't shit a motherfucker can do. You know what I'm saying?"

"But, dude, this just happened and you know there's that *little thing* in there."

"I know, I know, I know. But ain't nobody, nobody can't do nothin' right now."

"Dude, they ripped my door off and dragged me out of the house, butt-naked," Daimon said, chuckling.

The smug look on Daimon's face when the S.W.A.T. officer handed him over meant something. I was guessing that after all these years, he always knew if the cops came banging at the door, he'd come out *butt-naked* as a sign of defiance. It was like a game to him, like the signs he put up around the courthouse. Like mad-dogging. Daimon liked to antagonize authority figures for fun.

"Dude, I need to get bailed out."

"But they said on the news there was supposed to be a murder involved or something," Bobby said. The way he said it, he didn't sound puzzled by the thought.

Daimon laughed and said, "Whatever."

One of the local news reports had said the police were in Daimon's neighborhood investigating a murder when we stumbled onto his cache. I have no clue where they obtained that misinformation, but it's routine nowadays for the news media to get stuff wrong in the race to be first on a scoop. The only part that bothers me is how many people turn on the TV and accept what the media says as gospel.

The manager at the last storage unit business was contacted the next day. Daimon had provided a Texas driver's license as identification when he rented the unit. The manager had no reason to suspect the validity of the ID, but indeed, it was a fake.

The manager was shown the mug shots of Daimon's associates. When she saw Bobby's, she recognized him as the other person on the lease. The rental agreement listed him as "Robert A. Leiander." The manager took the detectives to the storage unit.

Like the others, this storage unit was filled with a vast quantity of items, including autographed sports memorabilia, autographed movie-star memorabilia, and other types of expensive collectibles. A couple of months earlier, other detectives had seen some of the sound equipment and sports memorabilia found here during their search involving the Wynn Resort investigation. There was a sound-mixing board worth around $30,000, fifteen expensive guitars and a large, framed, autographed picture of President John F. Kennedy.

In the storage unit, a ROP detective found an item of special interest in a trash can, buried halfway down amongst unopened bottles of expensive shampoo. It was a .38 caliber revolver, stolen in the burglary of a doctor's office. The doctor had kept the gun in his desk for protection. Someone had tried to grind the serial number off but didn't do a good job.

A trash bag contained bank documents in Bryan's name. They were similar to bank documents found in Bryan's Explorer. These were large accounts. I wondered if it would be possible to seize the bank accounts as crime proceeds.

The forensic lab found no fingerprints on the gun. Whoever handled it had probably wiped off their prints. I decided DNA testing would take too long and be too expensive. At best, DNA testing would confirm what we already knew: Daimon put the *little thing* in there. At worst, DNA testing would be inconclusive or show multiple people had handled it.

I told Sandy about the gun and the phone call from Daimon to Bobby. After our conversation, I went to the jail to rebook Daimon for being an ex-felon in possession of a firearm, another count of possession of stolen property, and possession of a firearm with an obliterated serial number. I didn't bother trying to talk with him—it would've been a waste of time. He wouldn't say anything incriminating. I'd given him plenty chance to come clean, anyway. I didn't need a confession from him.

Daimon now had three cases in the system; the car-stop case, the big property case, and the gun case. A lot of effort and long hours had paid off and I thought things would finally slow down. Oh, how wrong I was. <>

16

////////

THE VICTIMS

Wisdom is not acquired save as the result of investigation.

—SARA TEASDALE

I began the grueling process of sifting through the mass of impounded property. I hoped it would be fruitful in reuniting victims with their stuff. A civilian Investigative Specialist, Lexie Mason, took lead with the mammoth task. Lexie had one of the best work ethics around. She was smart and always willing to go the extra mile for people.

Lexie spent countless hours comparing impound reports and crime scene photographs to old crime reports, searching for items with matching or similar descriptions. If Lexie found a burglary report possibly describing something we had impounded, she'd dig further.

Several times, Lexie obtained photos or paperwork— such as appraisals or receipts—from victims to confirm she was on the right track. Other times, when she was satisfied the victim had suitably described a piece of property, she'd email pictures to see if they recognized the item. The first couple of weeks of this process proved worthwhile. Almost two dozen more victims were identified, as were dozens of pieces of valuable stolen property.

One of the victims identified was an artist named Michael McNealy. Several valuable pieces of artwork were stolen from his warehouse in Las Vegas. Finally, the mystery of what a "McNealy" was had been solved.

A woman named Alana Perry called the police department, and said she might have property belonging to the victim of a burglary. She and Tammy had been friends, and she'd seen the story about the stolen property accompanied by Tammy's mug shot on TV. Tammy had given her a couple of expensive paintings several months earlier, as a housewarming gift. Alana turned the paintings over to the police; they were tied to a commercial burglary from 2002.

Experts in computer forensics examined the computers from the house and the storage units, checking the hard drives for anything related to the investigation, including information deleted long ago. The computer from the loft in Daimon's house was probably the most interesting.

Someone had been visiting the police department's website and the map of the police substation boundaries. Internet research on night vision equipment, encrypted communications equipment, satellite phones, police scanners, radio frequency counters, debugging equipment, and listening devices was found. There were engineering diagrams for burglar alarm systems. It seemed as though someone had been doing homework.

Someone had also researched large caliber sniper rifles with long-range scopes on the computer. It didn't make sense why burglars would be interested in sniper rifles. Maybe this was how Mr. Chen would "go swimming." I knew this information would probably never see a courtroom since proving who was actually on the computer when those images were viewed was unlikely.

A computer impounded from a storage unit had email traffic on it exclusively to and from Bryan. The Internet history showed dating websites were commonly visited. There were several emails from someone purporting to be a woman in Russia. This supposed woman was affectionate with Bryan and claimed to want a relationship.

Didn't Bryan know 99.9 percent of those websites are scams? At some point they end up asking for money, "So I can come see you," or because, "My mother is ill." Sure enough, in some of the later emails, this "woman" started asking for money so she could visit.

I let Sandy know about the victims we had discovered, and how we had identified around a couple hundred pieces so far.

"How many counts are you going to charge in this case?" I said.

Sandy said, "Here's what I'm thinking. It doesn't make sense to charge one count for each piece of property. If I do that, the complaint will weigh ten pounds. If I charge one count of stolen property per victim that makes it simple and has the same effect."

"How's that?" I said.

"If they're convicted on a couple dozen counts of stolen property, it will carry the same weight as a hundred counts.

The judge will understand what lies beneath the case."

Sandy said she would take the big property case to the grand jury in the next week or two. Criminal cases make it to District Court for trial in two ways: Indictment from the grand jury or through a preliminary hearing in Justice Court, heard by a judge. The grand jury can be less complicated for prosecutors, especially in cases teeming with exhibits and witnesses. It gives the prosecutor the ability to streamline the information.

"If you keep finding more victims, I can always charge those counts later, if we need to," Sandy said.

Her idea made perfect sense. Sandy started working on the complaint to charge Daimon, Bryan, Tammy, and Bobby with criminal conspiracy and twenty-six counts of possession of stolen property.

Despite all we knew, it would be almost impossible to prove who committed any specific burglary, other than at the crystal shop and dentist office. Sure, everyone knew Daimon did the burglaries, but proving it in court was an entirely different matter. Most of the burglary crime scenes had no identifiable fingerprints lifted, and those that did were fingerprints of people who were supposed to be there. Most prosecutors don't like cases where the prospect of a conviction boils down to a coin-flip, and rightfully so. I don't want people going to prison on coin-flips, either. <>

17

////////////

FULMER

If you tell the truth, you don't have to remember anything.

—MARK TWAIN

A major element in proving possession of stolen property on Daimon would be to prove he lived with Tammy, since that's where much of the stolen stuff was found. It seemed easy enough, but Daimon claimed on the jail phones that he lived with a woman named Christy and he said she was his sister. Years before, when he registered as a felon, he even used Christy's address on the paperwork. I didn't know for sure if they were related, and my research to that point provided no answer.

The house Daimon and Tammy lived in was owned by a guy named Steve Fulmer. He'd spent time in prison at about the same time Daimon had one of his stays. I figured they knew each other from prison as Daimon often called Fulmer

"Bunkie" on the phones. Guys who've done time together often call each other "Cellie" or "Bunkie."

Daimon kept his name off the utility bills and any other house paperwork in order to stay "off the grid," as they say. I figured the easiest way to show he lived there would be to have the landlord testify. But if Fulmer knew Daimon from prison, would he cooperate and tell the truth?

I called Fulmer to ask if he could come to my office for an interview. He agreed and we met the next morning. Steve was a big man in his fifties with wire-framed glasses and thinning, gray hair. Once you hear his voice and see him, you think he'd be comfortable wearing a cowboy hat. He's a little odd-ballish, though—he thinks the government is out to get everyone and still feels his time in prison was an injustice.

We went into an interview room and I turned on the audio recorder.

"Mr. Fulmer, do you rent a home out to Daimon Monroe and Tammy Tremaine?"

"Yes."

"How did you come to know Daimon?"

"We met at the Tonopah Conservation Camp in 1994."

"You were serving time on a, what kind of case was that?"

"It was assault with a deadly weapon. I got probation and my probation was violated, so I ended up spending twenty months in the Nevada Department of Prisons."

"Okay. So you met Daimon; what do you know him by?"

"Uh, Daimon, at that point, Daimon. I mean, since then he uses Devon. That's his standard go-by name now."

"What do you do for a living?"

"I'm a draftsman or designer. I've got a really strong computer background and I've had drafting in my past, so on and off since 1987."

"Tammy and Daimon have been living in your home that

you're renting to them since when?" I said.

"November, 2003."

"How do they pay their rent?"

"They've always paid me in cash—six months in advance—$9,600."

"Did that ever draw some curiosity from you? Like, where's this $9,600 cash comin' from?" I said.

"Oh, I know Tammy's always worked and according to Daimon, Devon, he's always worked at doing one thing or the other. He said he was pressure, pressure washing, uh, in the kitchens in the hotels on the strip. Doing pressure washing, cleaning the kitchens and the last two years, he's told me that he steadily had a job with this, uh, this black fella, cleaning carpet," Steve said nervously.

"Look, you guys have known each other for a long time," I said. "You're in a tight spot this friend put you in because you've seen some things over the years that are just not right. You're not the kind of guy that's gonna help get your friend in trouble. If your friend gets himself in trouble, you're not gonna volunteer to help keep him in trouble. So, you're in a very uncomfortable spot and I understand that clearly. You're aware that a search warrant was served on November sixth at your rental. An enormous amount of stolen property was found."

"I believe it," Steve said.

"When was the last time you were in the home?"

"Let me try to nail that down for you. Okay, probably May or June of, it's the first half of 2004. I could probably narrow it down a little closer than that, but the first half of 2004 was the last time I was in there."

"That's over two years ago," I said, as I raised my eyebrows. "Have you ever been in the garage or outside?"

"The procedure was always the same," Steve said. "I'd call him on my way home from work and say, 'I'm heading that way.' I'd stop by because some of my mail still goes there. And he'd come out and bring me my mail and we'd sit there and visit for a minute or two in the street. But I've never been in the house, I do promise you."

"Let me make something clear," I said. "Even if you had been in the house and ended up seeing anything in there, that doesn't constitute a crime on your part. It doesn't constitute possession or conspiracy."

"I have no guilt. I mean, I may have the guilt of ignorance, the guilt of knowing that I'm associating with somebody who is less than an upstanding citizen. And of course, knowing his past, it's not surprising. You know, I feel real bad about it."

"Why do you say it's not surprising?"

"Well, because, evidently he just can't get away from the stuff, you know? There was two of his associates, and I'd told him and told him that he'd be in trouble with them. One was this Bobby Holmes, and the other one is a fellow named Chris something. His name that he always goes by is Matthew."

A light went on in my head when Steve mentioned Matthew.

"Had Daimon mentioned anything to you about the stuff going on since he was first arrested?" I said.

Steve said Daimon had become paranoid and thought the police were always watching him. "They're investigating him and all these cars are following him. Everywhere he went they were following. And he told me how he found a tracking device on his van."

"What did he have to say about that?"

"Oh, he was freaked out. He called and said, 'We found a tracking device.' He asked what he should do about it."

"And what did you tell him?"

"He asked me, 'Should I smash it, or what?' I said, 'I

don't think I'd touch it.' "

At this point, I confronted Steve with knowledge that he'd recently been in the home and had to have seen all the stolen property. "I heard your voice in the background when Daimon was on the phone one time with Bryan. I can quote for you what you said to him. You were giving him advice on what attorney to get. He was talking to Bryan on the phone when you were at the house."

Steve said he remembered the conversation, yet swore he wasn't in the house when it took place. He thought maybe he was on a speaker phone. I knew better, but Steve's denial was meaningless. He thought he might get in trouble, so I didn't push too hard—I only needed Steve to help prove Daimon lived there, and he complied. I didn't want to lose that, so I concluded the interview. <>

18
///////////

60 MINUTES

Lawyers spend a great deal of their time shoveling smoke.

— OLIVER WENDELL HOLMES, JR.

*I*n Nevada, if a person is detained for an investigative stop, the police have sixty minutes to either arrest them for something or release them. Most other states don't set a specific time limit, but use a *reasonable time* standard. In the car-stop case, if Daimon and Bryan were detained longer than sixty minutes before being arrested, the arrests would probably be deemed unlawful and anything discovered as a result of those arrests could be invalidated as "fruit of the poisoned tree." All of the phone calls I'd been listening to could potentially be ruled inadmissible.

The preliminary hearing in the car-stop case was a day away. I examined the dispatch logs from that night and the arrest report by Officer Salisbury. Some ambiguity in the arrest report about the sequence of events and the time of the arrest caught my attention. To prevent Sandy from being ambushed in court by the defense, I called Officer Salisbury. If I found the sixty minute rule had been violated, we'd have to live with it and the case might die with it.

I said, "I'm going to ask you some questions about the Daimon Monroe case, and I don't want you to tell me what you think I want to hear. I want you to tell me what you remember about that night."

"Okay, that's easy enough," Salisbury said.

From the dispatch logs, I already knew the car stop occurred at exactly 02:17 a.m.

"What time did you arrest Monroe and Fergason?" I said.

"What time did I write on the booking sheet?"

"03:00 a.m."

"Then it was 03:00 a.m."

"How do you know for sure?"

"I have the habit of looking at my watch when I arrest someone because I know I have to put it on the booking sheet."

I continued, "It seems from the dispatch printout that the owner of the crystal shop wasn't even there yet to identify the property. So, what did you arrest them for at 03:00 a.m.?"

"For possession of stolen property and the burglary at the crystal shop."

"With what probable cause did you arrest?"

"I could see the property through the windows of the van, in plain view. I spoke to the officer at the crystal shop on the phone and the descriptions I was getting of the stolen stuff were identical to what I was looking at. I didn't need the owner there to identify the property. I already knew it was his stuff."

The defense might claim Officer Salisbury wasn't telling the truth, although something else in the dispatch logs backed him up. At 03:02 a.m., one of the officers reported that the car stop and the dentist office call were related to the burglary at the crystal shop. Linking the two calls together meant they knew Daimon and Bryan had done the crystal shop burglary, and they were going to jail. This was precisely forty-five minutes after the van was first stopped.

But my guess was, the defense would still make this a key argument and hope for traction. It's not always about the truth for them; it's about what they can get people to believe.

The next day, when I arrived at the courthouse, Tammy was in the hallway. She'd been released from jail after one day since she had no prior record. She wasn't a defendant in the car-stop case, so I guess she showed up to see Daimon and show her support.

Tammy was with Daimon's friend, Carlos. I recognized him from his mug shot several years before for a stolen property conviction. He was an average looking Hispanic guy in his forties—short, medium build with dark hair, and a heavy mustache. He looked like he could be in a Mariachi band. He shot his eyes in my direction a couple of times.

We sat outside the courtroom, only a few feet apart. I was friendly with Tammy and asked about her kids. She said her mom came in from Kansas and got them from Child Haven. She added that her mom was probably taking the kids back to Kansas with her.

The patrolmen, Mr. Chen, Mr. Hopkins, and the other witnesses were called to testify, one-by-one. When they were done, I was called into the courtroom. Bryan and Daimon were seated at the defense table wearing orange and blue jail clothes. Sandy was standing by the prosecution table. I was sworn in and gave my name.

Sandy asked questions about the follow-up I'd done on the car-stop case. She brought out the pictures I took of Matthew, and I explained how I'd used the tool to open the doors of the businesses.

When Sandy was done, I was first cross-examined by Daimon's attorney, Joel Mann. Mr. Mann is small and in his late thirties with a shade of bronze hair directly from a bottle. Still, he was a sharp dresser, as are most attorneys. His always emotionless face never flickered a smile.

I was also cross-examined by Bryan's attorney, Cynthia Dustin. She's an attractive, smart looking woman in her late thirties with reddish-brown hair past her shoulders. A self-made woman, she's intelligent and confident—so much so that she tends to be a bully in the courtroom.

Neither Mr. Mann nor Ms. Dustin asked anything remarkable of me; this wasn't the day for a big battle. Their best fight here would be with motions to suppress evidence. When my testimony was complete, Sandy rested her case. The defense called no witnesses.

Judge Zimmerman decided there was more than sufficient probable cause to bind the case over to District Court. Sandy made an argument for higher bail on Daimon. She informed the judge about the alarming conversations on the jail phones about Mr. Chen. She also said Daimon had access to Mr. Chen's home address and phone number from the police reports we found in his house.

When the prosecution provides discovery materials, the defense attorney is responsible for redacting that sort of information before giving it to their client. After all, defense attorneys are supposed to be officers of the court and bound by a code of ethics. I don't think Mr. Mann failed to redact the information with intent to help Daimon carry out some sinister plan. No, I think it was carelessness. Nevertheless, Judge Zimmerman was concerned. The look on her face was of surprise and displeasure. The judge admonished Mr. Mann for a minute or two in open court and more than doubled Daimon's bail. <>

19

//////////

THE MONEY

The man who damns money has obtained it dishonorably; the man who respects it has earned it.
—AYN RAND

When Daimon called Tammy from the jail, she wanted to talk about the kids or pretty much anything besides the case. Daimon would pacify her for a moment or two and turn the conversation back to himself, how lonely he was in jail and how desperate he was to get out. He didn't seem equipped to comfort Tammy and her fears; he simply kept talking about the case and things he'd do to get out of trouble.

Tammy said, "Your attorney said talking about the case on these phones is hurting the case and he's going to withdraw if you don't stop. But, the other thing I worry about is if we would have a freeze, you know what I mean?"

Daimon played it off like Tammy was talking about getting a new freezer and said he wasn't worried about it.

It seemed clear they had bank accounts, too. I suspected the clock was ticking before the bank accounts would disappear.

Even though Daimon knew I was listening, he couldn't stop himself from talking about the case. To him, silence must be deafening. From that point forward, Tammy accepted fewer and fewer of Daimon's calls. She was obviously languishing, crying unstoppably and she wouldn't speak more than giving Daimon one word answers. Finally, Tammy stopped accepting Daimon's calls entirely.

I contacted Detective Fielding to help with the financial investigation. He's an experienced undercover detective assigned to a Federal Task Force that works money laundering investigations. He's built like a fireplug and likes to wear his hair in a long ponytail. When I explained what I was working on, he was eager to help.

I started communicating with the local financial networks, trying to find bank accounts for Daimon, Tammy, Bryan, and Bobby. It took several days for the information to come in. Under subpoena, Bank of America confirmed Bryan and Tammy both had accounts, and Bryan also had a safe-deposit box. The bank wouldn't reveal the balance of their accounts without a search warrant, although they said each had well over $100,000. Nothing came back on Daimon or any of the other people involved in the case. I collected the necessary information and started writing warrants to seize the bank accounts and safe-deposit box.

Sandy filed a motion in court requesting a source hearing before Daimon's release if he posted bail. It meant Daimon, or whoever might post bail for him, would have to prove the money was from a legitimate source. The judge granted the motion.

I completed the warrants and took them to the Chief Judge of our District Court, Kathy Hardcastle. In chambers, Judge Hardcastle greeted me with a smile. She read the affidavits, swore me in and authorized the warrants. I later met Detective Fielding at the main Las Vegas branch of Bank of America.

On top of seizing the accounts as proceeds of crime, the warrants ordered the bank to produce documents showing movement and expenditures of money—transaction histories. Where was the money coming from and where had any of it gone to? The bank manager came back after a brief time with cashier's checks and records. The check for Bryan's account was over $124,000. The check for Tammy's account was over $26,000. I thought the check for Tammy's account was light.

"Too bad you weren't here the day before yesterday," the bank manager said.

Transactions showed Tammy had withdrawn, spent, or transferred more than $200,000 in the previous two days. Approximately $145,000 was in cash withdrawals. The withdrawals were made at the same branch as Bryan's safe-deposit box.

On the way to the other branch, I called my sergeant and advised him I thought Tammy was trying to hide money. I knew from the jail phones that Tammy stayed back at the house for at least a couple of nights. Detective Schoening started working on another search warrant for the house in hopes that Tammy, the money, or both were there.

At the other branch, I spoke with the tellers who handled the withdrawals. They remembered Tammy and how they'd given her the large cashier's checks but, after a few minutes, Tammy walked back into the bank and demanded cash instead of the checks. They expressed concern for her to be walking out of the bank with that kind of cash.

Bank records showed Tammy completed several other transactions. She'd wired about $18,000 to an account in Kansas belonging to her mom. Mr. Mann, Daimon's attorney, was given $10,000. Another $45,000 was wired to a second attorney for Daimon, Alan Kreech. That amount seemed high, and I wondered if an attorney might be helping Daimon and Tammy hide money. Considering Mr. Kreech was practicing out of an office the police had long suspected of having ties to organized crime, it wasn't so far-fetched.

Tammy had paid $18,750 to a bail bond company before Daimon's bail was increased and the source hearing motion was granted. The source hearing motion must've narrowly halted the plan to bail Daimon out of jail since they didn't want to reveal the bank accounts to the judge.

A teller brought us Bryan's safe-deposit box, and we took it to a private room. When I opened the heavy, metal box, I found a mini version of one of the storage units. It contained a large quantity of gold coins, old silver dollars, and U.S. Silver Certificates—all later determined to be worth enormously more than their face value. There were also two large, well-preserved teeth from the long-extinct giant megaladon shark, worth several thousand dollars each. I took pictures of the contents, counted the money, and bagged it all up as evidence.

Surveillance was fired up at Daimon's house though it didn't appear anyone was home. We contacted Daimon's next door neighbor, J.R. Fulmer, who is also Steve's dad. J.R. said the last time he saw Tammy was a couple days before, when Tammy and her mom were at the house. Tammy mentioned something about going to Kansas for Thanksgiving.

The search warrant for the house was authorized. Once inside, we found nobody home—not a surprise. The place wasn't in much different condition than when we'd seen it last. There were still piles of stuff lying around; yet, I could tell Tammy or somebody had been cleaning up.

Even though Tammy wasn't there, we thought maybe she stashed the money in the house. We searched as best as we could, but there was only so much we could do. We weren't going to knock holes in walls to try and find the money. And it wouldn't be easy to put $145,000 under a mattress and have it go undiscovered. Nevertheless, we left the house without finding the money.

I went back to my office and met Detective Fielding. The federal agents he was working with on the task force were agents from Immigration and Customs Enforcement (ICE). I wondered if they could use their federal authority to do something if Tammy took the money over state lines. Finding her would be the key. I spoke to Agent Sampilo and gave him the details and the address for Tammy's mom. He gathered some information and contacted his counterparts in Kansas. They started developing a plan, and Agent Sampilo said if anything happened, he'd let me know.

Trusting the Feds wasn't so easy. Over the years, I'd had dealings with agents from several different federal agencies, and many of those dealings didn't turn out well. But in their defense, it usually wasn't their fault. The assistant U.S. attorneys to whom they report tie their hands and over-scrutinize their every move. Federal agents usually can't do much without pre-approval from an assistant U.S. attorney. However, this ICE agent was a little different—something about him convinced me he'd do everything he could.

Something you should know about ICE is, yes, they're the immigration enforcement arm of the U.S. government. However, they're responsible for much more. ICE is the principal investigative arm of the U.S. Department of Homeland Security (DHS) and the second largest investigative agency in the federal government, behind the FBI.

Detective Fielding and I finished the documentation on the bank seizures and the evidence found in Bryan's safe-deposit box. The evidence and the cashier's checks were secured in the evidence room and we were done.

It was simply another crazy day in this twisting investigation. I went home and straight to bed. Family had come to town for the holiday, and I had to get up in the morning to deep-fry a bird for the Thanksgiving feast. <>

20

////////////

THE TURN

Each betrayal begins with trust.

—UNKNOWN

The next morning, I woke to the wonderful smells of the Thanksgiving feast being prepared. I hoped four good days of rest would free up my head.

Halfway through the meal, Detective Fielding called.

ICE agents were at Tammy's mom's house. They found Tammy there, and she said she didn't have the money. She claimed she left it with someone in Vegas but wouldn't say who. The ICE agents thought Tammy was scared and on the edge of giving up the name, but when pressed, she asked for a lawyer. Tammy's mom was cooperative and consented to a search of her home. The ICE agents didn't find the money.

Monday morning, I met Sandy at her office, and we were speaking about what I'd learned. My cell rang and a woman's voice said, "Hi, this is Tammy. I need to talk."

I stepped into the hallway and cupped my free hand over my other ear. "I'm not supposed to talk to you without your attorney."

"I told him I was going to call you. He said I shouldn't, but I told him I was going to anyway."

Tammy agreed to meet at the Detective Bureau.

I said, "Bring your attorney if you want. Call me again when you get there and I'll meet you in the lobby."

As I drove to the Detective Bureau, I thought about the questions I wanted to ask. Ordinarily, I would've made a long list of things and hit them methodically. However this unexpected twist would have to be dealt with on the fly. I didn't know how much Tammy would say, but I'd at least try to hit the most important stuff. The money was the most pressing item on my mind—where was it? If the money wasn't found soon, it probably never would be.

When I met Tammy in the lobby, she seemed scared—a deer-in-the-headlights look. Later, I realized the look was a combination of scared *and* determined. Scared about what would happen but determined to do the right thing. She didn't have her attorney with her, and I walked her back to an interview room where we met another detective who stayed for the interview.

"Okay, you understand that you don't have to talk to me and you're here on your own free will. If at any point you want to leave, you can. Just walk right back the way we came in here and nobody will stop you. You understand that, right?"

"Yeah, I know," Tammy said.

"Let me be clear: if you provide information to me, I can't make any promises to you. I can tell the prosecutor what you've said and how you've cooperated and the District Attorney's Office will make any determinations about what happens. There's no guarantee that this will do anything for you."

"I understand."

"What is it you want to talk about?" I said.

Tammy's voice cracked and she started to cry as she explained she was afraid of losing her kids. The Feds coming to her mom's house on Thanksgiving Day was a frightening wake-up call. Federal agents don't simply show up at people's homes on Thanksgiving unless it's serious. Nobody threatened to take her kids away, although she knew she'd be without them if she went to prison.

I asked where the money was and she said she gave it to Bobby Holmes. She spoke to Bobby on the phone and he *volunteered* to hold the money for her.

"He said he couldn't do anything for *Devon* at that point, but, if he were in the same situation, he'd want someone to help his wife," Tammy said.

"I notice you called Daimon, *Devon*."

"I've always known him as Devon."

Tammy continued talking about the money. She said Bobby had the idea to get the money out of the bank and for him to hold it. When she made the big withdrawal, she took it in cashier's checks as the bank teller suggested. But when she got out to the car, she called Bobby, and he said to take the checks back and get cash. Bobby's intent seemed clear. I figured Tammy would never see that money again.

I said, "If you're able to get your hands on the money and surrender it for seizure proceedings, it would probably look good for you. It would demonstrate you're cooperating and trying to turn over a new leaf. When you leave here, I'd like you to call me if you get the money back or talk to Bobby about it."

I advised Tammy the grand jury was convening the next day, and she had the right to appear. "That would probably go a long way to showing your cooperation, too, if you did that. Talk to your attorney, and he can help you decide what to do."

Tammy wanted to explain how her life had turned out this way. She met Daimon after he was released from prison the first time and his girlfriend Regina had just left him. "I've been with him since I was fourteen and the only time I wasn't is when he was in prison, you know? When he was in prison, I spoke with him on the phone almost every day. Finally, when I turned eighteen, I told Devon, 'You have to promise me that things will be completely different once you get out of prison.' Even on the phone from prison he said, 'No, I won't promise you that. It will be exactly the same.' So at that point, I just stopped answering his calls. But when he got out of prison again, I was just feeling really desperate, and he went right back to doing what he'd done before. Things are so complicated, and you don't know how to get out of it. Devon told me things where I should've known better. I should've walked away—but I didn't." Tammy's eyes dropped and she bit her lip.

"He'd say things like, 'I'm involving you on purpose and I'm gonna make sure that anyone around me if they were ever to say anything, they'll be taken down too.' And he'd say, 'If you ever do anything with the money I'll kill you.' He said a lot of things like that. I'm smart enough, you know? I should've made better choices, but even now, it's like I'm still making justifications. Finally, I took everybody's advice and stopped talking to him. After I don't have him in my ear for a few days, I realize again that I can have a life away from him. I just felt responsible, you know? It's like I didn't know right from wrong anymore. I mean, he's the father of my kids. It's like I didn't know whether it was right or wrong to help put him away for the rest of his life. It's just, when I get to this point, it's hard to know what to do."

Tammy's hands had been trembling since we sat down.

The trembling subsided and she was more comfortable by the minute. She revealed some of the code words Daimon liked to use. Some of what she said confirmed what I'd already figured out, while other stuff was new and helpful. Tammy explained how Daimon might refer to any black person as *Bobby*, since Bobby was black. But if he was talking to someone about the real Bobby, he might use *black man* or *dirt*. She said Daimon liked to refer to Mexicans as *Carlos*. When Daimon spoke about doing a *walk-through* she said it meant doing a burglary. And, *pressure washing* also referred to doing burglaries. Tammy volunteered to listen to anything on the jail tapes and tell me what she thought was being said.

I said, "How often did they do burglaries?"

"He and Bryan would go out every weekend, like it was their job, and he's also gone out with Engel. There was a period for a long time where Engel, he and Engel were going out every weekend. I mean, those are the two people he's gone out with to burglarize places, but not with Engel in a couple years. The other people Devon hangs out with are just buyers of the stuff he stole. If we were to drive around town, I could pick out some of the places he'd burglarized. I know he's been at these places because he told me. But I can't match everything to where it came from because I wasn't there to see it, you know?"

I said, "So he'd go out to commit burglaries almost every weekend?"

"It was *every* weekend. Like every Friday and Saturday and then if it was a holiday weekend, he'd figure he had an extra day. If Monday was a holiday, then Friday, Saturday, and Sunday they'd go out."

"But never on week nights?"

"He was just supposed to go play pool, but they'd go play pool for maybe a game or two and then they'd just be right back out doing it, you know?"

Daimon had been out of prison for about six years. Do the math—two days per weekend, times fifty-two weekends per year, times six years—the numbers are staggering. I think a person could conservatively say Daimon had gotten away with committing three hundred burglaries. The actual number will never be known but is probably closer to six hundred.

"Oh, and you know about Sonitrol, right?" Tammy said.

Sonitrol is a burglar alarm company that uses advanced listening technology. When an alarm is tripped, sensitive microphones are activated and the alarm company can hear conversations or other sounds that can indicate whether it's a false alarm and what part of the building the sounds are coming from.

Tammy said, "Devon got a kick out of setting them off everywhere. He figured it would piss them off and waste their time with everybody coming out. He thought maybe if you do it long enough then they won't show up anymore. All I know is, he set those off all the time." Obviously, the *Old Sony* that Daimon talked about on the phones was Sonitrol.

"Did Steve Fulmer know?" I said.

"More recently Devon told Steve he had stopped doing burglaries. However, Steve had already received, you know, property . . . guitars, at least guitars, but sort of more recently where he said that his company needed a new whatever it was . . . oh, I remember, it was a projector. The company needed a new projector."

"So, he was ordering it from Daimon like he'd order something from a legitimate store?"

"Right. People would call him and like you said, basically put in an order. And he'd go out looking for specific things."

I added, "And then he'd break into a place and get that thing and if there was other good stuff he'd just use that to come home with?"

"Right, and you know sometimes Devon would say, 'I don't want anything here,' and just lock it back up."

"How long has it been since he had a real job?"

"At least five years."

Tammy then confirmed that Daimon met Bryan in prison.

Our conversation continued for a while, and Tammy said Daimon was always thinking only about himself. "You know, there's like a Taser thing in our house. He shocked the girls with it as a punishment. And it's something I knew about and I let him justify it, you know? He stopped doing it, but he had done it a few times and he tried to say, 'Well uh, it's on low battery,' and, 'I've done it to myself.' And he even shocked himself to show it wasn't so bad, you know what I mean? That should've been enough to make me walk out the door, but I didn't, you know?" Tammy sobbed. "But I didn't."

I remembered the stun-gun device found in one of Daimon's kitchen drawers. I clinched my teeth and felt the anger well up. I gave Tammy a moment to wipe her eyes and compose herself.

"There's one other thing you should know," Tammy said. "From the time I first met him, he kind of justified things. He'd tell me about how horrible his childhood was."

I was still disturbed about Daimon using the stun-gun on his kids, so I wasn't interested in his justifications and moved on. "Do you think he's capable of harming people? If he thought he could kill somebody and get away with it, would he do it?"

"I don't think he's like a violent or overly violent person. I don't think he'd hurt people just for the sake of hurting people. But in time, how do you know? He'd said, 'If that's what I had to do to beat this case, I would.' The original case wasn't even that huge. I mean, maybe he could've gotten prison time out of it. But at the same time, it wasn't that big of a case compared to everything now. I immediately told him, 'I don't care, that's never okay. That option is never okay.' But Devon came back with, 'Well, I just wanted to tell you about it.' I think if it would make the case go away, he'd do it."

"Are you afraid he'd harm you if he gets out because you're speaking with me?"

Tammy nodded and pursed her lips. "After hearing a tape like this one? Yes, I'm afraid."

"What would you do if Daimon got out of jail?"

"I truly made a decision that I'm done, you know? I'm not going to flee. I want to get this over with. My mom's in Kansas. My kids are enrolled in school there now. And that's where I'd like to go. But if he were out then I'd be worried. My mom and I even spoke about whether we need to change our names or something."

"So he couldn't find you?"

"Right. When he sets his mind to something, he won't sleep until he's accomplished whatever it is. It could be something small, like even something as small as a sprinkler was broken in the yard. Nothing could come before the sprinkler was fixed. You know, like if we had to eat dinner, it didn't matter. Anything could've been going on; that sprinkler, he was gonna go get it, and it was going to be fixed before he was gonna move on to anything else."

"Why did they call that screwdriver Matthew?"

Tammy chuckled. "It was a joke between them because Matthew was Christopher Clayland. He said they should call it Matthew. He's always been called Matthew. And uh, I think the bent thing is like trying to make a joke saying like Matthew has a bent dick."

The silence in the room was noticeable for a moment. I grimaced and looked at Tammy. "Okay. So they think the bent tool, they refer to that as a bent dick and Matthew has a, is supposed to have a bent dick or something?"

"Right, right. So calling it Matthew was a ha-ha thing," Tammy said.

Tammy revealed things Daimon would do while committing burglaries. "He'd take some of the surveillance tapes from businesses that he had been in. I mean because if he saw they were caught on camera, he'd pull out the videotape. He got a kick out of watching them at home."

"He took them as a memento?"

"Right."

The videotapes were probably in Daimon's house when we searched it, although I couldn't have known some old videotapes might be valuable to the case. With those, I might've been able to prove Daimon actually committed some of the burglaries, not simply possessed stolen property from them. Still, several weeks had passed and it was safe to say the videos were moved or destroyed already. Steve had been working on cleaning up the house and had removed much of the property that remained.

Tammy said, "One of the reasons they liked to do dental offices is that Bryan had been on probation. When he got arrested he was almost done with probation. They'd get tons of drugs—prescription drugs from dental offices or places that do day surgery and just hoard the drugs for when he got off probation. He figured he could use them then, when he didn't have to get drug tested anymore."

"Would they case these places?"

"They'd drive around like different places, some of the places they'd go immediately into, other places, they'd plan it."

"There were several thousand dollars wired to your mom's bank account. What's that all about?" I said.

"That was purely for her having the three kids. I didn't know how long they'd be there. I thought that was . . . I didn't know what amount to come up with. But I wanted to give her, you know, something for supporting my kids."

I drew the interview to a close and said, "I think it would be best for you to talk to your attorney before doing anything else. But do call me if you speak to Bobby about the money."

I walked Tammy out to the lobby and bid her goodbye. Everyone in the office was pretty amazed about what had just happened. Nobody ever thought Tammy would flip and confess.

I called Sandy and gave her the Reader's Digest version. "I told Tammy that the grand jury is tomorrow, too, and I think she's interested. You might want to talk to her attorney about it."

Tammy called that night, just as I arrived home. I knew my family was already in bed. I sat in the dark on the phone, hoping this would be the last business for the day, as I was exhausted.

Tammy said she called Bobby. She asked him to meet with her and bring the money. When they met, Bobby said he wouldn't give her the money until he spoke to his attorney. My earlier hunch was right. When the ship's going down, it's each pirate for himself. Tammy didn't expect to be double-crossed. She said Bobby was acting weird, so she got out of there.

I said, "Don't worry. You did what you could. Don't meet with him again; you don't know what he might do. How did so much money get into your account to begin with?"

"When Devon sold the stolen property, he'd put the money in my account at the ATM. Sometimes I was with him, but sometimes I wasn't. But he used my account so they couldn't trace the money back to him."

"All right, well, get some sleep. You've got my number. Call if you need anything. I'll be in touch with you again soon."

I wondered if Tammy was trying to pull a fast one. Maybe she still had the money. I thought maybe Daimon was coordinating events from inside the jail. <>

21

///////////

CHASING
DOLLARS

*The man of character, sensitive to the meaning of
what he is doing, will know how to discover the
ethical paths in the maze of possible behavior.*
—EARL WARREN

The grand jury convened the next morning. Sandy needed
me to testify and help sort out the many witnesses and
victims. There were hundreds of crime scene photographs
that had to be cross-referenced with impounded property,
which in turn had to be mated with burglary victims.

When I arrived, Tammy was in the hallway, seated next to
a man in a brown tweed suit. This was Tammy's attorney—
Jonathan Lord, an averaged sized man in his thirties with
light brown hair. Mr. Lord had been a prosecutor in Arizona
before entering private practice in Vegas.

Steve Fulmer showed up, complying with his subpoena,

and we made small talk for a few minutes. Tammy was nearby, and I could sense uneasiness between the two even though they didn't speak to each other. After all, Steve was buddies with Daimon, and now Tammy was helping bring Daimon down.

Tammy was one of the first people called to testify. Good thing she and Daimon had never married. If they had, Tammy would be barred from testifying about anything Daimon said to her. It's known as *spousal privilege.*

Tammy was in the grand jury room for about half an hour. When she was done and preparing to leave, I told Sandy I'd like the chance to interview her again. I was better prepared to ask additional questions. Sandy spoke to Mr. Lord and called me over. At the end of our conversation, Tammy said she didn't have a problem doing another interview. She added I could call her anytime if I had questions. Tammy's attorney concurred and they left.

Steve was called into the grand jury room and came out after a few minutes. I could tell he was happy to be out of there as he hustled out of the courthouse. I hoped he was honest with Sandy and the grand jury, otherwise, things would go south for him.

Witness after witness, victim after victim, law enforcement officer after another gave their testimony. It seemed like an endless assembly line. At the end of the second day, I testified. When I was done, the presentation of evidence was complete. The grand jury extended their session a third day for deliberations. The volume of evidence and number of witnesses was unprecedented for a case involving burglaries and stolen property.

The grand jury returned a true bill on Daimon, Tammy, Bryan, and Bobby for criminal conspiracy and twenty-six counts of possession of stolen property.

The next day, I finally had time to call Detective Fielding.

"Robert Holmes is supposed to have the money that Tammy took out of the bank and according to her, he won't give it back."

Detective Fielding brought some of his Fed compadres with him, and we met up near Bobby's house.

Diana answered the door and I asked to talk to Bobby. Diana is an attractive, petite, Filipino woman in her thirties with long, flowing dark hair and a nice smile. She was pleasant, yet unusually casual for having two cops and some Feds at her door. She invited us inside and said Bobby wasn't there. She called Bobby on his cell and told him we were at the house.

"Tell Bobby we're not here to arrest him, we simply want to talk," I said.

Bobby said he was across town and would be home in about twenty minutes. I agreed to wait for him there.

While we waited, Diana said, "Can you tell me what's going on?"

"I believe Bobby is holding a lot of money that doesn't belong to him, and the money was recently ordered seized from a bank account by a judge."

Diana acted like she was mad at Bobby; yet, so casual it seemed trouble with Bobby was commonplace for her. After forty-five minutes had passed without Bobby showing up or calling, Bobby's attorney, Sean Sullivan called. He asked to speak with me.

I advised Mr. Sullivan that ICE agents were considering opening a money laundering investigation on Bobby over the $145,000 that Tammy gave to him. I explained if Bobby surrendered the money, the ICE agents wouldn't try to indict him.

Mr. Sullivan said Bobby only had $70,000 of the money left, which he'd turn over. Bobby claimed he used the rest to pay off bills.

"Well, your client is going to have to agree to come up with the outstanding balance of the money within three months or the Feds will possibly indict him," I said.

Mr. Sullivan said they'd meet at my office later in the day to surrender the remaining money. I thanked Diana for her time and we left the house.

When I got back to my office, Mr. Sullivan called my cell. He said Bobby wasn't able to produce the money *that* day. "I can't say why, it would violate attorney-client privilege. The only thing I can say is the place where the money is wouldn't let him have it today. They said he could get it tomorrow."

I said, "So what you're telling me is, Bobby put it in a safe-deposit box and the bank is closing, right?"

"I think you must be pretty smart," Mr. Sullivan said.

The next day, Mr. Sullivan came to my office. He looked like an Ivy School law grad. I soon learned he was smart and a little arrogant, although he hid it well in this situation.

Mr. Sullivan said Bobby was afraid to come because he thought I'd arrest him for something. He had the money in a brown paper bag and was prepared to surrender it for Bobby. We went back to an interview room. Agent Sampilo joined us.

Mr. Sullivan produced a document titled, "Agreement Not to Prosecute" and asked me to sign it. The document said if Bobby gave up the $70,000 cash and promised to pay the remaining $75,000 in three months, the Feds wouldn't pursue an indictment on him.

"Neither I, nor Agent Sampilo, have the authority to make such an agreement," I said.

"I had to try," Mr. Sullivan said as he handed the bag over.

I opened the bag and found it contained $70,000 in crisp, bundled one-hundred dollar bills. When we were done counting the money, I asked Mr. Sullivan to remind Bobby the agreement included coming up with the rest of the money within three months.

"Why don't you tell him yourself? He's in the lobby now," Mr. Sullivan said.

I was surprised, wondering why the cloak-and-dagger act?

Agent Sampilo and I met Bobby in the lobby with Mr. Sullivan. I told him I wasn't there to ask questions, but I wanted to tell him to his face he had three months or the Feds would put him under a microscope. Agent Sampilo reinforced what I said. With that done, Bobby and Mr. Sullivan left, and Agent Sampilo and I went back to the interview room to complete the paperwork.

I asked Agent Sampilo if we had any real leverage to get Bobby to give up the rest of the money and he said probably not. But Bobby didn't know that.

I called Sandy and we spoke about the money trail from Tammy's accounts to Daimon's attorney, Mr. Kreech and the bail bond company. I thought we might be able to get a judge to authorize warrants to seize the money from those accounts. After all, we knew it was dirty money, it already had been ordered seized. And just because it changed hands didn't mean it was somehow washed clean—at least not without the scrutiny of forfeiture proceedings in court.

Sandy thought the idea seemed plausible but wanted to check with her superiors. After all, seizing money from a defense attorney's client trust account was unprecedented in Nevada. In the legal arenas in Las Vegas, attorney-client trust accounts have always been viewed as off-limits for law enforcement.

Sandy made the case with her superiors, and they gave her the green light. I drafted the warrants and took them to Judge Valerie Adair. I wasn't sure if she'd take the bold step I was asking, but it was worth a shot. One thing I knew, though, Judge Adair had been a District Attorney in charge of major fraud cases before being elected to the bench. The sometimes complicated realm of bank accounts and dirty money wouldn't be anything new to her.

Judge Adair sat at her desk, reading the affidavit. With a finger to her chin, I could tell the gears were turning in her head. "Very interesting," she said, as she continued reading.

When she finished, I said, "I think the court should find it outrageous that someone charged with crimes could use the fruits of those very crimes to pay for an attorney and bail."

Judge Adair swore me in and signed the warrants.

I went to the bank for the bond company where I met Detective Fielding. The warrant ordered the seizure of $18,750 from the bail bond account. There was only $5,600 remaining, so the bank manager gave the entire balance. Later, Detective Fielding and I served the warrant at the bank for Mr. Kreech. The warrant ordered the seizure of $45,000 from the account. There was only a little over $30,000 remaining, as some had been spent or moved. The entire balance of that account was seized as well.

About half an hour later, Sandy called. "Guess who's been trying to call me?" she said.

Alan Kreech, Daimon's attorney, left an angry sounding voice mail on her phone saying, "Hello Sandy, it's Al. I'm calling to find out why you are taking food out of my family's mouth," and hung up. Sandy said we would probably hear from people about this.

Sure enough, a couple of days later, there was activity in courtrooms and discussions in chambers between attorneys and judges. The end result? Mr. Kreech withdrew from the case. High-priced attorneys don't work for free. He wasn't getting the $30,000 back.

The court appointed private attorney Martin Hart to represent Daimon in the big property case and the gun case.

Marty Hart had spent several years as a prosecutor in the D.A.'s Office. Although he's only about five-nine, Marty is a large, heavy man. He's balding, with a fringe of graying black hair around a shiny bare dome, reminiscent of Friar Tuck from *Robin Hood.*

Over the course of several days, Sandy communicated with Daimon's other attorney, Mr. Mann, and Tammy's attorney, Mr. Lord. She informed them about the attorney-client trust account seizure. They both agreed to surrender the money they'd received from Tammy since it was tied to the dirty account. It was good to see there were some ethics left in the defense bar. In fact, Mr. Lord continued to serve as Tammy's attorney pro bono, a noble act.

Mr. Mann withdrew from the car-stop case when the money dried up. The judge appointed private attorney, Susan Burke, to take his place. Susan Burke grew up in Indiana and earned her law degree from Indiana University. She'd been practicing law for twenty years as either a public defender or a private defense attorney. A petite woman in her early fifties with a pleasant smile, she had red hair, and wore red framed glasses.

Daimon would still have solid private attorneys; the taxpayers would pick up the bill. <>

22

///////////

THE BREAK

Depending on the reality one must face, one may prefer to opt for illusion.

—JUDITH GUEST

One of the victims at the grand jury identified some furniture stolen from her store in a photo taken inside Daimon's house. We hadn't seized that property, as it seemed to be just ordinary furniture. But the victim described markings on the back of the furniture. I wrote another search warrant for Daimon's house.

Judge Adair was available and I met her in chambers. She reviewed the warrant, swore me in and granted authority to search the house for the third time.

Steve Fulmer met me at Daimon's house with a key. Another detective and I went to the master bedroom and inspected the furniture. Sure enough, just as the victim said, the markings on the back of the furniture were there.

We loaded the furniture into a truck to be taken to the evidence vault. One of the courts had already granted a motion for no additional property to be released without order from the court. Daimon asserted that Sandy and I stole his things and held a "garage sale" with the property. As I did every other time at the house, I left a copy of the warrant on a table in the living room.

As I prepared to leave, I took Steve aside. "I don't know what you said to the grand jury, but I know the D.A. didn't play hardball with you. If you have to testify again, you might be asked some tougher questions about Daimon, and you might want to make sure you tell the truth. I *know* you were in the house and I *know* about the guitars and the projector for your employer."

He started to say something. I raised my hand to cut him off and said, "I don't want you to say anything. I'm not here to interrogate you. I just wanted to let you know in case you have to testify again."

Sometimes, seeds planted grow into fruit-producing vines. That day, Steve would argue, minimize, or deny. But let that seed germinate and it might bear fruit. At a minimum, Steve would probably go home and toss anything he ever acquired from Daimon for fear of a search warrant coming to his door. With the amount of time and effort I'd put into the investigation, the only thing I wanted coming from anyone's mouth was the truth. The truth is simple, uncomplicated. The truth doesn't unwind and take down innocent bystanders. The truth only takes down those who hate the truth.

A few weeks passed and Daimon was still using the phones, calling Carlos, Steve, and Christy. He also called Bobby, but Bobby wasn't accepting the calls anymore—

probably heeding the good advice of his attorney. Or maybe trying to dodge questions from Daimon about where the money went.

Daimon knew Tammy had spoken to me and testified at the grand jury. He had the transcript of her statement and the grand jury testimony. He told his friends I must've threatened Tammy and forced her to lie. He talked about it so much I thought he might start believing it himself.

Most normal people live free from criminal behavior because they know it's wrong. But those with criminal minds don't care whether it's wrong or what the consequences are to anyone. They have no remorse and often have a validation, a reason, an excuse giving them the right—in their own minds—to commit crimes. It's always something other than taking responsibility. Some sex offenders blame terrible things done to them when they were young. Some people who steal from credit card companies blame them for "ripping people off" with high interest rates. Some people like Daimon do commercial burglaries, but claim it's not so bad because they don't break into people's homes. They all have some kind of justification, unless they're a sociopath.

When Daimon tried to convince people Tammy was lying and the cops "made her say those things," there had to be a conflict in his head. He knew what he'd done over the years. He couldn't deny the memories of all the break-ins. But the Daimon on the phones was trying to convince himself and others of things he knew were untrue. Over time, I believe this birthed a real psychological fracture in his mind. He knew he faced substantial prison time—maybe life in prison—and had no way out. He became more and more paranoid in his conversations.

Daimon said he was thinking of complaining to Internal Affairs about what the cops were doing to him. He believed we searched his house illegally and there were no warrants.

He thought the search warrants were forgeries. He said he wanted to talk to the news media, and he wanted to file a civil rights complaint in federal court. He'd done that back in the early 1990s, but the complaint was dismissed without merit.

Daimon had been calling Carlos, asking about Tammy, "Does she still love me? Are the kids okay?" Carlos said Tammy was okay and was probably forced to tell on him. But it was obvious Carlos wasn't in contact with her. He could never give specifics about anything she said. He only told Daimon what he wanted to hear. Much easier to do than argue.

Every now and then, Carlos went to the jail and put small amounts of money on Daimon's books. He used it to buy snack foods and shampoo from the inmate canteen. Daimon complained about not having the right kind of soap and shampoo. Tammy had said how important it was for him to always have his hair bleached blond, that he was obsessed with his appearance. In the house, there were dozens of bottles of professional shampoo and other hair and skin products in quantities that made it apparent Daimon had been burglarizing hair salons.

Daimon spoke often with Christy about how Tammy must've been forced to lie. He was confident Tammy would eventually come to court and tell everyone she lied, and he was innocent. He pressed Christy into trying to get in touch with Tammy.

A few days later, Christy told Daimon she spoke to Tammy's mom on the phone and was asked not to call anymore. Tammy confirmed the conversation with me, saying, "I don't want to talk to any of those people. I'm moving on with my life."

In one phone call to Christy, Daimon was distraught and crying on the phone. "Do you think I should just end it?" he said.

"Don't you even think about it. You can't even talk like that. I won't be able to live with myself if you do something stupid like that," Christy said.

I immediately left the phone room, called the jail and told the booking sergeant about the call. I said, "Listen to it for yourself and make your own judgment." I had to let the jail know Daimon might do something rash.

The jail had routine procedures for things like this. If the corrections officers (C.O.'s) believe an inmate is a danger to himself, he's put on suicide watch. The inmate is placed in a special isolation cell designed to prevent him from hurting himself. They remove the inmate's clothing, so he can't hang himself, and give him a special anti-suicide blanket and sleep mat. The inmate remains there until a mental health professional determines he's no longer a danger to himself.

The jail put Daimon on suicide watch. But after a couple days, he was back in general population. Someone must've decided he was no longer a danger to himself. In hindsight, I don't think Daimon would've hurt himself. He loved himself too much and was too self-important. I think he talked about ending it simply to get sympathy and attention.

Shortly afterwards, Daimon called Steve and told him about the suicide watch. He said the cops were listening to his phone calls. He also said he got into a fight with another inmate and the C.O.'s broke it up. Daimon had a tooth knocked out and said, "I'm going to make someone pay for all of this." The way he said it, it didn't sound like "pay" had anything to do with money. And it didn't sound like he was referring to the inmate. <>

23

////////

CHRYSALIS

Success means having the determination and the will to become the person you believe you were meant to be.

—GEORGE A. SHEEHAN

*I*n January of 2007, a hearing was held in Judge Michelle Leavitt's court on the big property case. Tammy flew in from Kansas to appear with Mr. Lord. Daimon and Bryan were brought from the jail and Bobby showed up with Mr. Sullivan. Daimon was standing there in shackles with his long hair slicked back in a ponytail.

Judge Leavitt was trying to figure out who each defendant was and called them by name. When the judge called Daimon, she referred to him as "Ms. Monroe."

One of the attorneys gracefully said, "It's Mr. Monroe, Your Honor."

"You're Mr. Monroe? I apologize," the judge said.

"That's okay," Daimon said. He was obviously embarrassed.

The judge ordered Bobby into custody, but that lasted only a few days, until he made bail. When he made bail, Mr. Sullivan showed that Bobby had taken a note out on one of his houses—a legitimate source.

At one point, Mr. Sullivan approached Sandy about a deal and asked if Bobby could stay out of prison if he produced the rest of the money. Sandy said no way. She didn't think twice about her response.

Since Tammy was back in town, I called and she agreed to meet at my office, so I could tie up the loose ends on the interview. We started talking about Daimon and I wanted to know more about the fabric of the man.

"What's supposed to be his real name?" I said.

"Supposedly it was Whitfield, I believe. That's what he told me was his real name, but I don't know."

"Devon Whitfield?"

"Right."

"How long ago did he tell you that?"

"Um, oh, when I was fifteen years old," Tammy said.

"How'd you guys meet?"

"We met through . . . I mean we met at Bobby's mom's house. Which now is in Bobby's name, I guess."

"Bobby, meaning Robert Holmes?"

"Right. Uh, at the one on Virgin Street."

"Did you know Daimon's family?"

"No."

"Do you know Christy?"

"I've spoken to her on the phone maybe once or twice, but I've never met her in person," Tammy said.

"She's Daimon's sister?"

"Well, that's what she calls herself, but I don't know. I have no way of knowing what the actual relationship is. I think she's maybe like a half-sister. But I'm not sure and I, I've never known any family."

"Do you know anything at all about Daimon's parents, where they are?"

"As far as I know, both of his parents are dead," Tammy said. "His father's been dead for longer and I believe his mom died while Devon was in prison this last time."

Tammy went on to explain how Daimon wasn't originally from Las Vegas.

I said, "How do you think he ended up in Las Vegas?"

"He and Bobby would both come out here. They've known each other from when they were little and living in southern California."

"Do you recognize the name Frank Pearson?" I said. Daimon had placed phone calls to Frank while in jail.

"Yes. He's another person Devon sold a lot of property to. More recently, I'd say the majority of stuff was sold to him."

"Did Frank ever come over to the house?"

"Uh, yes. He'd come over to the house sometimes and pick up the stolen property and then sometimes Devon would drive it to his house. They'd kind of take turns."

"Did Frank ever put orders in?"

"Yeah, definitely. Sometimes he'd say, 'I want a laptop,' or, 'People want TVs right now, so get plasma.' "

"So Frank was selling stuff?"

"Right."

"Over the years, did you ever take any orders for these people?"

"You know, someone would maybe call and Devon wasn't home and they'd say, 'Hey can you have him pick me up this whatever,' you know?"

"Would they tell you about where it could be found? Where it could be stolen from? Did that ever happen?"

"Occasionally. Like, most of the time they'd just talk to him or they'd, like Frank—especially Frank—would. His thing was using code words, so I couldn't easily figure out what he was talking about. He'd say like "blood work" for the plasma TVs. Things like that. You know, they had code names for everything."

"Can you specifically think of anything where you knew someone had put in an order and then Devon went out and did the job and you actually saw the piece he brought home? You know, something like maybe Frank put in an order for a plasma TV and the next day or whatever, Devon comes home and says, 'Look, I got Frank's plasma.' Do you ever remember anything like that happening?"

"I do," Tammy said. "But at the same time, it's hard to remember specifics."

"Is that because there's so much that it's all just kind of a blur?"

"Right. I mean, it was a few times a week—every Saturday night, every Friday night and pretty much, usually all weeks, and at least one day in the middle of the week. So it would be usually at least three nights a week. And sometimes he'd go burglarize one place, bring stuff home, drop it off and then go do another place. So it's like, I couldn't keep up with it all."

"So, sometimes there were multiple jobs done in one night?"

"Right, right . . . you know, if he didn't fill up the van, he might do several different places before coming home. But if there was a place where it was more things, he might fill the van up, bring it home, unload it and go back to the same place and fill up again."

"Did he ever tell you exactly what happened the night he was arrested by the patrolmen?"

"Yeah, he did. He said he went in, I guess it was the

Crystal Palace first. And he stole some things from there and had those in the van and then he went over to the other place where he was arrested. What he told me was he had gone into the other business, but that he hadn't taken anything. And it sounded like he had locked it back up or, or something like that. He had used that tool he calls Matthew and gone in, but he said that he didn't take anything from that place. And then, I guess people saw him breaking in and they called the police."

I showed Tammy a picture of one of the bent screwdrivers and asked if she recognized what was in the picture.

"That's what he calls the Matthew and you know, he'd make those too. He had figured out some way to unlock doors using that tool."

"Did he tell you how he figured that out?" I said.

"Uh, no. I don't know exactly how he used it, but I'll tell you I was there when he'd make them. You know, take a regular screwdriver and turn it into that."

"He made those in the garage?"

"Right."

"Did he, what'd he use, a grinder and a torch?"

"Yeah, he took a grinder and then he'd just kind of bend it like, you know, put it up against something and bend it."

I pointed at the picture and said, "It appeared when I examined this item, it appeared on this curve, this is forged steel. Pretty tough to bend and a lot of times it will snap unless it's heated."

Tammy chuckled and said, "Yeah, that's happened to him before."

"You've seen it happen?"

"Well, I wasn't in the garage when it happened, but he'd be mad about it and come inside."

"Did he ever cut himself or anything doing it?"

"Yes," Tammy said as she chuckled again.

Tammy said whenever Daimon left the house, he'd always have his tools with him. She spoke about some of the other tools and said, "He'd have plenty of things, not just for getting into businesses, but also like for getting into their safes. He'd use like the big pry bars for getting into safes. Sometimes he'd do it there and sometimes he'd just bring the safe to the garage and break into it."

"So you've seen the safes he has stolen?"

"Right. And then he'd go dump them somewhere."

Not all of the stolen property we identified came from burglaries where it originally seemed like Matthew was used to get in. Some were rooftop entries and some were committed by breaking through the drywall from the business next door.

I said, "Did he ever do commercial burglaries where he'd go through a wall of another business?"

"Yes. He did that a lot."

"Did he do some where he'd go through the roof?"

"Yeah, he's done that," Tammy said.

"Through like, ventilation shafts and stuff?"

"Yeah."

"Okay. I'm gonna turn now to some information that came through the phones over this long period of time to see if I can clarify some of it. The date he was arrested with Bryan was September 24, in the early morning hours, around two or three o'clock. That morning, he called you at home and something he said to you struck my curiosity. He said, 'I'll take a month off or whatever, okay?' When he says, 'I'll take a month off or whatever,' what does that mean to you?"

"He meant he wouldn't go out burglarizing businesses for a month."

"Why? It seems almost like he's asking your permission. Why would he do that?" I said.

"Well, I mean, all of the time he was there with me, I had no say in anything. He didn't ask my permission for anything. But when he's in jail, then he acts like I had some faith in him."

"Is it because all this time you've been trying to get him to stop?"

"Well, it's not like I'd say every day, 'Please stop,' because I'd get the same answer if I did that. But I would try. I mean, there were many times where I'd say, 'When is enough, enough?' and I told him, 'I don't care. I wouldn't care where we were living. And I don't care about having all this stuff in the house. I'd rather that you don't go to prison.' But he'd never, he'd never tell me he was going to quit."

"When you started checking on bail for Daimon, you asked him what name he was arrested under and he said he wasn't givin' up Devon. What did that mean?"

"Well, what he meant was, as far as he's told me, Devon Whitfield is his real name. So, he'd rather that you guys have the wrong name for him, I guess."

Tammy explained how back in 1995 or 1996, Daimon had taken a death certificate for someone and changed the name on it. "He created a birth certificate from this death certificate and then I was with him when he went to the DMV. He actually got a DMV issued ID card and got an actual social security card issued to him in the name Daimon Monroe."

"When Daimon says, 'doing a walk-through,' what does that mean?" I said.

"It meant he'd break into the business and kind of walk through it to see what was there, see if there was anything he wanted. You know, just kind of see what's there basically; he'd literally walk through it."

"Would he be there to burglarize it or was he just casing the place?"

"Well, to potentially burglarize it. But if he said, 'I did a walk-through,' that would mean he went in there to see what was there and didn't take anything."

"That leads me to another question. Did he ever, that you know of, did he ever burglarize places without knowing about the place first?"

"He did sometimes. Sometimes he could see stuff inside the building or just thought it might be a good place to do. And if he felt like there was nobody watching or that he'd be able to do it without being caught, then he might do it right then. But sometimes he'd drive by places several times before going back there. Um, he'd sometimes wait for a holiday weekend thinking, 'Well, I gotta go in when everybody's out of the store for several days.' He thought it would help him if the police couldn't prove which day the burglary actually happened. If he did it Friday night, but it was a holiday weekend and they didn't find out about it until say, Tuesday, he thought it helped him if no one knew which day he actually burglarized it."

"That night he was arrested, what time did he go out?"

"It was always around like five or six. The sun was going down and usually around five thirty, Bryan would drive over to the house and park. And then they'd go together on one of their rounds."

"When Bryan was in jail, did Daimon go out and do any burglaries without him?"

"Yes."

"Solo?"

"Yes. He was alone for those," Tammy said.

"Did he do any with Engel?"

"No. He previously—it was a while back—Engel had done burglaries with him. But then he started going out with Bryan. And then it was like a loyalty thing, not taking Engel out while Bryan couldn't go out with him. But it was hard for him to not go out at all. So he did a few by himself, but Engel didn't go with him, as far as I know."

"During that period, do you know of any specific places he went to?"

"I know there was a Halloween store and the Sylvan Learning Center by our house," Tammy said.

I remembered the big barrel full of Halloween masks, costumes, and toys found in the garage. That made sense now.

I said, "The Sylvan Learning Center?"

"Yes. The Sylvan was the first thing after being released from jail. He was right into the house, and he wanted to see if he still had the balls to go in a place after just getting out of jail. So he just decided he'd go in there. And then he brought home all kinds of education books. He figured that I'd be able to use them for teaching."

"During this period, Daimon was going over to Bryan's apartment. What was he doing?"

"At first, he didn't want people to know Bryan wasn't there. He didn't want anyone to break into Bryan's house. So he'd go and turn lights on and off and stereos on and off and those kinds of things. Then he decided he was worried that the police would search Bryan's apartment. So he started to clear everything out."

"What does it mean when Daimon talks about 'pressure washing?' "

"It might help to have it in a sentence," Tammy said. "But I imagine it would be referring to, it would be him trying to act like he actually worked, maybe."

"Let me read this to you: 'I'm just trying to debate everything. Trying to figure out when we get back on track and stuff. Is it cool to go back to pressure washing?' "

"He'd mean to go back to working," Tammy said. "But the only work he did was burglarizing places."

"Has he ever done any pressure washing?"

"Um, he'd stolen pressure washers and told people he

did."

"But he never worked for a pressure washing company?"

"No," Tammy said.

"When he says he went and saw "Old Sony," what does that mean?"

"He went and, you know, set off one of those Sonitrol alarms because he got a big kick out of everybody showing up. He'd set them off just to amuse himself."

"What's the importance of Daimon saying he wanted to 'get a Big Montana?' "

To you and me, a Big Montana is a sliced beef sandwich at Arby's restaurant. So when I heard Daimon say that several times over the phones, I could tell there was something more to it.

Tammy said, "Well, we had those big pieces of meat in the freezers and he'd break into Arby's and other restaurants at night to steal food."

"So a Big Montana was a reference to burglarizing Arby's?"

"Yeah, that or probably any kind of restaurant."

When Daimon raided the restaurants, he only took some of their food, so when the employees came to work, they either wouldn't notice missing food or they'd think another employee was stealing. I wondered how many of them were fired over the years when their boss thought they were stealing, when indeed, Daimon was to blame.

I changed gears and said, "One of the things they were concerned about was the victim from the Crystal Palace— the one they called 'the Chinese guy'—they spoke about whether he'd show up in court."

"Yeah."

"Did Bobby go visit him at the store?" I said.

"Yeah, Bobby went to the store to get a feel for the guy, I guess. And they spoke about bribing him to not come to court. I heard Bobby and Devon talk about it."

"There was some talk about whether or not they should spend the money to make people go swimming for a little bit. What does that mean to you?"

"That, whether they should kill him is what I would take from it."

"What do you know about that?"

"He told me he'd . . ."

I interrupted. "*He* meaning, *Daimon*?"

"Yeah, he told me he'd rather kill him than go to prison for this."

"So he and Bobby actually spoke about it?"

"Yeah. Bobby said he told Devon, 'Forget about it.' And from what I know, Bobby went to see, kind of check it out. But Bobby told me that he was completely against that."

"Daimon became aware that ROP detectives were investigating the case. What happened then? What did that make him think?"

"He thought the house was being watched and so at that point, I don't think he burglarized anything else after. He was worried about being followed and people watching him."

"Would you say he became really alarmed and paranoid?"

"Yeah, he was definitely paranoid."

"There were plasma screen TV's, computers, autographed sports memorabilia everywhere, movie star stuff. How much of that stuff, if any, wasn't stolen?"

"Well, I guess to give you an idea, even down to toothpaste and meat in our refrigerator. I mean, there weren't many things that we would actually buy. He'd only buy things he really couldn't steal. We would go to the grocery store once a week and get produce and milk, things like that. But he wouldn't buy meat or cheese or anything ever from the store because he'd go to a restaurant, and he'd take all their meat and all their cheese and just fill up the freezers."

"In a kitchen drawer, oven mitts were packed full of money. Where did that money come from?"

"I don't know specifically where it came from. For a long time, any cash he had, he'd put in that drawer in the oven mitts. Every few days or so, he'd go deposit money in the bank."

"He'd deposit that money into your account?"

"Right. He'd deposit it in either the checking or the savings."

"The freezers in the garage were found to be stolen. They were packed full of food—steaks, lobster, other perishable items. All that was stolen from restaurants?"

"Yeah. There might've been a few things from the grocery, but basically all meat, all cheese. The majority of everything including the food was stolen."

"There were surveillance cameras at the house and they were operating, correct?"

"Right," Tammy said.

"Did he record that stuff?"

"He'd never recorded until he was all paranoid after he found out about the ROP guys watching him. So then he'd record and watch it."

"Why did he want surveillance cameras?"

"He was paranoid about someone stealing from him, like, someone breaking into our house. But also, he liked the idea, if the police came to the door, he could see them."

"A portable hyperbaric chamber was found in a storage unit. How long had it been in there?" I said.

"Oh, I'd say maybe a month. I don't think it had been a long time. Devon brought it to the house and he took it from our house to the storage unit."

"Why did he steal it?"

"I guess he just thought it was expensive. I think at first he wasn't even sure what it was. I can't remember what he thought it was, but I think he thought it was something else when he got it. And then he looked it up online."

"And then he put it in storage? What did he intend to do with it?" I said.

"Well, I think he looked up the price of it and it was expensive, so he was gonna hold onto it until he could sell it."

"It's my understanding that one type of store Daimon would hit regularly was hair salons—to steal shampoo and hair care products and toiletries—is that correct?"

"Yeah."

"He had cabinets in the garage and in the bathrooms that were packed full of those kinds of things?"

"Right," Tammy said.

"So, if he were to say to somebody, 'Yeah, I went into this one place, I went into this other place, I went into the hair,' that meant he had hit a salon, right?"

"Right."

I showed Tammy a photo of the gun found in one of the storage units and said, "This gun was found in a trash barrel being used to store a lot of these shampoos and hair care products and toiletries and stuff. Then down halfway into these bottles and things was this gun. Like someone was trying to hide it from being easily found. You'd have to actually dig to find this gun. Do you know anything about that?"

"What I know is Devon told Bobby he picked up that charge and he was mad because he referred to it as Bobby's gun. However, I'd imagine when they originally got the gun, Devon probably stole it and sold it to Bobby. I mean, I don't know exactly how the gun came about."

"There was a spa stolen from Cal Spas. It was huge. How did he get it home?"

"He came home one night with that spa actually on top

of the van," Tammy said.

I imagined a minivan with a spa strapped to the roof rolling down the road at two in the morning with a couple of guys from a Metallica concert driving.

I asked about the paintings Tammy gave to her friend, Alana Perry.

"Yeah, I know those are from a long time ago because they'd been in our house for a long time, and he was running out of wall space. He had new, more expensive paintings, he thought. So, he didn't want them anymore. We didn't know what to do with them, so Devon suggested I give them to Alana."

"Milton-Homer Fine Furniture recovered a large quantity of expensive furniture and home furnishings," I said.

"Yeah, he brought home a bunch of furniture and Bryan was with him for the first of however many trips. And then he was supposed to have been done, but it was either that night, or it was the next night, he actually had me and the kids in the car and went back to it."

"So you were actually there? You were there, and he went inside while you were waiting in the car?"

"Yeah, but it wasn't a normal thing," Tammy said.

"Did that scare the crap out of you?"

"Yeah. Because normally I was never there."

"Did you see him go in?"

"Yeah."

"How did he get in?"

"I think he went through the back. I'm pretty sure he went in through the back. He had us parked in front and then he went in through the back."

"What did he take?"

"Um, he took like, some more paintings and plants and, it's like he wanted the whole store. It was hard for him to stop without the whole store being empty."

"What time of day was it when you went there with him?"

"It was in the middle of the night."

"So he said, 'Hey, get the kids. Let's pack up the kids. Let's all go down and . . .' "

"Yeah."

I brought the interview to a close and asked Tammy if I could call her if I had more questions. She said I could call anytime and she'd tell me anything. I walked her out to the lobby and we said our goodbyes.

I called Tammy a few times over the next couple of weeks and asked mostly about different code words Daimon used. At the time, I was going over old phone calls to make sure I hadn't missed anything. During one phone call with Tammy, I asked if she was going to change her mind and stop cooperating. She said she wouldn't.

"What makes you so sure?" I said.

"I don't want to live like that anymore. I want to live the rest of my life not even telling a white lie. I want to just move on and be honest, even about the littlest things. I've always known at some point, Devon would go away to prison, again, probably for a long time. That's why I went to school to become a teacher. I knew someday I'd have to be independent of him."

Tammy had been with Daimon since she was fourteen years old. She was a good mother to her kids, except when it came to Daimon's behavior. Whether her timidity or his overpowering nature induced it, for many years, he totally controlled her. She didn't intervene when he used the stun-gun on the girls. She said something about it, yet allowed him to minimize the behavior and let it pass. There were deep-seated psychological issues from being in that kind of relationship for so long. When she was able to have a few days away from Daimon's domination, Tammy compared it to the clouds opening to bright sunlight, letting her see clearly.

My attitude toward Tammy in the beginning of this investigation was disgust and animus. She was a schoolteacher for goodness sake. In some ways, she was worse than Daimon. At least he didn't try to convince people he was some kind of angel. But as time went on, and my understanding of what brought Tammy into this moment grew, animus transformed into empathy. I began to hope Tammy would get through all of this in one piece, and these times would radically change her life and the lives of her kids for the better. Some of the greatest things in human history have been forged out of the heap of destruction.

I said, "I want you to know that I'm proud of you. I think you're doing the things it will take to make a new life for yourself and your kids. There's going to be a lot of times when you're scared and don't know if you're doing the right thing. If you ever need someone to talk to when you're feeling like that, give me a call. <>

24

/////////////

TRAGEDY

We can easily forgive a child who is afraid of the dark; the real tragedy is when men are afraid of the light.

—PLATO

February 15, 2007—Tammy called from Kansas and said her oldest daughter told a school counselor that Daimon had raped her. Tammy sounded broken. She asked what she should do.

"If she wants to talk about it, fine. Let her do it in her own words. Don't coach information. Probably the best thing you can do is just reassure her and make sure she feels loved. Let her know how much you love her and this doesn't change that at all," I said, my heart crushed.

"Okay."

"Do you know when or where this happened?"

"Well, it had to have been in Las Vegas. I'm not sure

when exactly, though," Tammy said.

"I'm going to have someone who specializes in this kind of thing get in touch with you."

I contacted Sergeant Shingleton in the Sexual Abuse Detail and advised her of what I knew. She made a report and assigned it to a detective in her unit. About a week later, Tammy called again and said now her younger daughter was also talking about Daimon sexually abusing her. Her younger daughter gave graphic details about what happened.

I said, "I'm going to let the detective who's handling this know what you've said and have her call you. Make sure you don't force your daughters to talk about things before they can be interviewed by someone."

"Okay. Child Protective Services are already involved here and I think they're getting the police involved, too."

I didn't ask for specifics in what Tammy's daughters were saying, as I wanted to keep my distance. I didn't want anyone to think I had influenced anyone. Plus, I had enough snapshots of the world's ugliness in my head already. Cases where kids are victimized have been some of the toughest ones to swallow.

Several weeks later, Bryan finally had his probation revocation hearing. The key element supporting the revocation was Bryan having had picked up the new charges. The defense argued the new charges were invalid, as the search of Daimon's van was illegal. Judge Wall examined the facts of the case and ruled the van search as valid. Bryan's probation was revoked. He was sent to prison to serve out his original sentence, which was only twelve to thirty months. He'd be eligible for parole in only a few months.

Bryan's attorney, Ms. Dustin, inquired about a deal on

the new cases. Sandy said any deal would have to include Bryan testifying. Bryan didn't want to do that.

Sandy said, "If I have to go to trial on Monroe, I might as well go to trial on the other defendants, too, unless they testify."

Bryan always had the option of pleading guilty and hoping the judge would show mercy. But, no, people think they're entitled to plea bargains. Another example of where our system of justice has gone wrong. It's the drip-drip erosion of personal accountability that our society has been ushering in for several decades, all in the name of expediency and cost savings.

Not long after this, Ms. Dustin withdrew from the car-stop case. The money dried up and the judge wouldn't appoint her at taxpayer expense. She was lucky, though, because she didn't have to surrender any money she had already received for defending Bryan—it wasn't directly linked to the seized bank accounts.

Same as what happened with Daimon and Mr. Hart, the court appointed a good private attorney with many years of experience to represent Bryan. Frank Kocka was the man for the job. He was a tall, thin, handsome man whose dark balding hair was turning gray. His distinguished appearance was offset somewhat by his fidgety habit of frequently tugging on his salt and pepper goatee.

Daimon had been trying for some time to make phone calls to Carlos, who would never answer the phone. Christy stopped accepting Daimon's calls, as she was mad over Daimon having her son do a three-way call when she wasn't home. She didn't want Daimon manipulating her son. Steve was the only person left still taking Daimon's calls.

In one call, Steve said he'd spoken to Carlos briefly and Carlos said something about the cops coming to his house, although Steve didn't have details. Right away, Daimon assumed the cops were harassing Carlos because of him, and that was why Carlos wouldn't answer the phone anymore. I didn't know anything about the police talking to Carlos or anyone Daimon knew. But Daimon was convinced I was having Carlos harassed simply because he accepted Daimon's phone calls and put money on his books.

Daimon seemed to be more and more paranoid all the time. He told Steve the C.O.'s had cleared everyone out of his housing unit. "They do it when they want to check the rooms for contraband. But I'm telling you, dude, they did it this time to cover-up what they were really doing. When they let us back in, they'd moved all my papers, and I know they copied all my stuff."

"Are they allowed to do that?" Steve said.

"Dude, they do whatever they want, but get this—they put a listening device in my cell. There's a little black thing in my ceiling vent that wasn't there before."

There was no listening device in Daimon's cell, but the conversations he had with other inmates afterwards must've made them think he was going nuts.

A few weeks later, Daimon told Steve he fired one of his attorneys, Susan Burke. He said Ms. Burke was acting weird one day, and he found she had a voice recorder. Daimon said he knew she was working with ROP, recording him so ROP would know what he's thinking.

What Daimon proposed was like something from a TV show. Defense attorneys don't work with the police to convict their clients. Daimon's behavior was becoming unpredictable. I hoped he wasn't going off the deep end. That could delay the case for a very long time.

Sure enough, a few days after the phone call, Susan

Burke withdrew from the case. She informed the judge she could no longer represent Daimon, as he refused to cooperate in forming his defense. Her request to withdraw was granted. Mr. Hart, Daimon's attorney for his other cases, was appointed to that case as well. Ms. Burke had no idea how fortunate she was.

Detective Jensen from the Homicide Detail stopped by my desk one morning. He worked one of Daimon's cases back in the 1990s. We talked about the similarities between his case then and my case now.

Detective Jensen said, "What do you think about him possibly being involved in the murder of Chris Trickle?"

Everyone knew about Chris Trickle. He was related to a famous race car driver and was an upcoming young star in motorsports himself. But on February 9, 1997, at around nine in the evening in Las Vegas, Chris Trickle left his house to play tennis. While he was driving, a car drew up beside him and someone fired shots. Chris was hit in the head. He died from his injuries a little more than a year after the shooting. The story was featured twice on the popular network TV show, *America's Most Wanted.* The case went cold; nobody was ever arrested for the crime. There were few leads in the case, but a witness had done a composite sketch of a possible suspect. Nothing ever materialized about who committed the crime.

Detective Jensen said he recently saw the sketch in the cold-case file and immediately thought it looked a lot like Daimon.

I said, "Well, from what I know about Daimon's personality, I wouldn't rule it out. I think he's capable of anything, if the circumstances are right. But I do know he was in prison somewhere around that time. I'll find out when he went in and when he got out."

I contacted central records for the Department of Corrections, and asked a secretary what Daimon's commitment and release dates were for that prison stay. Her database didn't have the information; it had been purged a few years back. Daimon's file had to be retrieved from archives, which would take a few days.

I started communicating with Officer Nagler, a C.O. in Jail Intel, about Daimon. Jail Intel handles things having to do with offender management, confidential informants (C.I.'s), escape prevention, gang enforcement, and dealings with contraband and problem inmates. I wanted to find out what it would take to monitor Daimon's mail if he was sending or receiving messages.

Officer Nagler said he was familiar with Daimon from the 1990s and remembered what a pain in the neck he was, always complaining and scheming. He said he'd stay on top of things and let me know if anything came up.

One day, as I spoke with Officer Nagler, I said, "Keep it to yourself, but we're checking into the possibility of Daimon being involved in the Chris Trickle murder." I told him it wasn't going anywhere, since we first needed to know if Daimon had been incarcerated at the time.

A few days later, the gal in prison records called. Without a doubt, Daimon had been in prison when the shooting occurred. It was impossible for him to be the guy in the sketch.

I informed Detective Jensen of what the prison said, closing the question for him. I sent an email to Officer Nagler, as well, letting him know Daimon couldn't have been involved in the Trickle murder.

Daimon continued talking with Steve about once or twice a week. He said he had to be real careful, as there was a snitch in his unit. He said the snitch was trying to make friends with him and had started talking to him little-by-little about his case. Daimon thought the guy knew too much, so he confronted him about it. The guy told him he was working with the cops.

A few days later, Daimon told Steve the cops were doing crazy stuff to try and frame him. He said, "The snitch said the cops are looking at me for killing some guy named Chris Trickle."

I couldn't believe what I heard. How in the world could these people have learned that? Daimon couldn't have been involved in the Trickle murder. He was in prison when it happened. But how could he know we even looked at the idea? The only people who knew about it were me, Detective Jensen, and Officer Nagler in Jail Intel. My shoulders slumped. I sighed. Could it be?

After thinking it through, it became clear. It's common for Jail Intel to solicit information from inmates about what's going on inside. When I've worked informants on the streets, I sometimes gave them a small bit of information to see if they could fill in the rest of the puzzle on their own somehow. You do it so the informant can have a starting point. It seemed Officer Nagler must've provided confidential information to a jailhouse informant, which made it back to Daimon.

Certain types of information are okay to give an informant and other types are not. This would definitely fall into the "are not" category. But I didn't have heartburn about it. It didn't affect my investigation, and we already knew Daimon couldn't have done the murder. This was a quick way to learn to never again trust Officer Nagler with confidential information.

What if Daimon was the Chris Trickle murderer, and he prematurely found out we were looking at him? That sure could put a bad wrinkle into a murder investigation. I didn't hold it against Officer Nagler for too long, though. I was angry at first, but time heals those wounds. Nagler was probably trying to do a good job and made a mistake. But I didn't like the idea that information I provided to someone in confidence could ever be given to an informant I didn't trust. <>

25

///////////

THE PLOT

Anger ventilated often hurries towards forgiveness;
anger concealed often hardens into revenge.
— EDWARD BULWER-LYTTON

It was unnerving when Johnny sounded panicked and told Rich that Daimon wanted me killed. But I didn't have time to worry about it. We didn't know if the plot was already in play and, with the possibility of the Aryan Warriors or the Sureños being involved, time was our enemy. Those groups have the ability to get things done quickly.

I called my wife, telling her to keep the kids inside. It's not every day a warning like this comes. The crack in my wife's voice revealed all I needed to know. She acted like she wasn't scared, but she was. I felt like going home and circling the wagons, but I knew the best I could do was help nail things down and get a solid picture of what we were facing. I went back to the phone room and put on the headphones.

Johnny said the cops didn't find all of Daimon's money, and Daimon's friend named Carlos could arrange for it to be delivered. Johnny also said Daimon wanted someone to kidnap Tammy and their kids and either harm her or take them to Mexico. Johnny said Daimon was furious that Tammy turned on him.

As I listened to the phone calls, it ate at me that I didn't know the identities of Johnny or Rich. I could tell Rich was probably someone in law enforcement or retired law enforcement by the way he spoke. I researched the phone number with no luck. It would take days for a subpoena to the phone company to provide information. I called the number Johnny was dialing, not knowing who might pick up. My caller ID was blocked, so they'd have no clue I was a cop. The same male voice answered the phone, "This is Rich Beasley."

I said, "Rich, I'm not sure who you are, but I'm a detective with Metro. I just listened to some jail phone calls between you and someone named Johnny. These phone calls sound pretty alarming and I need to know who you are and who Johnny is."

"I'm an FBI agent, and Johnny is someone who has given me information for several years. His name is Johnny Marquez."

Johnny Marquez was in jail awaiting trial on a violent domestic assault and rape case. Agent Beasley and I spoke about what was going on. I said, "Detective Joe Kelley in our Organized Crime Bureau is leading the investigation. I'll have him get in touch with you."

Detective Kelley was a senior and experienced detective—a great asset to the department. He was bald and kind of rugged looking, yet in a good and wholesome way. Mix that with his southern drawl, and you'd think he grew up on a ranch wearing cowboy boots. He was old school and didn't put up with a lot of modern-day politically correct hullabaloo.

For Detective Kelley, the investigation started when inmate James Mailer reported the plot to jail personnel. Mailer was the guy to whom Johnny leaked information. Mailer told Detective Kelley another inmate named Danny Butcher was talking about setting up a hit on Sandy. Butcher was a suspected associate of the Aryan Warriors.

I called Detective Kelley, bringing him up to speed on what I'd learned. I said I wouldn't interfere with his investigation while offering to provide any help or information he might need. He asked me to continue listening to phone traffic in Daimon's unit and to let him know if I heard anything worth knowing.

"At what point do you think we should let Tammy know that she might be in danger?" I said.

"We should do that right away," he said. "Why don't you do it, since you already have a good rapport with her?"

"All right, but I'll only give her the basics. I won't let her know about the threat to me or the D.A. and the judge. I'm not completely convinced she's not in contact with Daimon. I'd hate for him to get tipped off and make it harder for you to do your job," I said.

I called Tammy and told her about the threat.

"Do you think we should move?" Tammy said.

"Ultimately, you'll have to decide for yourself. Nobody can be right there with you all the time. Only you know what's going to give you peace to sleep at night. You said we found all his money and all of the storage units. So it seems he might not have the means to get something done. Just remember, though, Bobby didn't turn in all of the money you gave him. But if it were me, I wouldn't be that drastic yet. We don't have conclusive information that there's a plan in place. If we learn more, I'll keep you posted. And, as always, if you ever need something, call me no matter what time it is."

When our call ended, I called FBI Agent Bob Hunt. Agent Hunt was the resident expert on the Aryan Warriors. They call themselves *A-dubs*. I told Agent Hunt what I knew about the murder-for-hire plot and how it had been suggested that the A-dubs and the Sureños might be working together. It seemed strange because the A-dubs are white supremacists and the Sureños are almost exclusively Mexicans. Ideologically, the two groups are enemies.

Agent Hunt believed the Aryan Warriors had developed relationships with the Sureños in the past, and they had exchanged work. He described a hypothetical scenario where the A-dubs might carry out a hit on someone for the Sureños in exchange for the Sureños doing one for them. That way, it would be harder for law enforcement to tie the job back to who actually ordered it. It didn't mean the A-dubs and Sureños were allies, or even liked each other, it was just business. Many times, it's business first—loyalties and ideologies somewhere after. That concept didn't give me a good feeling.

I brought the information to my superiors, and they sat on their hands. They'd never dealt with anything like it before. I took the initiative and made sure the other detectives in ROP knew about it, too. They were potentially in danger, as well, since we were all at Daimon's house and many of our names were on his paperwork.

When I got home that night, I told my family the bare minimum. They didn't need to stare darkness in the face like I had done for years. We spoke about different safety measures, which I won't discuss here for obvious reasons.

I already had my home address protected from public records several years before in case something like this ever happened. Even today, if people do an Internet search on me, they'll find nothing besides old addresses and disinformation. I've been dealing with the worst of the worst criminals for years, and many of them have a long time in prison to think about how to lash out. I've taken steps to get off the grid, just like Daimon did. The irony isn't something I take humor from at all. <>

26

////////////

TAIL-CHECKS

The question is not whether I'm paranoid, it's whether I'm paranoid enough.

--UNKNOWN

I started checking my mirrors on the way home from work and, many times, I took different routes home. I'd watched bad guys tail-check for years, so I used some of their tricks. I ended up doing tail-checks of my own if I noticed the same car behind me for too long. It seemed twisted that a cop had to tail-check for bad guys when it's supposed to be the other way around.

Something in particular that gave peace of mind was knowing if someone ever showed up at my house with bad intentions, it would be war. He'd better get it right with the first shot, as that was the only one he would get. I was prepared psychologically. I was expecting something to happen and wouldn't be caught off-guard. It wouldn't matter if I had a gun on me at the moment or not. If something happened at my home, the perpetrator would quickly find he should've tried somewhere else. I had seen and investigated extreme violence. It wouldn't be hard at all to embrace it, to protect my family. Sure, I've got plenty of firepower, although you'd be amazed at what human beings can do to one another with their bare hands, given the proper impetus and kick of adrenaline.

I learned that when the FBI first started looking at the threat, they were alarmed because there's a Federal Magistrate in Vegas with the last name Leavitt. They thought it might be their Judge Leavitt and not our Judge Leavitt who was being targeted. With the plot possibly involving the A-dubs, Agent Hunt was also considered a potential target since he'd recently engineered a huge investigation that decimated their leadership. I once heard that Agent Hunt was briefly sent to an FBI safe house in Utah for protection, but I've never been able to confirm that piece of information. It's not like the Feds go around advertising their methods.

After my episode with the two men on the freeway, in which I was sure I was about to be ambushed, I drove home with my thoughts abuzz and relieved I hadn't shot anyone. In the house, I put my shotgun away and kept the story to myself. It was nothing. It wouldn't do any good to tell about something that was make-believe—this time. My family was already nervous enough. Adding to it wouldn't help ease the tension.

Not long after, I had a high-tech burglar alarm installed on my house that would at least give us some warning if someone tried to bring Daimon's wrath to our door. I kept a fully loaded AR-15 tac-rifle with extra 30-round magazines next to my bed every night.

There were a couple of nights when the burglar alarm did go off. The first time was about two in the morning. I jumped out of bed in my underwear, grabbed the AR-15, and made my way to the stairs. The house was dark and the alarm was blaring. I quick-peeked every corner down to the room where the alarm panel was located. I looked for anything out of place or any sign of movement. Had I seen someone who didn't belong in my home, he'd have been greeted with merciless .223 rounds.

The flashing red lights on the alarm panel told me the exterior garage door had been tripped. I silenced the alarm, and a female's voice from the alarm panel asked if everything was okay. I said I wasn't sure yet, and she asked for my password. I gave her my password, and asked her to remain on the line.

I went into the garage and saw the exterior door was closed. I scanned the area, checking all of the places where someone could hide. Nobody was there. A gust of wind came up and shook the garage door. Right then I knew it was a false alarm. The wind must've shaken the door enough to trip the door sensor. I was relieved until I thought about how Daimon intentionally tripped burglar alarms to test them and make people mad. I wrote it off and went back to the alarm panel. I told the alarm company rep everything was fine. She said she was canceling the call she'd made to the police.

Almost everyone in the house was awakened by the false alarm. They were a bit unnerved, and I was disturbed the alarm had blown a good night's sleep. There were a few more false alarms over the next few weeks until the alarm company installed a different kind of sensor on the garage door.

For further safety, I developed good relationships with my neighbors. I told them what was going on, and if they ever saw anything strange at my house, they should call the police. I asked them to trust their instincts and look out for people or cars that didn't belong.

One day on the phone with Sandy, I mentioned my burglar alarm going off and told her the story. She gave an uneasy chuckle and said her alarm went off once or twice too, which gave me pause. Sandy obtained a concealed weapons permit and was keeping a gun in her purse. The D.A. gave her special permission to carry it in the courthouse.

Things were serious enough for a squad of detectives in our Organized Crime Bureau to conduct surveillance on Judge Leavitt for a few weeks. They acted as a covert security detail, following the judge wherever she went.

When Sandy found out about it, she said, "Hey, how come we aren't getting bodyguards?" Her question came out sounding like a joke, but we would've welcomed the protection had it been offered. Apparently, we weren't important enough. <>

27

///////////

THE GIRLS

Courage is grace under pressure.

—ERNEST HEMINGWAY

The detective in the Sexual Abuse Detail submitted the case to the D.A.'s Office for multiple felony counts, including sexual assault with a deadly weapon and child abuse with a deadly weapon. The investigation showed not only did Daimon use the stun-gun on his daughters, but he put a gun to one of their heads and threatened to kill them if they ever said anything about the sexual abuse.

Tammy called a few days before the preliminary hearing in the sex-abuse case. She was scared to bring the kids back to Vegas, especially in light of Daimon possibly wanting to do them harm. I offered to take her to and from court. She said it would make her feel better knowing I was there and could protect her if something happened. I called Detective Kelley to ask if he was interested in helping. He said it would be his pleasure.

On the morning of the preliminary hearing, I picked Tammy up from the lobby of her hotel. She had the girls and her son with her. We drove to the courthouse and went around the block to see if anything looked out of place. The dark tinted windows on my unmarked police car made it impossible for anyone to see inside.

I called Detective Kelley on his cell and advised where I was parking. He was on foot nearby, surveying the vehicle and foot traffic bustling all around. He had a good view of the surrounding area and operated as a covert escort while Tammy, the kids, and I walked up the steps of the courthouse and into the building. Once inside, we went through security and on to the courtroom.

As we waited outside the courtroom, Tammy introduced me to some family members who had come in from California to be with her. Detective Kelley went into the courtroom and sat inconspicuously, in case Daimon tried to pull something in there.

The prosecutor was Lisa Luzaich from the Special Victims Unit of the D.A.'s Office. This arm of the D.A.'s Office specializes in sex-crimes, and the prosecutors have experience in dealing with victimized children. Lisa was in her forties with dark, spirally curls and a great smile. She was one of the best sex-crimes prosecutors in the region.

Tammy's younger daughter was first to be called into the courtroom. She must've been in the courtroom giving testimony and being cross-examined for close to an hour. While Tammy's younger daughter testified, I taught her older daughter how to play slap-hand, a child's game. I also played peek-a-boo with Tammy's son, who was about four years old. At one point, he came up with a smile on his face and said, "You're not my Daddy."

Surprised, I said, "I know, I never said I was."

I pondered the implications of this toddler's hunger for a father and the gravity of everything that had happened. What effect would it all have on the lives of Tammy and her kids? I hoped they'd figure out how to forge through it and turn out all right. I silently said a prayer, asking God to touch their lives and make them okay. They'd been through enough and needed his grace.

I had a conversation with Tammy, and encouraged her to get the kids into counseling. I explained how the Victim Assistance Office would probably pay for it. She said when she got home, she'd try to find someone for the girls.

When Tammy's younger daughter came out of the courtroom, she had a smile on her face and was obviously happy to be done. I thought of the fear she must've felt stepping into the courtroom to face the man who abused her and the courage it took to withstand the embarrassment of telling her story to strangers with him looking on. But at the same time, Daimon was her father, so the torn feelings must've been gut wrenching.

I said I was proud of her being so courageous, and I knew she'd be fine. She said it wasn't that bad and told her older sister she'd be okay, too.

Tammy's older daughter was called into the courtroom. She was in there less time than her sister. When she was done, she came out with a big smile. I could see she was relieved. I said I was glad she was so strong. She asked if I wanted to play slap-hand again, but, just then, my name was called. I went into the courtroom and saw Daimon seated at the defense table with his counsel.

Lisa asked about my involvement in the case. I didn't have much to provide other than the fact that Tammy informed me about what her daughters were telling school officials in Kansas. I advised the court I didn't investigate the case, that other investigators with special training and experience handled it. The important thing I was asked about was the stun-gun found at Daimon's house. Its existence corroborated some of the events from the girl's testimonies.

When Lisa was done questioning, I was cross-examined by Daimon's attorney for this case, Tracy Browning. Tracy was an attractive, thin, nicely dressed, red haired woman in her early forties.

When Ms. Browning started questioning, I studied Daimon. He was wearing orange and blue inmate clothing and his hair was noticeably longer and a little darker than when I'd seen him last. He had it in a ponytail falling past his shoulders. I thought about how he complained about not having the right kind of shampoo in jail.

The look on Daimon's face as I answered questions from his attorney was striking. He seemed to have a dark look of pleasure on his face; his mouth shaped into a mirthless smile, like a smirk, with real hate behind his eyes. His expression reminded me of the face of Heath Ledger, portraying The Joker in the Christopher Nolan Batman movie, *The Dark Knight*.

Ms. Browning didn't have any questions of real substance. However, she asked questions that implied I'd influenced Tammy and her daughters' statements. At one point, she said, "What's your relationship with Tammy?"

Lisa objected to the line of questioning, however the judge allowed Ms. Browning to explore.

I said, "I don't even know that I can describe there being a relationship. I'm a police investigator, and she's one of the subjects of my investigation."

Ms. Browning said, "How did you come about talking with Tammy about these allegations?"

"She called me out of the blue one day."

"How was it that Tammy had your phone number?"

"I gave her my business card on November 6, when she

was arrested at her house."

Several times when Ms. Browning asked questions, she interrupted my responses to start asking another question. When I'd had enough of being bullied, I said, "Would you allow me to answer the question, please?"

"Sure," was her response with a small grin. She was trying to push my buttons and was getting close.

When Ms. Browning was done with her cross-examination, I was dismissed. I escorted Tammy and the kids out of the courthouse and Detective Kelley followed nearby.

The sex-abuse case on Daimon was bound over to District Court and set for trial. <>

28

///////////

THE REC YARD

*Anger is a killing thing; it kills the man who angers,
for each rage leaves him less than he had been
before—it takes something from him.*
—LOUIS L'AMOUR

*D*aimon thought Johnny was connected with the Sureños,
and he wanted Johnny to connect him with a hit man.
Johnny looked the part to a tee. His dark hair reached his
shoulders, and he wore it pulled back off his face, his entire
forehead exposed. He had three dots tattooed in a triangle on
the web of his right hand, like many hard-core Hispanic gang
members. To some, the three dots stand for "mi vida loca"
or "my crazy life." But to others, the three dots represent
what the gang life leads to: the grave, the hospital, or prison.
A thin patch of hair on Johnny's chin added the final touch,
making him the stereotypical image of a man in the Mexican
Mafia.

Johnny and Daimon were in the rec yard together while other inmates were playing basketball nearby. Johnny said, "Bottom line is, I don't want to have conversation after conversation. We're not going to have this conversation again. Do you want to get these people murdered or not?"

"Yeah. But how we gonna do it? That's what I've been trying to tell you," Daimon said.

"Shhhh. Keep your voice down," Johnny said.

Inmate Angel Garza stood nearby, keeping guard so Johnny and Daimon could talk privately. Angel was Hispanic and rough looking. He had years of prison on his face. He always had a look in his eyes warning others not to mess with him. And he was big enough to back it up, too.

Daimon said, "How do you do it, though? I can't make the move." He figured his every twitch was being watched and every conversation he had in his cell was recorded. He was afraid if he tried to set up his plan, it would be discovered.

He talked to Johnny about sending out mail to his friends, hidden in mail from other inmates. He didn't want the cops to read his letters, so other inmates let him piggyback their mail for it to be resent on the outside.

Johnny asked what the problem with Judge Leavitt was and Daimon said, "Oh, Leavitt's a bitch, dude. Leavitt's a fucking bitch." Daimon explained how he had an argument with Judge Leavitt in court. He knew Judge Leavitt was tough, and he might get a long sentence from her. Daimon's anger with her might've started back when Judge Leavitt mistook him for a woman.

Johnny and Daimon spoke about payment for the hits. Daimon said the cops didn't find all of his storage units and, "When my cases get dismissed, I'll get all of the property back that the cops stole."

"If we were to go for the property, how much is it?" Johnny said.

"Millions, dude."

"What I mean is, the refrigerators and sofas are shit. I don't want no refrigerators or sofas. LCD's or something. What . . ."

Daimon cut him off. "All sorts of stuff."

"Good shit?"

"I didn't have anything that wasn't good. I couldn't count it in the millions if it wasn't good. You know what I mean? My refrigerators and freezers were $30,000." Daimon went on, "Bobby's got money, but he ain't moving. He won't move it because of the Feds. The Feds went to his house. The FBI, ROP, and a couple of other people went to his house."

Johnny said, "I mean, I got the people to do it. You know what I'm saying?"

"I know you do."

They spoke about communicating with notes, and Johnny said he didn't want a paper trail. "I send you a note or you send me a note and I wad it up before I flush it."

"That's why when I wrote that thing I crossed it out. You know?" Daimon said.

"Yeah, you crossed it out with black and all that," Johnny said.

"How do you make the move when you're locked down tight?" Daimon asked. "That's what I started to say last night. How do you make a move? It's not easy. It's truly not."

"You know your own people."

"I know my people. I don't know what to do. You tell me how to do it."

"I'm not going to tell you what to do," Johnny said. "That's your decision to make. You know what I mean? Think on it and if you don't want to do it, let's not play games."

"It's not a matter of playing games."

"If you want to hit these mothers, then do it. Especially

with all the shit I'm gonna take. You know what I mean? I already told you how it is. You know what I'm saying? I got people for this. You want to do this or no?"

"I understand. Yes. Money's not really the issue. The issue is making a move. I can't really do it on the phone."

"I'm giving you my bitch's number," Johnny said. "Whenever you need to call her, she'll help. You know what I'm saying? She's picked up money before. She's picked up 30, 50 G's before. It ain't shit to her. She's Chicano, you know what I'm saying?"

"She said she'd call Carlos for me if I gave her the number?"

"I spoke to her about this yesterday. Her name is Jazz. Her real name is Jasmine but call her Jazz."

Daimon was worried the cops might listen to the call. Johnny said he hadn't been calling Jazz directly from the jail. He said he was having other people call Jazz on three-way when he wanted to pass information to her.

Johnny said, "Nobody has called her number from here. So they don't even know if you called. That's what I'm saying. That number is only good for two or three tries and that's it. You can't be calling no more."

"Yeah, you can only call once or twice."

"Yeah, and then it's burned down. Because man, that's how the cops pick it up," Johnny added.

Daimon said his lawyer told him there were paid informants in the housing unit.

"How am I supposed to explain that to my people?" Johnny said.

"No, no, no! Don't worry. I know one of the guys. A guy on the street."

"What guy?"

"A cop," Daimon said.

Johnny sounded alarmed and said, "Cops? You know

cops? Oh, come on, homey. I'm here talking this shit with you and now you say you know cops?"

"I know dudes who were doing business with street cops. They brought cocaine and heroin into the south tower of the jail."

"Metro cops?"

Daimon said, "Like this fuck." He looked in the direction of one of the C.O.'s.

"Oh man, you're telling me you're fucking with cops."

"Dude, a guy named Richard I know and do business with. He never do me wrong."

Johnny said, "I don't get down with cops."

"I don't get down with cops, either, but I can get information from them. I can have your girl call Richard and say 'Hey, check this dude out.'"

"You can do what you want, but that number is good for one, two—three times, tops. And the risk is yours. You know what I mean? In calling her. You know what I'm saying?"

"They're gonna be watching who I call."

Johnny said, "This shit could take six months to a year or even two years."

"That's okay," Daimon said. "I'm going for ROP and that's it. I'm gonna try to shut them down. For real."

"What's that?"

"I'm gonna shut them down."

"I don't give a fuck who ROP is," Johnny said. "They are what they are, homey."

"I'm going to shut them down."

"Fuck the cops. I'm into money. I'm not into cops, homey. I don't work with cops. I don't snitch on cops. I don't do anything with cops. I don't get down with cops. I don't sleep with anybody. That divide and conquer shit, it don't come down on me, you know what I'm saying?"

"That's what I'm talking about."

"You lead the way; I like you because you're hard. You haven't broken and shit. You know what I mean?"

"Yeah," Daimon said.

"That's why I'm willing to get down and do this shit for you. If not, then forget about it."

"Well, the thing is, I'm not gonna burn you, ever. But the thing is, my people are so hesitant, you know, as a group. The last time I spoke to Frank, about two weeks ago, he was like, 'Yeah, we got people to deal with it right now,' and, 'The cops are still checking you now.' But I'm not supposed to talk about it."

Johnny said, "I don't even know why they're putting so much heat on you, you know what I mean? So what, they got $300,000 from you? There's still what—about a million dollars worth of property?"

"No, more than that."

"Whatever."

"More like six million," Daimon said. "I just gotta figure out a way to get a hold of Rob."

Johnny walked off and acted like everything was normal.

But everything wasn't normal. Daimon had no idea Johnny was wearing a wire. Detective Kelley and an FBI agent taped the recording device to the inside of Johnny's leg near the groin in preparation for the meeting in the rec yard.

When Daimon talked about needing to get a hold of Rob, I knew he was talking about Bobby. I thought about the $75,000 still floating around out there.

I knew who Richard was whom Daimon spoke about. Tammy said he fenced stolen property for Daimon. Richard Church—part Japanese, I think. I also knew if Richard was messing with cops on the take, Tammy would've known about it. Daimon would've bragged and I think she would've told me. Or would she?

Detective Kelley's case was supposed to crescendo with

Daimon making arrangements for money to be exchanged. Johnny gave Daimon the phone number to call "Jazz." What Daimon didn't know is Jazz was actually an undercover detective. Johnny said Jazz was his girlfriend in Southern California. The phone number even had a Southern California area code to make it appear legit.

Daimon was supposed to call the number and connect Jazz to Carlos or someone to supply the money. But if the money never came through, it didn't matter much. The case was already solid for soliciting murder. That bridge was crossed when Daimon began asking Johnny to provide a hit man.

During this time period, a software upgrade to the inmate phone system was being installed and tested. There were bugs in the system that caused problems. The inmate phone calls weren't free and the person receiving the calls had to have an account set up with the service provider. Many inmates were having their calls rejected as the system wasn't recognizing some of the paid accounts.

I discovered several call attempts from Daimon's housing unit to the undercover number. On a couple of the recordings, I could hear Daimon's voice right next to the mouthpiece, speaking to another inmate while waiting for the system to complete the call. But the system didn't recognize the account and the calls never went through. I alerted Detective Kelley, and he scrambled to fix the problem, to no avail. After a couple of days, the call attempts stopped.

I wish those calls had gone through. It would've been interesting to hear what Daimon would say to Jazz. That surely would've sealed Detective Kelley's case. It was good already, but a conversation with Jazz might've made it bulletproof.

When the phone system had trouble, Daimon somehow figured out Johnny was snitching. Maybe Johnny pushed too hard for information or something. Maybe he panicked when the calls wouldn't go through to the undercover number and said something that tipped Daimon off.

Daimon wasn't stupid. Being smart *and* paranoid might be the perfect blend that helped him detect something about Johnny. Or maybe someone on the outside told him Johnny was snitching. Daimon said he had contacts. Or maybe he was still in contact with Tammy through another inmate. Or even worse—maybe a certain loose-lipped C.O. said the wrong thing to somebody.

This ended Johnny's involvement with the investigation. Detective Kelley had jail classification move Johnny into protective custody. He needed to be kept safe. It wouldn't take long before the entire inmate population knew at least some of what was going on. Detective Kelley's next move was to interview Daimon and see what he had to say. <>

29

PAINT

The search for truth is more precious than its possession.

—ALBERT EINSTEIN

*D*aimon would likely deny everything and claim he was set up. But even then, a good detective can paint a man into a corner, so he can't later change his story without exposing his deceit. At a minimum, Detective Kelley wanted to look straight into Daimon's eyes and let him know the game was up. Probably the best way to push Daimon into ending his pursuit of having people killed—at least for now.

Detective Kelley and his sergeant interviewed Daimon in a private room at the jail on November 11, 2007. After the introductions and niceties were over, Detective Kelley said, "We've received what we believe to be at least marginally credible information that you may be attempting to cause harm to either a police detective or a District Court Judge."

His eyes pierced the air between him and Daimon.

Daimon laughed.

"So you can see from our standpoint as police officers, we're going to react to it pretty conservatively and in the best way . . ."

Daimon interrupted. "That's what this is about?"

"That's exactly what this is about."

Daimon laughed again.

"If you'd like to make a comment, you're more than welcome to. If not, then we just want you to know the . . ."

Daimon interrupted again. "I know. I appreciate it."

"So until we investigate it all, the best thing is to isolate you. That way we don't have to worry about things."

"How in the world would I do that?" Daimon said.

"I don't know. You tell me how you would do it," Detective Kelley said. "You'd save me a lot of time and trouble if you'd tell me you know a way to do it."

"Honest to God, dude. Metro's fucking with my mail. They've threatened everybody I know. I can't call anybody any more. Everybody's scared to come by me. This whole thing is psychotic. They have everybody under the sun, you know, like rats and C.I.'s working on me. I actually thought this was something completely different. This is even more bizarre than what I thought I was coming in here for. Because I mean, there's a C.I. out there on the floor named Johnny Marquez, and he came to me and said they were looking at me for murder."

Johnny wasn't the inmate who told Daimon about Chris Trickle. Daimon just threw it on the table like a trophy to show Detective Kelley that Johnny was burned. Daimon had made the first move in their invisible chess match.

Daimon continued, "I thought the dude was a psychopath. I mean it was just . . . dude! I'm charged with things that are just ridiculous, okay? So this guy was, he would come to me and he would say he was Mexican Mafia and he was this, this and this. So I just listened, 'cause most of these people are, are kind of losers, you know?"

Daimon was trying to break down Johnny's credibility and make him look like a liar. But he didn't know about the covert recording in the rec yard.

Detective Kelley said, "Well, the information we got is you are actively trying to pursue someone on the outside who will cause harm to either one of the detectives investigating your case, the district court judge hearing the case or the prosecutor prosecuting you."

"What's the point of all this?"

"Well, I don't know, but you know when we get allegations or accusations like that, we take them seriously."

"You should," Daimon said with a smirk.

"Is there any chance you may have said something to someone that could've been misconstrued?"

"Are you kidding me? Dude, are you kidding me? Listen to me: I've never done a drug in my life. I don't drink and I don't smoke. My head's pretty clear. People I'm locked up with are uh, I don't want to say—they all got their issues—you understand? But dude, you don't say shit like that in jail. I'm not stupid."

"I know you have to be in a very frustrating situation. And I know sometimes you just get to the point you're ready to, you know, to just scream. So, I mean, I could understand if a person were to off-handedly say something that was misconstrued."

Detective Kelley was trying to soften Daimon up. Goad him to admit something he couldn't take back, yet at the same time, let him minimize and claim he didn't mean anything by it. Paint him in a corner.

Daimon responded by telling a long story about the weird stuff he'd seen in the jail and how a snitch was put in his cell. He spoke about a conversation he had with this supposed snitch: "He said, 'Look man,' these are his exact words: 'ROP fucked up. Careers are on the line and they're gonna fuck you to put themselves in the clear.' "

The interview went on for several more minutes and amounted to nothing more than a long series of denials from Daimon. Not surprisingly, Daimon volunteered to take a lie detector test. Lie detector tests—more professionally termed polygraph examinations—generally aren't admissible in criminal proceedings; the courts recognize they lack a necessary degree of certainty. They aren't much more than a tool to motivate someone to tell the truth. There's some science to it, although not enough for conclusive results. If I wasn't sure before, I was sure of it now—Daimon is probably a sociopath who could pass a lie detector test without a qualm or flinch.

Jail Classification moved Daimon into isolation to make sure he wasn't able to shop his plan around any longer. It made it easier to monitor his phone activity and eliminated his ability to have other inmates secretly send out mail for him.

After a couple weeks, Detective Kelley called and said his investigation was almost complete. He still had a few loose ends to tie up. One was to interview Carlos, but he couldn't be found. Carlos had quit his job at a casino, and his neighbors hadn't seen him in a couple of months. Carlos wasn't taking Daimon's calls, and I was out of leads to help Detective Kelley find him.

I called Tammy and asked if she could guess where Carlos might go. She said he had family in Mexico and sometimes went there for a couple months at a time.

I suggested to Detective Kelley he could apply for a warrant and ping Carlos' cell phone for GPS coordinates. But the idea was put on the back burner so other, more traditional methods, could be tried first. <>

30

//////////

LOOSE ENDS

*Accursed who brings to light of day the writings I
have cast away.*

—WILLIAM BUTLER YEATS

A week or so later, Detective Kelley submitted his case to
the D.A.'s Office for review. He wasn't sure whether the
screening D.A. would approve the case, but he had submitted
it for three counts of soliciting murder. The investigation
showed Daimon hadn't found someone to do the hits—yet.
But Daimon had solicited Johnny, who kept him occupied
and thinking he was Daimon's go-to guy. Thankfully, this
kept Daimon from soliciting someone else who might indeed
try to carry out the murders.

In Detective Kelley's investigation, Johnny turned over
the handwritten notes he had received from Daimon. Starting
with the most incriminating, the notes from Daimon read
[sic]:

Go with killing levit, nicols, hold digiccamo I had
someone who came to me yesterday asking who I want
killed, and they would do it for free, and if I new anyone
Here who could get things done on the streets. I just didn't
answer then he said He had a new DA on his case named
(digiacomo) they asked if I new where to find someone
to get info on there (case). So I just didn't answer, Im
going to get my people to Run this guy. Or do I let you
handle It, you where 100% WRight, my mouth is Shut
thanx foR keeping my head together.

Listen my attorney told me they have2 people
On the Cotts trying to extract info- apparently
there concerned with, 2 people in here, she said
that they purposley Seperated these 2 people for
concern of them getting together, they supposdley
think these people are connected! She told me to
be careful because these people could be wired for
sound if the opportunity presents itself, she also
said they might try to talk to people these people
talk to! So obviously it will be good to keep your
eyes and ears to the ground!

Checkyour vent. Mine has a little black like pin thing
in the back now, and they went through my paperwork.

Set it up with the hit,S.$ your attorney if you can

How to do it! You Figure a way on that you would
be better with that since your talking to your lawyer
Ill see what I can do on the Brady Bunch. No Mas
Hablendo (no more talking) Yo peinsa este bueno
ahora mismo (I think this good right now)

I tried to get ahold of my paisa to see whats up and
for $ I talk to a friend who said he got some
info for me. And trying to see if my buddy put my
song book at his house. I'll let you know what's up .
Talk to Jazz, to see if he put $ on my books for me.

I tried the # not working yet, Im going to call Christy,
she knows what's up. We may also need someone to
go by Carlos, work, to see what is the word, need
him to grab some "$ for books?" and see what isgoing
on? Im trying to stay low, and relax, and I'll talk to you
at rec.

These aren't all the notes that Johnny turned over, but
they're the most important. Handwriting analysis was done
on the notes and compared to Daimon's known handwriting.
Some of the results affirmed Daimon as being the author
and some were inconclusive. But none of the notes were
conclusively *not* Daimon's handwriting.

Handwriting comparison is not like you see on the
popular TV show, *CSI*. There has to be enough of a sample for
the examiner to note distinctive features in the handwriting.
The note with the scribbled out text was one of the notes
confirmed to be Daimon's handwriting. The note was put
through a spectrum comparator using different infrared
filters that separated the lead obliterating the actual writing.
The comparisons were made with other writings Daimon
had sent making complaints or requests to jail personnel.

Near the end of January 2008, the D.A.'s Office approved
three counts of soliciting murder against Daimon. He was the
top story on the local TV stations that evening and the next
morning, the newspaper gave him the front page. For a few

days, the news media scrambled to get their facts straight and their coverage focused on the judge being targeted.

A reporter from the Associated Press kept leaving messages at my office. He wanted a scoop. I thought about calling him back, but there was no benefit in it. The press often writes what they want with barely enough truth sprinkled in to call it legit. I trashed the guy's phone number.

A couple of days later, Detective Kelley found Carlos at home. Carlos invited Detective Kelley inside and they sat around a coffee table. The house was in a dilapidated neighborhood where most kids don't play outside after dark, but the house was well kept and had a splash of traditional Mexican décor. Most notably, though, there was no evidence visible of grandiosity or hoarding of stolen riches like there was in Daimon's house.

Carlos said he didn't know anything about the murder-for-hire plot. He had been in Mexico for a couple of months and had just returned to Las Vegas to resume his job at the casino. He said he didn't want anything to do with Daimon anymore, which is why he stopped taking his calls.

Detective Kelley said, "He has made some statements about giving you something like half a million dollars in cash to hold for him. Is there any truth to that?"

In his Spanish accent, Carlos said, "No, it's no true. You can check my checkbooks and everything. I got my—matter of fact, I got my statement from the bank. I have like $2,100 in there." Carlos leaned over and sifted through a stack of mail on the table. "I got a loan for my—I got that second mortgage—I got some money but I spent it already. I went to Mexico for a couple of months."

"Do you have any money that belongs to Daimon?"

"Not at all. He never give me any money, and I don't know how he can give it to me."

"Do you know who Tammy is?"

"Yes, but not too much."

"Do you know where she is?"

"As far as I know, she's in Kansas. As far as I know."

"Okay, do you know where in Kansas?"

"No. I talk to her a couple times when Daimon is in jail. It was about over a year."

"Okay. You haven't spoken to her in a year?"

"No. And to be honest, I call once and her Mom answer the phone and she say, 'Please don't call here anymore.' So I stop calling."

Detective Kelley said, "Okay, well one of the things he said—and we kind of intercepted some paperwork he was writing—your plan was to kidnap Tammy and the girls and take them to Mexico, so they couldn't testify against him. Is there any truth to that?"

"I don't know about what you said. I was in Mexico a couple months. I just got back. To be honest, I open a nightclub over there."

"In Mexico?"

"In Mexico. The money—I tell you, I don't have nothing to hide—and the money that I use for that was my loan, which was $47,000. And to be honest, it's not—I cannot kidnap anybody, and I say I don't want to risk my life or risk my freedom for something that's not worth it."

Carlos dug his cell phone out of his pocket and said, "He used to call me on this phone. And to be honest, I have nothing to hide. I stopped taking his calls because he got to the point—annoying. He tell me the same thing, over and over."

Detective Kelley said, "About?"

"'Did you see Tammy?' No, I didn't see Tammy. 'Can you please talk to her?' No, I cannot talk to her because she don't want me to talk to her. And, he never called for nothing else so, to me, it got to the point that I cannot—he is my friend, and I don't want to be like that because I cannot say, he is not my friend. And for whatever reason, I stop the calls for that reason. It's for that reason because he was—call me a lot. And my phone bill start getting high."

Carlos said he even stopped opening the mail Daimon was sending to him. He gave Detective Kelley several unopened letters from Daimon and said he didn't want them. He said if he received more from Daimon, he'd be happy to turn them over.

Detective Kelley asked Carlos how he met Daimon.

"I met him like because of the music; I used to have a band. We used to play it right in the garage. That's fifteen years ago. So one time, Daimon stop and hear and, just starting to listen to us. We were playing Mexican music. Latino music. And, he sit down, he told me, 'Do you mind if I sit and listen to music?' I said, 'No, you're welcome.' And I think he was a bass player, but I think he play rock music. Something completely different from my music."

The house Bobby grew up in on Virgin Street was only a couple of blocks away. For Daimon to be passing by at some point and hear the Mexican band playing made sense. Daimon always had a strong interest in music of all kinds.

Detective Kelley said, "Do you know Steve Fulmer?"

"I just hear his name but I don't know him."

"Daimon told Fulmer you quit accepting his calls because the police were over here harassing you about knowing him."

Carlos said, "They never—this is the first time somebody contacted me."

"Okay, so you had no problem with anyone from the police department?"

"No, not whatsoever. If there something wrong, I would have tell you or go straight to the police department to find out."

Detective Kelley ended the interview and gave Carlos

his business card. The final loose ends in the murder-for-hire investigation were tied up.

On January 25, 2008, Daimon was arraigned in Justice Court on the solicitation of murder charges. Judge Lippis said in open court that she found Daimon to be an incredible danger to the community. She set his bail on the case at over two million dollars. With the multiple cases against him, that brought Daimon's total bail to almost three million dollars.

Daimon was all over the local TV news that night. They had cameras in the courtroom when he was brought before Judge Lippis. There was some kind of dark colored writing on his arms. I took a closer look at the TV. Daimon had used something like a black marker pen to write "STOP" on his right forearm and "CORUPTION" [sic] on his left. Daimon made sure the cameras saw it. His smug face reminded me of The Joker again. It caused me to chuckle, especially since he didn't know corruption is spelled with two Rs. The news reported that Daimon claimed innocence and that he told the judge he was willing to take a lie detector test.

I thought, of course he's willing! Pathological liars consider taking polygraphs as the Holy Grail—the highest proof of their skill in deception.

Judge Leavitt removed herself from the big property case about a week after the story broke. Judges have to maintain the highest level of impartiality. That could be a problem with her making rulings on someone who had "allegedly" plotted to kill her. It would definitely create an appeal issue if she didn't step down.

The Chief Judge reassigned the case to Judge Bell, the judge who signed my first set of search warrants on the case. The bad thing for Daimon was Judge Bell had developed the reputation of being one of the toughest judges on repeat criminals in our District Court. And with Judge Bell's many years of experience in three different roles in the courtroom, he knew how to make sure a bullet-proof record would be preserved to stave off appeals. <>

31

////////

SHEEP AND
WOLVES

*Panic is a sudden desertion of us, and a going over
to the enemy of our imagination.*

—CHRISTIAN NESTELL BOVEE

*D*aimon filed a civil rights complaint in federal court.
"It names you, me, and the police department as
defendants," Sandy said.

In Daimon's thirteen-page handwritten complaint,
he claimed that under color of law we'd violated his due
process, illegally searched and seized his property, applied
unreasonable bail, and denied him an attorney. He wrote
about how the cops were harassing him and his friends,
illegally detaining him, and had knocked his tooth out. He
also asserted there were no search warrants for his house.
Daimon proposed relief of $48 million, plus $1,200 per day

for "illegal incarceration" and, "any other award the court deems appropriate."

After reading Daimon's complaint, I wasn't riled. Everything he claimed was fantasy, good only for amusement. Unfortunately, in courtrooms nowadays, it's about what lawyers can convince people to believe, which doesn't always mean the truth. It's asinine, when you consider the enormous taxpayer cost for our system to continually entertain such false and frivolous claims.

As I was about to leave Sandy's office, her investigator, Jerome Revels, took me aside. He said he was having trouble serving a subpoena on Sam Hopkins, the office manager from the dentist office. Mr. Hopkins had already testified long ago at the preliminary hearing, and Sandy would soon need him to repeat it before a jury. Jerome tried to contact him several times by phone and had been to Mr. Hopkins' home the day before. The housekeeper said Mr. Hopkins wasn't home, and she was less than cooperative in trying to find him. Jerome said Mr. Hopkins' car was in the driveway, and he was probably in the house, hiding.

I went back into Sandy's office and she was on the phone. With the phone by her ear, she pointed at it with her other hand and mouthed "Adams." She was on the phone with Dr. Adams, and they were having a discussion about Mr. Hopkins coming to court.

Dr. Adams told Sandy that Mr. Hopkins wouldn't be available to testify. Sandy couldn't get her to elaborate and finally said, "Then I'll just have *you* come in and testify."

I couldn't hear the response from Dr. Adams, but Sandy looked irritated. She glared as she held her breath and did her best not to say something petulant.

"Are you telling me you are going to come to court and lie?"

Dr. Adams said she wasn't sure if Daimon and Bryan

were supposed to be in her business that night or not. Shortly thereafter, Sandy ended the call.

Something was definitely strange. Ordinary people don't behave this way. Ordinary people come to court and tell the truth when asked. Ordinary people don't avoid subpoenas when someone has victimized them. Especially in cases lacking violence where there's no real fear of retaliation.

"I said, "Do you want me to help serve the subpoena? I've met them both and they were really friendly and cooperative with me then."

"Sure. Give it a try and let me know what happens. If you can get Hopkins or Adams served, either one will be fine. I'll just deal with her on the stand if I have to," Sandy said.

I called Mr. Hopkins on his cell. "This is Sam," he answered.

I was on the tenth floor of the D.A.'s Office and my cell signal was terrible. I moved to the window hoping for better reception.

"This is Brad Nickell. Are you in Las Vegas?"

Click . . .

I wasn't sure whether I had lost signal or he had hung up. I tried to call him back and it went to voice mail. I tried a few more times with the same result. I ended up leaving a message, asking him to call. I never heard from him.

I drove to the dental office to find Mr. Hopkins or Dr. Adams, so we could speak face-to-face. When I walked in, I showed the receptionist my badge and asked to see Mr. Hopkins. The woman said she hadn't seen him in about three weeks. Dr. Adams was out for lunch.

"Could you call Dr. Adams on her cell and see if she'll meet with me?" The call was made and Dr. Adams said she'd be back in ten minutes. As I waited, I filled out some information on the subpoena I was about to serve.

Dr. Adams arrived and took me into a small room with a

table and a couple of chairs. She closed the door, sat down and folded her hands together. "Mr. Hopkins isn't going to be available for court."

"Why is that?"

"He's going out of state on a family emergency. His mother is ill and is going to have surgery."

"Can you appear? We only need someone who can say these men didn't have permission to be in your business that night."

The skin on her face tightened and her voice went up in volume and tone. "I wouldn't be a good witness for you."

"Why not?" I said.

"A lot of our employees have keys and there are cleaning people and others who come in and out of the office. I don't know who might've been allowed to be in there that night."

I wrinkled my brow and said, "But all those people would have a key and the alarm code, right? They would've deactivated the alarm and probably would've still been there when the cops showed up, right?"

Dr. Adams said, "I don't even know if anyone really was in the business. We're a dentist office for children, and we have a lot of balloons floating around all the time. They sometimes set off the alarm at night."

"But a witness saw two men enter your business by using some kind of burglary tool."

"*I* wasn't there and *I* didn't see it happen," she said with a snotty tone.

At that moment, I realized Dr. Adams had already thought through this question and answer session. She wasn't about to budge.

Finally, Dr. Adams said she could ask the office manager at her other office to testify. I asked Dr. Adams to call and let her know I'd be coming. We walked out into the common area of the office and the tension seemed to subside for a moment.

I said, "Was this woman an employee of yours when the burglary actually happened?"

"No."

"Then how can she come in and testify that these two people weren't allowed in your office if she didn't work for you then?"

"I don't know," she said with a specious tone.

"Well, this cat-and-mouse game is going nowhere," I said as I handed her the subpoena.

She put it down on the counter and said, "I'm not accepting that."

"You can't *not* accept it, you've been served." I said, as I almost chuckled. The situation had eroded into something close to humor, yet not funny.

Dr. Adams looked at me, grabbed some other papers out of my hand and ripped them into pieces, right there in front of everyone on her staff.

"What are you doing?" I calmly asked.

Everything in the office stopped—everyone was watching. Dr. Adams was embarrassed and with a startled sort of look, she quickly glanced at her staff. She took me by the hand and marshaled me back into the small room, where I made sure the door was kept open.

Dr. Adams had to be acting so frantically for good reason. She kept rambling about how I wouldn't be able to change her mind. I asked her to let me speak. When she finally did, I said, "Have you been contacted by someone? Has someone threatened you?"

"No, I just won't be a good witness."

"So you're going to come to court with a clear conscience and testify like you just told me?"

She looked me plain in the face and said, "Yes."

I saw fear. It was undeniable. I've seen fear in the eyes of people many, many times. We talked for a few more minutes, and Dr. Adams said, "I am not risking my life over this."

I could tell she wanted to reach out and grab the words back. Despite further attempts, Dr. Adams wouldn't elaborate. I left the dentist office with the subpoena sitting on the table.

I sat in my car and collected my thoughts. I wondered what happened to make these people behave like this. I wondered if someone had paid them a visit and made threats, or maybe someone called or wrote a letter. Bobby was out on bail, and Tammy said he visited Mr. Chen at the crystal shop to get a feel for him. Did Bobby visit someone at the dentist office? Or maybe they'd seen the news coverage about the murder-for-hire charges on Daimon, and they were overreacting. Either way, I understood their fear. I found it contemptible, but I understood it.

After I drove away, I called Dr. Adams. "If Mr. Hopkins truly is going to be unavailable and out of state for the trial, the D.A. might be able to get his testimony from the preliminary hearing introduced into the record in his absence. But he'd truly have to be out of state, and we'd have to be able to prove it."

She said, "What do you want, medical records for his mom?"

"No, is he flying? A plane ticket or something showing he's going to be gone would work great."

"He was planning on driving, do you want him to fly?"

"No, no, no. I want him to do whatever he was already going to do. We just need some proof that he truly is unavailable."

Dr. Adams said she'd talk to Mr. Hopkins and get back with me.

As I drove home, I thought of the contrast between me, Mr. Hopkins, and Dr. Adams. They wanted this whole Daimon

Monroe thing to simply go away, so they could continue, uninterrupted, in their lives. They wanted to act as though nothing had ever happened. I can't blame them, though, as they didn't have anything stolen or damaged. What was in it for them other than headache and worry? I, on the other hand wanted to see Daimon and Bryan brought to justice for their crimes. They'd victimized too many people without restrain. I have no doubt they were one of the greatest crime-waves to ever hit this town. They needed to be held accountable.

I thought of a lecture I'd attended a few years before. The speaker was retired Lieutenant Colonel Dave Grossman, former West Point psychology professor and Army Ranger. He was also a Pulitzer Prize nominated author and one of the world's leading experts in the psychology of killing. During his lecture, Colonel Grossman used a great story to illustrate the difference between ordinary citizens, bad guys, and cops or soldiers.

Colonel Grossman said, "Most of the people in our society are sheep. They're kind, gentle, productive creatures who only hurt one another by accident. Then there are the wolves, who feed on the sheep without mercy. Last, there are sheepdogs and I'm a sheepdog. I live to protect the flock and confront the wolf."

Colonel Grossman went on to explain how the sheep generally don't like the sheepdog as he looks a lot like the wolf. He has sharp teeth, cunning, and the capacity for violence. "The sheepdog must never harm the sheep. If he does, he'll be punished and removed."

"But the sheep are bothered by the sheepdog nonetheless. He's a constant reminder that there are wolves in the land. They would prefer the sheepdog didn't tell them where to go, or stand at the ready in our airports in camouflage fatigues with rifles or write them traffic tickets."

"What the sheep would really prefer to see is for the

sheepdog to turn in his fangs, spray-paint himself white, and say, 'Baaa.' That is, of course, until the wolf shows up! Then the entire flock cries for the lonely sheepdog and desperately wants his protection."

Colonel Grossman finished the story by explaining how we must understand there's nothing morally superior to being a sheepdog. It's just what he had chosen to be. The sheepdog is a funny animal, always sniffing around somewhere, checking the breeze, barking at things that go bump in the night, and hoping he'll soon find a wolf stalking the sheep.

It's this very thing that illustrates how the sheep and the sheepdog think differently. The sheep act as though the wolf will never come, but the sheepdog lives for that day. After the attacks on September 11, 2001, most of the sheep, that is, most citizens in America thought, "Thank God I wasn't on one of those planes." But the sheepdogs thought, *"Dear God, I wish I could've been on one of those planes. Maybe I could've made a difference."* <>

32

////////////

THE FIRST TRIAL

I consider trial by jury as the only anchor ever yet imagined by man, by which a government can be held to the principles of its constitution.
—Thomas Jefferson

On February 19, 2008, the Clark County Grand Jury convened to hear the case about the murder-for-hire plot. I was brought before the grand jury primarily to put a victim's face to the crime and provide motive for Daimon's fury. When my testimony was complete and I left the grand jury room, I saw Johnny Marquez sitting in the hallway waiting to testify. This was the first and only time I'd see him in person. He was seated next to a C.O. and was wearing orange and blue jail garb and belly chains. Someone must've told him who I was. We didn't speak to each other, yet when our eyes met, there was a message. I nodded to him as a thank-you for doing the right thing. He pursed his lips and nodded back.

When the grand jury was done hearing from the witnesses, they deliberated and returned a true bill for three counts of soliciting murder. The case was sent straight to District Court.

Daimon and Bryan's jury trial for the crystal shop and dentist office burglaries began that same day. Sandy and Deputy D.A. Sam Bateman teamed up to handle the trial. I didn't know Sam well up to that point. He seemed to be a sharp, young prosecutor who spoke well and came across as a pro. Sam's brownish, clean-cut hair, and boyish appearance made him look much younger than he was.

On that first day, Mr. Chen was the only witness to testify. Other court matters took longer than expected. The second day, the patrolmen, Mr. Hopkins, and a few other witnesses testified. Sandy had learned that Mr. Hopkins was friends with Bryan's attorney, Mr. Kocka. She said Mr. Hopkins was a difficult witness—even a little argumentative—but he testified truthfully and provided what was necessary, a victim.

The next day, I checked Matthew and the other burglary tools out of the evidence vault and went to the courthouse. With court in recess, I spoke with Daimon's attorney, Mr. Hart, for a few moments. I was acquainted with him from his days as a prosecutor. I asked why he left the *good guy* team. He said politics in the D.A.'s Office had caused him to leave, although he added that the money was a lot better now. We talked and laughed for a few moments until the jury was ready to be brought into the courtroom.

Daimon and Bryan were dressed in suits that their attorneys had provided. Many attorneys actually have a small wardrobe of different sizes to fit different clients. The courts like to make sure the in-custody defendants are dressed nicely for trial. They don't want juries to convict based on appearance, so they disguise the fact that defendants are in jail for fear of it being prejudicial.

Daimon's hair was longer again, down past the middle of his back and all brown except on the ends. The bleached blonde look was almost gone.

Neither Daimon nor Bryan made eye contact with me. I looked at Daimon a few times and could tell he was fighting the urge. There was a sort of thickness in the air. Maybe like when a wolf knows he's being watched by a sheepdog.

I was called to the stand and sworn in. During my testimony, I explained how I used Matthew to open the doors of the crystal shop and the dentist office without damaging the doors. I described the motions it took to make the tool work; how I unlocked the door and pulled up on Matthew to disengage the locking mechanism. While I was talking about it, Sandy displayed the demo photos I had taken, on a video screen.

From the witness stand, I noticed Daimon leaning over with his hand over his mouth, whispering to Mr. Hart. Daimon seemed excited about something.

Sandy played portions of seven jail phone calls from the hundreds of calls to which I'd listened. When the phone calls were complete, it was time for the defense attorneys to cross-examine me. During both cross-examinations, there weren't any tough questions or anything I felt might confuse the jury.

Mr. Kocka asked how I knew it was Bryan and Daimon on the phones. The explanation was simple. His last question was, "So, you believe this is my client talking on the phone?"

I paused for a moment and said, "No, I'm certain it is."

My testimony was complete and I was dismissed.

The defense didn't put on a case. Daimon and Bryan

didn't testify and their attorneys called no witnesses. They had nothing to refute the evidence and saved their case for closing arguments. Their strategy was to persuade the jury that the state failed to prove guilt beyond a reasonable doubt.

I stayed in the courtroom to watch the closing arguments of the trial. My experience all those years with courtroom happenings had always been simple: show up, testify, and leave. I'd never observed closing arguments before, but wanted to see it for myself this time.

D.A. Sam Bateman presented the closing for the state. He did a good job and was obviously well prepared. Sam had a Power Point presentation with photographs and point-by-point information about the elements of each crime. When he finished his closing, I thought he had done a great job of addressing anything that might be a foothold for reasonable doubt.

The defense made their closing arguments and, when Mr. Kocka spoke, he brought up a few minor inconsistencies in the testimony of some of the witnesses. His mantra was about holding the state to its burden of proving guilt beyond a reasonable doubt. Defense attorneys aren't allowed to directly tell the jury to hold the state to the burden of *no doubt*. But he hit the idea of reasonable doubt so hard I thought the jury might get confused about the distinction. Insert the names Casey Anthony or O.J. Simpson here. Same idea.

When Mr. Hart made his closing arguments, he put up a photograph on the video screen. One of the demo photos of the Matthew tool at the dentist office was on display. I wasn't sure what he had planned. He approached the jury and reminded them of my testimony about the motions I'd made using Matthew to unlock the door. He emphasized how I said I pulled up on the tool during the process. He gestured just as I had with his hands and made a face that implied confusion as he pointed at the screen. He showed the jury it was impossible for the door to be unlocked by pulling up. Of course, he didn't elaborate and tell them that pushing down would do it. He merely wanted to highlight that what I said was impossible.

A wave like a hot-flash rolled over me. Mr. Hart was right. My memory was wrong about how I opened the doors. I must've pushed down rather than pulled up. But I'd only used Matthew to open doors a couple times in my life—and that was more than a year before. My memory was faulty. But Mr. Hart tried to create the belief that I'd lied. If the jury thought I had, they might disregard my entire testimony. I probably should've done the Matthew demo on video rather than still photography. But that was hindsight.

Mr. Hart was smart to address this issue during his closing arguments. Had he questioned me about it during his cross-examination, Sandy would've easily cleaned it up on her re-direct. But he didn't want me to have the opportunity to clean it up. It seemed clear what Daimon had been whispering to Mr. Hart earlier. He knew I was wrong. After all, he's the world's foremost expert on how Matthew works.

Sandy presented the state's rebuttal to the defense closing. She started with probably the best statement she possibly could. "Hold the state to our burden of proof beyond a reasonable doubt? *Absolutely* hold the state to that burden."

Sandy refuted the points Mr. Kocka and Mr. Hart had made in their closing arguments. She addressed the issue of pulling up on Matthew instead of pushing down and said, "Don't be swayed by some confusion in how the lock works, because the tool still opened the doors."

When Sandy was done, the jury was taken to the deliberation room.

Outside the presence of the jury, Judge Wall said he would only keep the jury about another two hours, as he had promised they'd be done by 5:30 p.m. each day. If the jury hadn't completed deliberating by then, the judge would send them home, and they'd have to come back the next day to continue. The court recessed and Daimon and Bryan were taken back to the jail.

I approached Mr. Hart and said, "Good job!" extending my hand to shake his.

"What for?"

"That was a good catch. Obviously, my memory was faulty about the tool, and you picked up on it. I hope the jury can get past that."

It's almost like playing chess, congratulating an opponent for taking advantage of a false move.

We finished our discussion and I left the courtroom. But I decided to stay with Sandy at least until the jury came back or was released for the day. If it were to happen that day, I wanted to see the verdict come in.

About an hour and a half later, Sandy received a call from the court clerk. The jury was coming back. We went to the courtroom and the jury was brought in. The jury foreman presented the verdict forms to the court clerk. Judge Wall instructed Daimon and Bryan to rise and told the clerk to read the verdicts.

Daimon and Bryan were found guilty of both burglaries, grand larceny from the crystal shop, and possession of burglary tools.

When the verdicts were being read, Daimon and Bryan were silent. Bryan was expressionless. Daimon's face was flushed, and his expression looked like he was holding back tears. But they wouldn't have been tears from a man who was wrongly convicted. They would've been tears from a wolf who knew some dumb old sheepdog had foiled him.

Sandy, Sam Bateman, Mr. Kocka, and I later met with the jury while they were downstairs, collecting their jury pay. This is something prosecutors and defense attorneys often do for feedback on how well they did their jobs. I didn't want to miss the opportunity to talk with the jurors and answer questions they might have.

One of the jury members said finding Daimon and Bryan guilty was easy and the longest part of their deliberations was filling out the verdict forms. The jury foreman piped up, saying everyone in the jury wanted to come back faster with the verdicts, but he settled them down, made them go through each element of each crime, and made sure they did it as they were instructed by the judge.

Another juror said, "You can tell us now—this whole thing has to be part of something a lot bigger, right?"

Sandy said, "Well, you've probably seen on TV the story with someone wanting to murder a judge, a D.A., and a detective? That would be us." She pointed at herself and me.

The eyes of a couple of the jurors widened, and they seemed astonished they hadn't figured it out on their own. Sandy also did her best to embarrass me by saying, "And if it weren't for this detective putting in tons of work, none of this would've ever happened. These guys would probably have gotten misdemeanors."

I revealed that Daimon was a nineteen-time convicted felon, and he'd been doing this for years. That seemed to give the jury considerable satisfaction, to know they'd done their part to help make the community a better, safer place.

My final words were, "I really want to commend you for not buying into the B.S. this guy tried to feed you," as I put my hand on Mr. Kocka's shoulder. I said it in jest, although it wasn't an illusive statement. We chuckled about it.

Mr. Kocka feigned offense. "Wait a minute, B.S.? I thought I did a pretty good job!"

After a few days, I checked on Daimon's calls to see if there was reaction to the guilty verdicts. I knew he'd be more desperate than ever—who knows what he might intend to do. He might slip up and say something that would help prove his guilt in his remaining cases.

Daimon had called Steve a few times and lamented about being found guilty. He said, "We were doing real good until the last day. Then the detective came in and lied. You know, my attorney did a real bad job on cross-examination. We had them beat but my attorney messed up."

I did extensive searching on Bryan's phone activity. I checked every phone call made from his housing unit and searched a full, two-month time period. I manually scanned over twenty-five hundred phone calls and never once heard Bryan's voice or anyone talking about Bryan. Either Bryan was smart enough not to use the phones or he didn't have anyone who would take his calls. <>

33

///////////

PAPER
TERRORISM

Guilt has very quick ears to an accusation.

—HENRY FIELDING

*I*n April 2008, Charlie Waterman of Las Vegas died of a heart attack at age seventy-nine. Charlie had been appointed to represent Daimon in the murder-for-hire case. He was a prominent defense attorney who was known as a hardnosed, no-nonsense, get-it-done kind of guy with juice. He had access to old Las Vegas power and influence. He had been the Chairman of the Democratic Party in Clark County for more than twenty years. He was so well known and respected that U.S. Senate Majority Leader, Harry Reid (from Nevada) released a public statement regarding Charlie's passing. Charlie would've been a formidable adversary in the courtroom. Daimon had no idea what he missed out on in Charlie. Nevertheless, the ride ahead would still be rough.

In the sex-abuse case, the defense would probably try to make my teeny-tiny involvement seem colossal. To whip up the whole corrupt police conspiracy theory, someone would have to be the center of it. Making it seem as though I coerced Tammy and the girls into saying what they did would be the key. Perhaps Daimon's only chance was an all or nothing proposal. But this is Las Vegas and people are used to that. "Roll the dice, baby. I'm all in."

Daimon continued sounding paranoid on the phone. I wasn't sure if there was a real element of psychosis to it or if Daimon was simply playing the game. His collection of conspiracy theories and false accusations about police misconduct could've been just a smoke screen for the phones.

I wondered how long it would take for Daimon to come up with the idea that ROP had Charlie killed. That sure would fit into his conspiracy theories. He told friends his life was in danger in jail. He told people one of his attorneys was working with ROP. He claimed I didn't have search warrants and was covering it up. It would be too easy for him to think the cops killed Charlie, as we were afraid of facing him in court.

May 1, 2008—Tammy called to ask about court dates. We discussed whether or not she'd need to travel soon. It was hard for her to find someone to watch the kids and make the necessary arrangements to travel on only a few days' notice so many times.

"I have some other news," Tammy said.

"Lay it on me."

"I got married."

"Wow. Congratulations! That's awesome."

"He's a pretty good guy and he even thinks he might want to be a cop someday."

"You're like a butterfly, changing from one life into another."

"It hasn't been easy," Tammy said. "I've been scared a lot and just worried about what I'm going to do."

"Have you checked into getting back into teaching?"

"Yeah, but it just doesn't seem to be working out, so I've been waiting tables. The hours make it easy for me to be with the kids."

"Speaking of the kids, how are the girls doing?" I said.

"They're good. I have them seeing a counselor, and that's helping them sort out a lot of stuff."

Tammy had been in touch with the victim assistance office who took care of the cost of the counseling. She said she wouldn't have been able to pay for it otherwise.

"Well, no matter what happens, they're the ones most important in all of this," I said. "You have a huge job ahead of you in making sure they turn out all right. But I know you love them. Just live your life, showing that to them every single day, and the rest will sort of take care of itself."

I gave Tammy what news I had about the cases and congratulated her again before ending the call. This was an unexpected turn of events. I wondered how Daimon would react when he found out.

Sandy was busier than ever with Daimon's big property case. Prepping for trial isn't easy for a D.A. when so many witnesses and victims will testify. Each day for over two weeks, Sandy had five or six meetings with different witnesses, so they could read over their grand jury testimony and undergo some brief questioning. It's normal for witnesses, including officers and detectives, to have their memories fade to one degree or another. This is compounded when the testimony takes place months or years later.

Daimon and Bryan were set to be sentenced on May 5 for their convictions in the car-stop case. The hearing had been postponed a couple of times already for paperwork problems and another delay occurred when Daimon wasn't transported from the jail. When that happened, Sandy asked the C.O.'s why he wasn't there. They said Daimon didn't feel well and refused to be taken to court.

How can a jail inmate wake up one morning and tell the C.O.'s he's not going to court? How weak has our system become? Are we so afraid of some civil rights group filing a lawsuit over an inmate with a tummy ache being forced to appear before the judge?

Paper terrorism. I didn't invent the term. But it sure fits what it describes: inmates who file grievances, lawsuits, frivolous motions and meritless appeals for the dumbest things. Things like not being able to eat a certain kind of food, not having a certain book in the inmate library, being brought to court when they don't feel well, or having to wear a certain kind of inmate clothing. They bury the courts with so much paperwork that sometimes it seems easier to simply give them what they want. It has become Pandora's Box with a jackpot mentality thrown in.

If the C.O.'s had brought Daimon to court when he said he was sick, he might've sued, claiming his rights were violated. For him to prevail in such a matter is unlikely, but how much time and taxpayer money would the police department have to spend defending such a silly claim?

As an attorney once explained, "Our society has made the determination that we'd rather have the courts open to those who might not have cognizable claims than close them to those that do. So, there's leniency when it comes to filing even those lawsuits that have no hope of winning." The courts give a wide berth when it comes to filing patently false claims and others that can never be proven. The once shining ideal of a man getting his day in court has been corrupted by people who shape-shift illegitimate accusations into smoothly crafted legal arguments.

At the sentencing, I walked into the courtroom hoping Daimon would be there this time. As I sat down, the prisoners were being marshaled in. Daimon saw me and smirked. The C.O.'s had Daimon and Bryan chained together in the prisoner area with about fifteen other inmates.

The case was fourth or fifth on the docket and when called, Daimon and Bryan stood up. Sandy began with her argument on Bryan. She asked Judge Wall to sentence Bryan under the small habitual statute, with a sentence of eight to twenty years. She reminded the judge how Bryan was on probation when he committed the crimes. She stated that the number of commercial burglaries dwindled in the same part of town after Daimon and Bryan were arrested. Sandy spoke about the enormous cost they'd imposed upon the community, and how Bryan demonstrated he had no intention of stopping his criminal behavior.

"This was not the usual, 'I have a drug habit and it made me do it,' situation many criminals cry about," Sandy said. "No, his job was to steal."

Sandy discussed Bryan's previous felony convictions and had the prior judgments entered into the court record. The judge asked Bryan if he wanted to say anything.

"I don't understand how I got convicted on the case. I didn't do anything; I just got pulled over in a car," Bryan said.

The judge knew better; he had presided over the trial and had heard the testimony.

Bryan also complained—incorrectly—he had never been offered a deal. I'd met with Bryan at the jail and told him if he cooperated, the D.A. might take that into consideration for what kind of deal he'd receive, but Bryan declined. Several months later, Bryan's attorney asked Sandy about a deal, and was told Bryan would have to testify, which he refused. No, Bryan had been offered deals—although not to his liking. As he continued speaking, the closest Bryan came to showing remorse was when he said, "I'd like to ask the court for mercy."

Mr. Kocka argued for leniency and only a small prison sentence.

Judge Wall said he wouldn't treat Bryan as a habitual criminal, sentencing him to six to twenty years. Not terrible, not strong—especially when knowing the sentence will be virtually cut in half with automatic credits the inmates receive. Legislators trying to trim budgets by emptying prisons rather than ending wasteful spending elsewhere—a discussion best left for another time.

Next, Sandy argued sentencing on Daimon. In Daimon's interview with Parole and Probation, he tried to blame his demise on Bryan. He said Bryan hopped into his van with a bag full of stuff before the cops pulled them over. Sandy pointed out how ludicrous this was, especially with two pieces of the stolen property being large and heavy.

"This was his way of life," Sandy said. She went through Daimon's criminal history and pointed out how Daimon had been convicted of doing these same types of crimes for fifteen years. Judgments for Daimon's nineteen prior felonies were introduced into the record.

Sandy described how Daimon thought it was fun to do counter-surveillance on detectives and how he spoke on the jail phones about the jobs he had done and others he was planning. She reminded the judge that Daimon spoke on the jail phones about trying to take Mr. Chen for a "little swim" for $10,000. Sandy asked the judge to sentence Daimon under the large habitual statute and give him life without the possibility of parole.

Judge Wall quickly lifted his eyes from his paperwork and peered at Sandy through his reading glasses. The look on his face was of consternation. It seemed the judge was telegraphing that he thought Sandy was asking for way too much. That was his prerogative. It was his court and, even if people disagree, the law provides him great discretion in sentencing. If the public doesn't like it, they can always vote him out of office.

Judge Wall asked Daimon if he wanted to speak. Of course Daimon wanted to speak. His own voice was the sweetest sound he'd ever heard. Or maybe he simply hated silence. Either way, this would be Daimon's moment to shine—at least in his own mind. He could talk his way out of anything, or so he'd always believed. "I'm not a bad guy," he began, and admitted committing crimes in the past. He tried to minimize it by saying, "But everyone has done something wrong in the past, even you have," referring to the judge. When Daimon said that, the judge gave him the same look through his reading glasses that he had given Sandy.

Daimon continued, "All of these other cases were all set up by the ROP detectives. I don't understand this strange love affair that ROP has with me."

I could not fathom why Daimon didn't understand that we recognized him as a career criminal, and rightfully regarded him as a top-shelf pro. At least once he'd said he wasn't the ordinary bird. Why should he be so surprised, then, we didn't treat him like the ordinary bird?

Daimon said, "This case in your court is the only one that has any meat . . . I want to be able to raise my kids. ROP did a good job of painting me as a bad guy, but I am not that guy."

Same as Bryan, Daimon complained about not being offered a deal. As with Bryan, this wasn't correct. The morning of the search warrants, I urged Daimon to assist in helping identify what property was stolen and to whom it belonged. He said nothing was stolen; he was innocent. I suggested coming clean might help him at sentencing, but he held fast. In the later months, Sandy offered Daimon the deal to plead guilty to one count and stipulate to ten to life on the sentence. He refused, again saying he was innocent in spite of the massive evidence of his guilt. If he was truly innocent, why would he complain about his perceived lack of a deal? If the police had illegally searched his van and forged search warrants and covered it up, he wouldn't care about whether he received a deal.

Daimon said, "I have never had probation before. If I get convicted in the other cases, giving me probation here wouldn't mean a thing because I'll be going to prison anyway."

Mr. Hart began his remarks. "This is a *non-violent* crime."

I thought about Mr. Chen. What if Daimon made good on his idea of killing him? Is that what it would take for people to understand that Daimon needed to be in prison for a long time? I think we all knew Daimon was capable of any kind of crime if faced with the right circumstances. Daimon was God in his own world. He had and did anything he wanted without sacrifice or repercussion. That is, until the day he went to jail in a pair of sweatpants.

Mr. Hart asked the judge to reject habitual criminal treatment for Daimon and sentence him to sixteen to seventy-two months in prison.

Judge Wall announced he was sentencing Daimon under the small habitual statute. Daimon's shoulders slumped when those words came out of the judge's mouth. I think mine did too. Daimon's did because he thought he wasn't going to get "bitched" and mine did because I thought he'd get a large habitual instead of a small. Judge Wall gave Daimon eight to twenty years.

On my way out of the courtroom, I walked with Sandy. As Mr. Hart approached us, I remembered how Daimon commented about how he wanted to be free, to raise his kids. I asked Mr. Hart, "Does Daimon really believe Tammy hasn't turned on him?"

The look he gave was priceless; like a confused dog with his head cocked. He said nothing and walked away. <>

34

///////////

THE BIG
PROPERTY TRIAL

*In all debates, let truth be thy aim, not victory, or an
unjust interest.*

—WILLIAM PENN

A few days later, while working on the big property case
and putting things together to help Sandy prepare for
trial, she mentioned Robert Holmes. Bobby's attorney, Mr.
Sullivan had suggested Bobby would testify against Daimon
and Bryan if he could get probation. Sandy countered that
Bobby would also have to come up with the $75,000 still
outstanding from the money Tammy gave him. Mr. Sullivan
said he'd get back to her.

Sandy didn't need Bobby to testify. If he received
probation, he'd be getting more than he was giving. He could
only give the state something it already had in Tammy—a

star witness who would tell the inside story.

Bryan needed an attorney for the big property case. The Public Defender's Office had a conflict and couldn't represent him. As luck had it, Cynthia Dustin was on the rotation and was appointed by the judge. That was good for Bryan—Ms. Dustin was already familiar with him and the substance of his cases.

A week before the trial on the big property case, Ms. Dustin filed a motion to sever Bryan's trial from Daimon and Bobby's, citing a potential conflict of interest. Judge Bell reluctantly granted the severance.

Mr. Sullivan also tried to have Bobby's trial severed from Daimon's, although he didn't have a conflict or significant legal basis. Judge Bell denied the request. I guess nobody wanted their clients to be anywhere near Daimon when he went on trial.

The last day before trial, Mr. Sullivan pressed Sandy hard to give Bobby a deal. He proposed that Bobby testify against Daimon, agree to pay back the $30,000 stolen at the Wynn Resort and agree to come up with the $75,000 he had culled from Tammy, in exchange for the state not opposing probation as his sentence. Sandy told Mr. Sullivan, no, Bobby would have to agree to two to ten years in prison. The counteroffer was rejected.

Mr. Sullivan also wanted to talk to Tammy prior to the trial. Sandy told me of the request, but I already knew what Tammy's response would be. I called her anyway and told her what was going on.

Tammy said, "I don't see any point in talking with the other attorneys because they don't represent my best interests. They'll get the opportunity to ask me whatever they want when I testify."

The following Monday, Daimon and Bobby's trial for the big property case began. Shelly Small was the D.A. assisting

Sandy. Shelly was smart, energetic and highly motivated. An attractive, petite woman who resembled Farrah Fawcett in her younger years, Shelly signed on to assist Sandy only a week or two before the trial. She did a fantastic job of soaking up the huge amount of information needed to understand the case.

Bobby had been out of custody for months on bail. Unexpectedly, he didn't show up in court when jury selection began, and a warrant was put out for his arrest. The implications were huge. Now there was no chance of trying Bobby with Daimon since jury selection had begun. Bobby could be tried with Bryan, but only if we found him before Bryan's trial began the following week. This giant trial might have to be put on three times.

Hiding out was Bobby's best move. Since the prosecution was planning on having more than one hundred witnesses testify and several of them lived out of state, Bobby must have believed his chances of getting a deal might go up. And in this trial, sitting next to Daimon as a co-defendant was probably bad for anyone. Daimon was the mastermind.

I spoke with a security supervisor at the Horseshoe Casino. He said Bobby was on vacation until June, but if they saw him on the property, they'd detain him and call me right away.

Other detectives and I went to the neighborhood where Bobby lived, taking note of the cars parked at his house. After a short time, Diana arrived, alone, in Bobby's Corvette and went inside.

I left the surveillance team and drove to the other houses Bobby owned. There was no movement at either house, but Bobby's twenty-seven foot cargo truck was parked in front of one of them. It looked like it hadn't been driven recently—leaves and other debris had collected under it. One of the front wheels was missing and the axle rested on a cinder block. The truck looked like someone had been using it for some kind of business once upon a time. Markings on the side and on the roll-up door advertised a pizza business in town. Or maybe simply a disguise for the best burglary vehicle I'd ever come across. After making sure nobody was watching, I took pictures of the truck.

The jury was brought into the courtroom and sworn in. Daimon sat next to Mr. Hart. Sandy began her opening remarks. She explained how this trial would lay out a series of events leading to the service of several search warrants on which the charges were based.

"You are going to hear the big picture in this case because what we have is an overriding conspiracy that's charged between four individuals," she said. Sandy named Daimon, Bryan, Tammy, and Bobby, while showing their pictures on the big screen. She spoke about the role of each one of the coconspirators and their relationships with each other. She explained that Tammy was Daimon's ex and she was charged in the case.

Sandy described how the case started with Daimon and Bryan arrested by the patrolmen after doing the crystal shop and dentist's office burglaries. She went through bullet points covering everything that led up to search warrants being authorized.

Sandy said, "When detectives got into the house on November 6, 2006, they weren't prepared for what they found." She described the massive hoard of stolen property found in the house and storage units. The jury was shown a long list of victims on the video screen. Sandy also revealed Tammy would testify, admit her guilt, and implicate the others.

"When we get to the end of everything, the charges we have are conspiracy and possession of stolen property, the property belonging to each one of those victims. At the end of everything, the state is going to prove its case beyond a reasonable doubt and ask you to convict the defendant."

The judge asked Mr. Hart if he had an opening. Sometimes, the defense will hold their opening remarks until they get to present their case. They don't want to reveal much of their strategy, and they'd rather evaluate the state's case first. But this time, Mr. Hart said, "Yes, Your Honor. Very briefly."

Judge Bell said, "My two favorite words."

"You've been instructed by Judge Bell that you have a duty: to follow the law. You've been instructed not to come to any conclusions about the case until it's complete. You're supposed to wait and hold your decisions until all the evidence comes in. You've heard a list of a hundred witnesses, over a hundred witnesses coming in—victims, the police. But keep in mind, the state holds the burden of proving each and every count and charge.

"You have twenty-six different counts with different victims in front of you. As you will find in the instructions, and as you are well aware, the standard is proof beyond a reasonable doubt. You need to fill out the puzzle, ladies and gentlemen. If the pieces aren't there, you don't have proof beyond a reasonable doubt and the state has not met its burden on the counts. Do not confuse the *quantity* of information provided to you with its quality. Keep in mind, the items were found in six different places. My client's name is not on a number of those places.

"Probably the star witness in this case will be his ex-girlfriend who is, as you now know, a state's witness. Please keep in mind where that could cause a possible prejudice in her decisions to testify and how. The requirement of yours is to hold the state to their burden. Everyone is entitled to a fair trial. Everybody knows the standard set over two hundred years ago is beyond a reasonable doubt. I ask you to hold that standard.

"When you compare the items they claim were found to those items in the reports, you will find discrepancies. You'll find some people testified under oath: 'That's mine,' and then later testified, 'No, it's not mine, that one's mine.' Please keep these considerations in mind when you're going through this. Thank you."

Sandy worked her way through several witnesses and then had Officer Salisbury on the stand. She asked if he saw Daimon in the courtroom. Daimon was leaning back in his chair with his feet sticking out from under the table. He was wearing the suit, tie, and matching dress shoes Mr. Hart brought for him, but Mr. Hart had forgotten socks. Daimon wore the bright orange jail-issue socks with his cool duds.

In answer to Sandy's question, Officer Salisbury gestured toward Daimon and said, "He's right over there and he has orange socks on."

Mr. Hart smiled.

Later, and outside the presence of the jury, Mr. Hart objected to the description offered during the in-court identification and asked the judge for a mistrial. Mr. Hart said he believed when Officer Salisbury brought attention to the orange socks it also led the jury to know Daimon was in jail. He argued that knowledge was too prejudicial and the jury might be more likely to convict Daimon because of it.

Judge Bell said he believed none of the jurors had ever been in trouble and Daimon wearing orange socks would have no meaning to them. He denied the request for a mistrial and the court adjourned for lunch.

After lunch, more testimony and exhibits were presented. Near the end of the day, the jury was excused for the evening.

Outside the presence of the jury, Daimon was admonished about his right not to be compelled to testify. After the admonishment, there was a discussion about Daimon requesting toothpaste and shampoo. Apparently, Carlos had stopped putting money on Daimon's books, and he couldn't buy anything from the canteen in the jail. Mr. Hart asked if he could be allowed to put twenty dollars on Daimon's account.

Judge Bell didn't understand why Mr. Hart needed permission. Months ago, Mr. Hart explained, Daimon was in a fight and lost a tooth. He was sent to the dentist and now had a dental bill to pay. If anyone put money on his books, it would pay down the outstanding debt before he could buy snacks or shampoo.

Judge Bell granted Mr. Hart's request. It's my understanding Mr. Hart used his own money to help Daimon out. Either a noble gesture, or Mr. Hart was already tired of sitting next to the stinky guy.

During a recess the next day, Sandy brought a motion for the jury to learn what the acronym ROP stands for. Some of the jail phone calls she wanted to play had Daimon and Bryan talking about ROP in them. She couldn't remove those parts from the recordings without removing other parts crucial to her case. The jury would learn the meaning of ROP, Judge Bell ruled, but it didn't mean the jury would hear Daimon's long criminal history as a repeat offender.

When the third day of the trial came, Mr. Hart was visibly ill with food poisoning or stomach flu. The judge granted a one day delay in the trial and the jury was sent home.

The next day, Mr. Hart was back in court and objected to some of the phone calls Sandy wanted to present as evidence. One of the calls was the "take a swim" phone call. Another was where Daimon and Bobby spoke about the news media reporting $2 million dollars of stolen property being recovered at Daimon's house. The judge overruled the objections and the jury was brought in. More witnesses and victims testified and exhibits were presented.

The lunch break came. Outside the presence of the jury, Mr. Hart raised an objection. He didn't want the jury to know the S.W.A.T. team had executed the warrant at Daimon's house. He believed it would prejudice the jury into thinking Daimon was a dangerous person.

Judge Bell overruled the objection and said, "Using the S.W.A.T. team to execute the warrant is part of their normal business."

After lunch, several more witnesses and exhibits were presented. In all, thirty-two witnesses testified that day. Sandy thought it must've been a new record for one day during a trial in Las Vegas.

At the end of the day, the jury was excused for the weekend. The next week would bring the final group of officers and victims in to testify. The state was nearly finished with their case. The second week would also bring the grand finale, which would include testimony from Tammy and me.

<>

35

//////////

FOLLOWING
THROUGH

*In golf as in life, it is the follow through that makes
the difference.*

--UNKNOWN

*T*ammy flew into Vegas on Sunday, prepared to testify
Monday morning. I picked her up from her hotel and took
her to the D.A. Office for a pre-trial conference with Sandy.
Even though the danger had been quelled with everything
in the light, the necessity remained for Tammy to *feel* safe.
I didn't want her to walk alone or take a cab from the hotel
to Sandy's office—especially with Bobby's whereabouts
unknown.

When Tammy met with Sandy in her office, I waited
in the hallway. When the meeting was over, Tammy turned
back and said, "Oh, one other thing—Devon used to break

into, like, dermatologist offices and steal the chemicals they use for peels and, like, for skin treatments. He liked to give himself peels at home and used the chemicals to bleach his skin."

I stood there with a puzzled look on my face. Daimon said he wasn't the ordinary bird.

The next morning, Jerome picked Tammy up at her hotel and escorted her to the courthouse. Sandy had just finished having one of the bank managers testify. She called Tammy to the witness stand and the bailiff walked Tammy in from the hallway.

Daimon grinned. He hadn't seen or spoken to Tammy in many months.

The clerk asked Tammy to state and spell her name for the record. Tammy gave her new married name. Daimon's grin died of shock. It was the first moment he learned Tammy had married.

Sandy asked Tammy about what other names she knew Daimon to use.

"He goes by Daimon, Ashton, Dinkie, and Devon, but Devon is what I always called him." Tammy seemed scared on the stand and she didn't look at Daimon the entire time she testified.

Tammy then described in detail, the conspiracy between herself, Daimon, Bryan, and Bobby, much like she did when I interviewed her.

Sandy continued, "Did Daimon ever come home with property he hadn't paid for?"

"Yes."

"Did you or Daimon ever pay for any of the furniture found in the house?"

"No."

Sandy asked about Alana Perry, Tammy's friend who had been given stolen artwork. Tammy said Alana one time had seen the expensive things on display in every room of their house. She told her they could afford all of the stuff because Daimon was a successful self-recording musician.

"Objection, hearsay," Mr. Hart said.

Judge Bell said, "She can testify about what *she* said, not what Alana said."

"Did you ever go shopping with Daimon?"

"He took me to the grocery store once a week for, like, milk and fruit. He paid for those things."

Tammy testified that the sports memorabilia, freezers, commercial ice-maker, flat screen TV's, spa, guitars, and electronics in the house were all stolen.

"What items did you buy?"

"Not many," Tammy said. "Some clothes, no furniture. It was not more than one, maybe two items."

Tammy also testified about how she withdrew a lot of money to pay for the attorneys and gave $145,000 to Bobby to hold.

Sandy said, "Why did you do that?"

"We spoke about the money on the phone after I got out of jail and also Bobby thought I should do it."

Mr. Hart objected.

Judge Bell sustained the objection and said, "She can't testify to what Bobby *thought* because we don't know what Bobby thought."

Sandy worked her way around the objection by asking Tammy if she had a conversation with Bobby prior to her giving him the money.

"Yes."

"Based on that conversation, did you decide to give him the money?"

"Yes."

Sandy asked if Daimon had a job.

Tammy said, "Only when we first moved in together."

Mr. Hart objected as to relevance.

Judge Bell sustained the objection and said, "I do believe it's relevant but I don't want that line of questioning to go any further."

Sandy was leading toward asking how many nights a week Daimon would go out to do burglaries, performing the math to show how many he got away with over time. But she never got the chance.

Sandy quickly moved on and brought up the federal agents in Kansas, asking about the money on Thanksgiving Day.

Tammy described what happened, explaining how, afterward, she decided she wanted to meet with me. "I took the initiative and decided to talk to the police even though I had an attorney."

Throughout most of Tammy's testimony, Daimon sat motionless and seemed inattentive. But at this moment, he rested his chin on his hand with his elbow on the table. He covered his mouth with part of his hand. He was furious that Tammy had caved, just like his old girlfriend Regina years ago. I think Daimon covering his mouth was a subconscious sign that right below the surface, he was holding back screams of anger.

"Were you truthful when you spoke to Detective Nickell?"

"Yes."

"At some point, were you offered a deal in this case?"

"Yes, after I spoke to Detective Nickell the second time."

"Do you know what that deal consists of?"

"I pled guilty to one felony and one gross misdemeanor and all the other charges are dropped. I haven't been sentenced yet on the charges."

Sandy asked about the rest of the deal.

"I come and testify truthfully . . . I guess that's basically it."

Sandy said, "Is there also an agreement involving successful completion of probation?"

"Yes. The felony charge will be dropped and I'll be left with the gross misdemeanor conviction."

With that, Sandy passed Tammy to Mr. Hart.

Mr. Hart began his cross-examination by saying, "Let's talk about this real quick." He asked Tammy about the deal offered to her and asked if I promised her anything.

Tammy said, "Detective Nickell told me he couldn't make any promises."

"But Detective Nickell did tell you he would speak to the District Attorney and see if he could help you, right?"

"Yes."

Mr. Hart continued with this line of questioning for a few moments, trying to make it look like Tammy was coerced into talking with the offer of a deal. The tone in his voice and his manner of questioning made it look like Tammy thought she was owed something for her testimony. He was condescending. "You went in there and it's safe to say there was no formal deal in place, correct?"

"Yes."

"But you did go in there with the idea that hopefully things would be reduced, correct?"

"I went in with the idea that I wanted to basically do what was right: tell the truth. I had no idea what the outcome would be. You know, hopefully I didn't want to spend time in prison or be away from my kids."

"You had been arrested, your kids had been taken away from you, you had taken approximately $250,000 out of the bank, about $150,000 hasn't been recovered, correct?"

"I'm not sure how much money has been recovered."

"And you're going to get a gross misdemeanor at the end of all of this?"

"Yes."

"Originally you were charged with twenty-six or twenty-seven—dozens of counts?"

"That sounds correct."

"And you gave multiple statements, correct? And each one a little more damning?"

"I gave two statements to Detective Nickell."

"And you testified at the grand jury?"

"Yes."

"Is it safe to say that every time, your memory got a little better? It was a little more damning?"

"I wouldn't say that my memory got better. I was maybe asked additional questions."

Mr. Hart said, "You are the one—the cars were yours, they're in your name. The accounts were your accounts—they're in your name. You could've left at any time?"

"Yes, I physically could have left."

Sure, Tammy enjoyed living off the spoils of Daimon's crimes, yet it's not what adhered her to him. Her fear kept her prisoner through the years. She was afraid of what Daimon might do if she took the kids and broke free. She was afraid of life without him—she had known nothing else since she was just fourteen. Her fear of moving on was greater than the fear of what he had done to her and the kids over the years. She became numb to it. She justified it to herself at the expense of her children. And when she stared it in the face, it broke her heart.

Mr. Hart said, "You were contacted about possibly speaking with myself and other defense counsel?"

"Yes."

"Your statement was that you didn't want to talk to anybody?"

"Yes, I asked whether I was required to, and since I wasn't required to, I decided not to."

Mr. Hart said, "So as we sit here today, you say you knew everything in the house was stolen but when this is all said and done, you're going to have a gross misdemeanor?"

"Yes."

"Do you know how much money you're going to get to keep?"

"At this point I don't have any money that I had before."

"Did you get the cars?"

"I did get the cars."

"And the rest of the stuff is just up in the air as far as how much?"

Sandy objected and said, "It's assuming facts not in evidence."

Judge Bell said, "What *rest* of the stuff?"

Mr. Hart said, "Well, like I said, she, you're still claiming you had $40,000 from an inheritance, right?"

Tammy said, "It's not like I got to keep $40,000 in the account or anything. Everything in the account was seized."

"And that's not done, said and over yet, correct?"

"I believe it is said and over."

"So you forfeited all that?"

"Right."

Mr. Hart said, "I just didn't see that it had happened. Nothing further from this witness."

Part of Tammy's deal in fact was that she forfeited all claims to the seized monies or seized property in the still pending forfeiture case.

Sandy rose from her chair for re-direct. "Defense counsel asked you, 'Well, you could've left at any time. You own the cars. You had the bank accounts with all the money,' and you said, 'I physically could have left.' Do you recall that?"

"Yes."

"Why didn't you just take the money and go?"

Mr. Hart objected.

Judge Bell said to Sandy, "I'm not sure I would go there. Do you know the answer?"

"I do. Can we approach?"

Sandy and Mr. Hart approached the bench and the speakers in the courtroom were turned off so the jury couldn't hear the discussion.

Sandy said, "The answer is in one of the statements she gave to Detective Nickell. I don't want to get into any of the abuse stuff, but the defendant told her if she ever took the money, he would kill her. And counsel opened the door by asking the question, 'You could've left at any time?' "

Judge Bell said, "I think you're right, but I wouldn't take the chance of spoiling the trial where you're at right now. Let's just move on."

The judge sustained the objection and Sandy finished her re-direct, saying, "Nothing further," as she sat down.

Judge Bell put the court into recess for a brief bathroom break. Tammy left the courthouse with Jerome to catch a cab for her flight home. I was up next. <>

36

//////////

THE MIND OF
MONROE

*No man, for any considerable period, can wear one
face to himself and another to the multitude, without
finally getting bewildered as to which may be the
true.*

—NATHANIEL HAWTHORNE

After the break, the court clerk swore me in. Daimon didn't
make much eye contact with me; he kept fiddling with
a laptop computer on the table in front of him. I guess Mr.
Hart brought the laptop to keep Daimon busy and create the
appearance that he was involved and percipient. If Daimon
had to be there for days, sitting on his hands, I think he'd get
bored and do something he shouldn't. Probably a good way
for Mr. Hart to keep him occupied. But it was just theatre.

Sandy asked about how I became involved with the case,

and then about my monitoring of the phone calls. I explained how I first heard about Mathew from a jail call recording but I didn't know who or what Matthew was until I saw the tool and figured it had to be Daimon's favorite. I described how I used Matthew to open the doors of the crystal shop and the dental office.

I testified as to how I discovered one of the storage units by showing Daimon's photograph to the manager and how the ROP surveillance team found another unit while they watched Daimon use Bobby's big truck. Daimon seemed agitated while I answered this line of questions. He kept switching from side-to-side in his chair. Maybe he was bothered because he hadn't realized the ROP detectives had followed him to the storage unit. Crooks don't like to find out they've messed up. It bruises their inflated egos.

Sandy started playing the first of twenty-six phone calls allowed into the trial. Around the tenth call, it was like listening to a broken record. Everyone in the courtroom seemed like they'd had enough.

Some of the phone calls played contained humorous comments between Daimon and Bryan. Several times, I noticed Mr. Hart fighting to keep a straight face. He sort of covered his face with his hand, so the jury wouldn't see him snickering. One funny call was from right after Daimon and Bryan were first arrested by the patrolmen. Daimon had bananas and a tub of sour cream in the van that night. The bananas and sour cream went with the van to the impound yard. Several hours later, Daimon bailed out and got the van out of impound.

"Dude, I got my sour cream and bananas," Daimon said.

"Um, good for you," Bryan said.

"That sour cream is still good, dude."

"It is?"

"I think."

"Uh, I don't know, dude."

"What would it do if it went bad?" Daimon said.

"I don't know."

"Taste, taste funny or . . ."

"I don't know if I'd even fuck with it, dude," Bryan said.

"I already took a big old spoon full of it."

"Did you?"

"Yeah."

"Well, you'll know if you get the shits later."

Mr. Hart and even some of the jurors chuckled. Everyone was trying to be serious and composed in the courtroom setting, but these inane conversations made it difficult. Daimon smiled and seemed to enjoy being the center of attention again.

By this time, I knew a lot about Daimon Monroe from studying reports about him, what his friends said about him, how he reacted to the police and courts, and much from his own words. Like I've said, he's vain and obsessed with his appearance. His hair was back to its natural brown color and he'd lost a lot of weight in jail. He often talked to people about how bad he looked, and it had him depressed.

Wherever he was, Daimon considered himself to be the smartest person in the room. He *was* smart and even taught himself to speak Spanish fairly well. But his hubris made it difficult for him to comprehend when he was wrong. He exhibited a strong drive to be successful—probably to the point of obsession—that would've served him well in a law-abiding occupation. However, he had chosen to apply his energy to the criminal trade, becoming an accomplished burglar who had gotten away with more crimes than he could remember. Stealing was habitual for him, and he got a high from it. Being the best thief he knew became his identity. There's nothing he couldn't steal if he put his mind to it—or so he seems to have thought. He was proud of his criminal accomplishments and acted as though it was his right to steal. His nature was to hate the police and defy any authority standing in his way; probably something rooted in his childhood.

Daimon's upbringing was cloudy, although I've learned his true surname is Hoyt, not Monroe or Whitfield like Tammy had been led to believe. But he'll forever be Daimon Monroe to me. Daimon had led Tammy to believe he killed his father when he was a teenager and he spent time in the California Youth Authority for it. The truth is, his father, Floyd, died of cancer in 1992 and his mother, Ruby, died in 1997 while Daimon was in prison.

Before Ruby died, she revealed things that Tammy would never learn from Daimon. His parents moved from California and bought a home in Las Vegas in 1973, not far from Nellis Air Force Base. Daimon had two siblings, Christy and a brother, Karl. Ruby said Daimon became anorexic when he was thirteen and it caused severe damage to his personality. She said Daimon subsequently tried to remake his entire identity. This is probably where the use of Devon and other names began in his life. This is also probably where the obsession with his appearance and over-controlling personality began to take shape.

I've heard whispers of information indicating substance abuse problems—possibly alcohol—in the family when Daimon was young, and it was an unstable upbringing. Tammy was led to believe Daimon moved to Las Vegas when he was a teenager and at some point lived with Bobby Holmes and his family, but that's probably part of Daimon trying to reinvent his identity. It's more likely that Daimon and Bobby met at school in Las Vegas, since they lived in the same school zone. Nevertheless, Daimon dropped out of school, and Bobby's family became a surrogate family of sorts, hence the long-term loyalty and partnership between the two.

Daimon was consumed with being right and with winning any argument. This characteristic evolved into him being able to convince himself of things that cannot be true. He believed the police searched his house without having a search warrant, despite incontrovertible evidence to the contrary. He convinced himself that a senior District Court judge helped the police cover it up by signing backdated warrants. When his false beliefs collided with undeniable evidence, Daimon's resulting behavior led many people to believe he was mentally incompetent and delusional. I don't think he was delusional, I simply think he was wrong.

Daimon likely had antisocial personality disorder and believed everyone's lives revolved around his own. He was certainly obsessive and may be the most narcissistic person I've ever encountered. His conversations almost always involved him talking about himself. He was not able to show genuine concern for others for any sustained period of time.

Daimon was all about self-aggrandizement. He found it exciting to think he was the center of a government conspiracy, and the FBI was coming to rescue him. He believed the Feds would arrest me, Judge Bell, and Sandy DiGiacomo. Interesting how he wanted us dead at first, but now wants us in prison instead. In Daimon's daydreams, people praised him for bringing the *corrupt* ROP team down.

"What you think about, you bring about," Daimon said to Bryan in one of the phone calls right after he bailed out of jail. He was trying to reassure Bryan everything would be okay. When the call was played for the jury, I saw a few funny looks on the faces in the courtroom. Daimon sounded like a motivational speaker preaching from a self-help book.

After the phone calls were done, I testified about the follow up on the stolen property and the bank warrants.

When Sandy was done questioning, Mr. Hart cross-examined me. He asked if I'd discovered some property was mistakenly released to people who weren't the owners.

"Yes, that did happen."

Mr. Hart said, "Did it happen a couple of times?"

"Yes."

"When you first interviewed Tammy, you told her you couldn't guarantee her a deal, correct?"

"I told her I wasn't someone who could give her a deal."

"You told her you would do your best to do something for her if she helped you, right?"

"No, I don't believe that's what I said."

Mr. Hart read from the transcript and said, "Did you say, 'What I can do is speak to the District Attorney and let the D.A. know what you've done, what information you've provided and that may carry some weight with the District Attorney?'"

"Yes, that's what I said."

"After that, she came and testified at the grand jury, correct?"

"Yes."

"And then she came in and gave you even more specific information later, correct?"

"That's correct."

"Was Mr. Monroe's name on the bank accounts?"

"No, they were in Tammy's name."

"What about the storage units—were any of those in Mr. Monroe's name?"

"Not in his name but he did use a fake name on one of

them," I said.

"Did you end up speaking to the district attorney on Tammy's behalf?"

"Yes, I told the district attorney about the information Tammy provided."

Mr. Hart paused for several seconds, sat down, and said, "Nothing further." The way he said it sounded like he was looking for a fight and was disappointed at failing to create one.

When my testimony was complete, the hour was late. I had been grilled for about four hours.

Judge Bell said, "Thanks, detective. It's hot, everybody's tired, let's go home." He put the court into recess, and the jury left the courtroom. <>

37

THE BIG GUYS

Ego: The fallacy whereby a goose thinks he's a swan.
—UNKNOWN

*T*he next morning, Sandy rested the state's case. Mr. Hart chose not to put on an affirmative defense. The only defense I could imagine him trying was the conspiracy theory, claiming I forged search warrants and coerced false testimony. But there was no foundation for it. He would come across looking like a lunatic in a tin foil hat. Mr. Hart must've known with the amount of evidence, and the number of people who testified, that it would be ludicrous for anyone to believe in some sort of a frame-job.

But, then again, there was the O.J. Simpson murder trial back in the 1990s. The jury in that case was led to believe in a conspiracy theory. An investigation later showed it would've required dozens of police personnel from investigators and crime scene personnel to scientists in the crime lab for that theory to have been true—not simply one supposedly bad cop. But the jury fell in love with the dramatic circus act. Maybe they'd been watching too much TV.

I'd been suspecting for some time that I'd be the person Daimon's defense team would try to leave holding the bag. Try to spin something up out of nothing and make me the next Mark Fuhrman. But Mr. Hart wasn't able to give that plan traction in this trial.

The jury came in from a break and Daimon tried to make eye contact with each one of the jury members. Not one of them would look him in the face.

Shelly made the closing argument for the state. She started off by saying, "They didn't think we were anything big." She repeated those seven words in a more deliberate, condescending way: "*They didn't think we were anything big.*" She was quoting something Daimon had said to Bryan on one of the jail phone calls. The jury had sat through probably the longest and most complicated trial for stolen property in Nevada's history. I think they got the message. These guys *were* big. They knew it. We knew it. The jury knew it.

Shelly used her Power Point to remind the jury of what they'd learned during the course of the trial. She said, "Who's gonna care five years later? We all know *they* cared," as she pointed to the long list of victim's names on the screen.

Shelly re-illustrated the conspiracy by showing how nine paintings stolen from Annie Lee were found in Daimon's house and two storage units. A sales tag from one of the paintings was found in Bryan's garage. An expensive Sub-Zero freezer was found at Bobby's house and an expensive, commercial, cook top taken in the same burglary turned up in Daimon's house. Shelly reminded the jury how the first phone call Daimon made after his house was searched was to Bobby, and how Daimon wanted Bobby to "clean the spot."

Shelly finished her remarks by repeating, "They didn't think we were anything big."

Mr. Hart objected and said, "They're implying other acts not proven."

Judge Bell overruled the objection. "I think she's referring to the quantity of stuff found in the house and the storage units."

Mr. Hart stood to make his closing arguments. "All you have seen can be overwhelming. Look at each count individually. Don't think because this is so big, each count must be true. How much were these items of property worth when they were found, not when they were stolen, is what you must determine. We've had no expert testimony about value for these items. The police raided six different locations and none of them were in my client's name."

Nothing being listed in Daimon's name or real name—whatever it might be—*was* important, yet not in the way Mr. Hart was trying to convey. Daimon deliberately kept things out of his name to better hide his activities. Rather than this indicating Daimon's innocence, it represents consciousness of guilt and planning for a criminal lifestyle.

Mr. Hart brought up the importance of value. Each count had to be proven greater than $250 to be a felony. This also revealed the brilliance in how Sandy chose to charge the case. With one count per victim, the $250 threshold was easy. There was no question that each victim's property represented more than $250. Some counts represented tens or even hundreds of thousands of dollars.

Mr. Hart reminded the jury how they learned that a few pieces of stolen property were released to the wrong people. "Maybe these items aren't so unique. That's reasonable doubt. Look at each element of each count."

Of course Mr. Hart failed to tell the jury why this occurred: these were expensive collectibles that had more than one owner over time, and they were released to the *wrong* previous owner.

Mr. Hart went back to the determination of value saying, "We don't know if the freezers were working, we don't know if the spa was working." Mr. Hart didn't put up the photograph of the freezers full of meat. That would've proven him wrong. He didn't tell the jury how the spa had to be drained before being hauled away by the spa company. Who would keep water in a spa that wasn't working? Half-truths cooked up to trick people into believing the unbelievable.

Mr. Hart said, "No appraisers have come in and told us how much the gold records or other valuable collectibles are worth. Value must be proven beyond a reasonable doubt. The defendant is presumed innocent unless the state proves every material element: value, possession, and knowledge it was stolen, beyond a reasonable doubt. The accomplice, Tammy—you must have independent proof. Please keep in mind her deal, the money she transferred to her mom that never came back. She said she wanted to do the right thing. Maybe she just needed the heat to go on someone else. The two storage units that were the fullest were in Tammy's name. Thank you."

Sandy delivered the state's rebuttal. "This is an overriding conspiracy. Legally, Daimon Monroe is on the hook for the actions of all of the parties. Remember the defendant's own words—the jail calls. The first call to Bobby after going to jail: 'Nobody's going to want to come to court.' They're all involved in the conspiracy. By law, the highest reasonable value may be used by the jury when considering value. The jury must use common sense."

Mr. Hart objected and stated, "The jury must determine the value of the property when it was found, not when it was stolen."

Judge Bell explained, "Art can go up in value and cars

can go down in value. The state can make an argument about what the value is and it's up to the jury to use their common sense to decide what the value of the property was when the police found it."

Sandy continued, "Hold the state to our burden of proof on each element of each count. You clearly have conspiracy. Things from one theft ended up in everyone's hands. You clearly have possession. You clearly have value."

Sandy ended her rebuttal, and the jury was taken to the deliberation room.

As soon as the jury was out of the courtroom, Judge Bell said, "Mr. Monroe, here's the answer: there are a couple of ways to know if sour cream has gone bad. If you open up the container and there's mold inside, it's bad, but you can probably get away with removing the mold and eating the remains. The second way to tell is, if a lot of water has separated to the top, you can mix it up and it might still be all right. But just remember, it's already sour. That's why they call it sour cream."

Daimon said, "Yes sir. Thank you, sir."

The attorneys and other people in the courtroom managed a small laugh in response to the judge's levity. The court went into recess.

Sandy, Shelly, D.A. Nell Keenan, and I went to lunch together while awaiting the jury's verdict. Right when our food was arriving at the table, Sandy's phone rang. A little over an hour had passed since the court recessed. The court clerk, calling for Judge Bell, told Sandy the jury was coming back. We inhaled about ten bites of our food and hustled back to the courthouse.

When we arrived in the courtroom, the jury was brought in. The foreman announced that verdicts had been reached. Daimon and Mr. Hart stood, facing the jury as the verdicts were read one-by-one. Daimon was found guilty on all twenty-six counts. Not a big surprise to anyone. Even Daimon appeared unaffected.

Judge Bell took time with the jury to explain some of the missing pieces to the puzzle that they weren't allowed to know during the trial—the history of the case and how the investigation developed. I thought the judge was exceptional for showing interest in the jury and what was in their heads. He figured they had unanswered questions and felt the duty to fill them in.

The judge thanked the jury for their service and hit hard on the fact that this was a long and sometimes tedious trial. Then he said, "Tomorrow, Mr. Fergason will be going on trial, right here, for the same charges."

There was a groan from the jury expressing sympathy for the citizens who would be filling their chairs in the next go around.

When the jury was cashing their vouchers for their jury pay, Sandy and I paid them a visit. I thanked them for their service and for the good job they did. A few of the jurors asked questions about what would happen to Tammy and her kids. Others were interested in knowing more about the whole story than they were told during the trial. They were clearly glad their long ordeal was over and felt satisfied in reaching their verdicts. <>

38

ANDROGYNY

But you can only lie about who you are for so long without going crazy.

—ELLEN WITTLINGER

I checked on Daimon's phone activity and found he had called Steve the evening after Tammy testified against him. To my surprise, Steve took the call. He hadn't accepted many of Daimon's calls for a while.

Daimon said, "I wish someone would've told me Tammy got married. She never would look at me the whole time. But when I come home, everything will be just fine. Maybe she just had to get married. It's just the situation. But everything I know is, she still loves me. Maybe it's not true. I gave her a good life."

"Nobody can give her the life you gave her," Steve said.

"Do you think she'll come back to me?"

"She's got her mom in her ear. She's a weak, weak person

but I think she'll come back to you if you plead your case to her."

"I saw the ring on her finger."

Daimon couldn't see the truth even when before him on the record in open court. This weak woman they were talking about was the old Tammy, now transformed into someone capable of making a new life for herself and her children—a life with no need or space for Daimon.

Another call to Steve was made the evening after the verdicts came in. Daimon told Steve they'd convicted him and said, "But they aren't playing fair. They coached them all how to say it was their stuff. And I read Carlos' statement. What they did to him is a shame. He was just scared of them. But some of the stuff he said hurt my feelings."

"You need to get a good ghostwriter when you get out. Your story would make a good book. You'd make millions," Steve said.

"All them other cases, they're just set up cases. And I know I can do better than Tammy. It was just a friendship, anyway, for the kids. She's probably with some dude she don't even want to be with."

I think Sigmund Freud could've spent his entire lifetime dissecting this phone call.

The next day, jury selection began for Bryan's trial. Bobby was still on the lam, so it seemed obvious this would be the second of three identical trials. After the jury was empanelled, Sandy delivered her opening remarks, which were pretty much the same as in Daimon's trial. When she was done, Ms. Dustin gave her opening.

Ms. Dustin asked the jury to sit and listen to everything before they make their decision. "I'm not gonna kid ya', there's a lot of stuff. But here's what you're going to hear. You've seen the conspiracy charges. You've seen the possession of stolen property charges. But you're not going to see a single burglary charge. You're going to hear testimony throughout the course of this trial from people who years ago had their businesses broken into; stuff was taken and years later it appears.

"And then you're going to hear testimony and the state's going to try to show through their case that every single piece of property at other people's houses or in other people's storage units is attributable to my client. He didn't live there. He didn't have a key there. He didn't have access there. But they're going to say it's this big giant conspiracy.

"And so what I'm asking you to do is to consider each and every count here separately because that's what's really important. Because you're going to hear stuff that makes you really question whether he really was involved in that particular set of items; whether he really possessed it; whether he conspired to keep it hidden knowing it was stolen, and that's where the distinction is. That's what the state's job is to do."

When Ms. Dustin was done, Judge Bell gave the jury their lunch recess. Afterwards, the carousel of witnesses and victims began, just as in Daimon's trial.

Meanwhile, back at the jail, Daimon made another call to Steve. They commiserated about how the justice system was out to screw people. Steve said all of the people in the justice system act like "sheeple" and they say "Baaa" when they know the police are breaking the rules.

I thought about Colonel Grossman and the sheepdog story. Steve didn't even know Colonel Grossman; yet, he twisted the Colonel's story to fit within his own dark view of the world. The wolves were complaining about the sheepdog and expecting the sheep to take their side. Unfortunately, every now and then, the sheep do join in and assist the wolf.

When Tammy returned to Las Vegas for Bryan's trial, I picked her up from the airport and took her to court. On a break, Sandy came into the hallway and said one victim moved out of state and wasn't able to come back for this trial. She had to concede that count against Bryan, since the burden of proof couldn't be met without a victim.

I said, "Looks like Daimon wasn't far from right. Who's gonna want to come back?"

Sandy gave the look she gives when she wants me to shut up. We also spoke about hearings and upcoming dates in the other trials set for Daimon.

"Does Daimon have a new attorney yet to replace Charlie Waterman?" I said.

Sandy said, "You haven't heard? It's Christina DiEdoardo."

The name didn't have meaning. I shrugged.

"He used to go by Christopher and now goes by Christina," Sandy said.

Daimon's new attorney was transgendered. I pictured Robin Williams in the Chris Columbus film, *Mrs. Doubtfire.* I thought for a moment about how some people think Daimon looks feminine, which reminded me of a jail phone call he made to Tammy almost two years before. Daimon was in lock-down at the time, so he had another inmate make the call. This inmate passed along Daimon's message, but then he asked Tammy if Daimon was a cross dresser. Tammy sounded bothered and said Daimon was straight. The inmate followed up with, "Well, you got a pretty-ass boyfriend. At first I thought he was a girl or a cute little fairy." Tammy quickly ended the call.

It seemed ironic. I wondered how Daimon would react to his attorney being transgendered. Outwardly, Daimon comes across as a bit homophobic, so this might throw him for a loop. Sandy said he had already asked someone in court if his new attorney used to be a man.

When I met Ms. DiEdoardo, her makeup was rough, and her dress, while feminine, didn't camouflage her body type or male body language. Even though she was a bit dramatic and used strangely-timed metaphors few people understood, she seemed to be an intelligent and respectful person. Professionally speaking, Sandy and I had the same opinion— it didn't matter in the courtroom whether Daimon's attorney was male, female, transgendered, black, white, or other. This was simply another defense attorney. <>

39

////////

BRYAN'S TRIAL

Better to be a nettle in the side of your friend than his echo.

—RALPH WALDO EMERSON

*T*ammy was called into the courtroom, sworn in, and asked to state her name. As she spelled her last name, Bryan seemed puzzled. The scene was almost a replay of what happened when Daimon first learned she had married. After giving her testimony, Tammy was dismissed. Jerome escorted her to a cab for her ride to the airport.

When my name was called, I walked into the courtroom and stood by the witness stand, where I was sworn in. My testimony and the playing of the jail tapes was virtually carbon-copy from before.

When I finished discussing the phone calls, a juror passed a note to the judge through the bailiff. This is a common practice in Nevada criminal trials. One of the jurors wanted to know if I'd checked to see if Bryan had a regular job or legitimate source of income.

"There was no extensive work for me to do in trying to find out if he had a job. I mean, 'No,' would be the basic answer to the question. But from my extensive work on the phone calls—and you're hearing only a fraction of the phone calls here—there was never any mention of any legitimate sources of income for these people except for when I could tell they were talking for the phones, trying to create disinformation about pressure washing, which I would later learn was a code word for committing burglaries."

Sandy followed up on the juror's question and said, "When the search warrants were executed, if there had been paystubs or any other such information in Mr. Fergason's name, it would've been impounded wouldn't it?"

"Yes."

On cross-examination, the only significant question Ms. Dustin asked was, "Is your inference about Bryan not having a job based on something other than the phone calls?"

"Most of my inference, in fact all of my inference, was made from what I was learning through the phones. Listening to so many phone calls really gave me a pretty good insight into the private lives of these people because they talked about everything and never once did I hear somebody say, 'Hey, I need to call your boss because you're not going to be at work next week.' I never heard any of them make any other job-related comment."

Judge Bell asked Ms. Dustin if she had anything further.

Ms. Dustin, still seated, said quietly with her hands folded, "No, Your Honor." She sounded disheartened, like she wanted to continue, yet couldn't find the path to do so.

After seven days of witnesses testifying, Sandy rested her case, and the judge instructed Ms. Dustin to call her first witness. She said, "Your Honor, the defense is not going to call any witnesses at this time."

Judge Bell recessed the court until the following morning.

After closing arguments, the jury began deliberating. The court recessed for lunch and Judge Bell warned the attorneys not to go too far.

Déjà vu: lunch time with the jury deliberating. Sandy, Shelly, Nell, and I went to lunch together again. On the way, the ladies joked about how I was *Charlie* and they were *Charlie's Angels*. They looked the part, but it was just silly talk between a bunch of overworked professionals.

We'd just finished eating when the call came from Judge Bell's clerk. We paid the bill and stormed back to the courthouse. After we arrived, the jury was brought in and the court went on the record.

"Has the jury reached verdicts on all charges in this case?" Judge Bell asked.

"Yes, Your Honor," the jury foreman said. The verdicts were read: guilty on all counts except the one the state conceded.

I looked at Bryan as he stood there. The sides of his face were pulsing from clinched teeth. He was placed in handcuffs and taken back to the jail.

Sandy and I walked out of the courtroom together while Shelly stayed for a moment, speaking with Judge Bell. When she came out, we once again went to the area where the jury was collecting their pay. One juror told Ms. Dustin she'd had the hardest job, defending someone whose guilt was so clear. After several minutes, we began saying our goodbyes.

Shelly approached and quietly said, "Judge Bell wants you to tell Sandy that Bobby got picked up and we're starting trial on him next week."

Bobby hadn't been picked up, but the judge wanted to razz Sandy with the idea of doing back-to-back-to-back trials. I had an idea.

I acted like I received a call on my cell and played like I was speaking to the sergeant in charge of the Fugitive Detail. When I ended my fake phone call, I told Sandy, "Hey, good news. Fugitive just got Bobby."

Shelly chimed in perfectly, saying, "Judge Bell just said if we got Bobby right away we would start trial next week."

The look on Sandy's face was priceless—sheer horror for about three seconds. Then her eyes narrowed and like an engine being started, she went back into trial mode. She was already starting to figure out the logistics of getting all of the victims and witnesses back to court for a third time on short notice.

Sandy said, "But Sean Sullivan withdrew when Bobby failed to appear, he won't have a new attorney by then."

Ms. Dustin unwittingly helped trap Sandy in the joke, saying, "No, he hasn't formally withdrawn yet, he's still the attorney of record."

Sandy froze and said, "We have to go let the judge know."

Sandy led the way and we bolted onto the elevator to go back up to the courtroom. She said, "Hey, call the sergeant back for me. I want to ask him something."

I looked at my phone and said, "My cell doesn't have service in the elevator."

"Well, give me his number and I'll call him."

"It came up private and I just got a new phone. I don't have him in my address book yet." I had an answer for everything. Sandy was so frantic she didn't realize we were pulling the wool over her eyes.

We made it back to Judge Bell's chambers. However, he and his secretary were already gone for the day. Shelly quietly made a quick call on her cell to the secretary and told her about the joke, then passed the phone to Sandy.

I whispered to Shelly, "When are we going to pull the plug on this?"

Soon enough, Judge Bell's secretary must've told Sandy we were messing with her. Sandy stood still for a moment and robotically turned to face us with the phone still to her ear. "You guys suck," she said, while rolling her eyes.

A few days later, Mr. Sullivan filed a motion to withdraw from the case, which was granted. Often times, defense attorneys want out when their clients fail to appear. Their reasoning is, they can't get their clients to cooperate in forming a defense. But I think it's because they've already collected a chunk of money and have an excuse to get out of doing the work.

A few weeks later, Bryan was transferred to the prison to begin serving his other sentences. He'd be back in a couple of months for sentencing on the big property case. <>

40

MAN HUNTING

Certainly there is no hunting like the hunting of man, and those who have hunted armed men long enough and liked it, never really care for anything else thereafter.

—ERNEST HEMINGWAY

Over the course of the next few weeks, detectives put a lot of hours into trying to find Bobby. He wasn't seen at the three homes he owned, but I figured if he was still in town, he'd probably have contact with Diana.

ROP Detective Britt went to Bobby's house and knocked on the door. Detective Britt, in his forties, had blondish hair and a devilish smile. He had the kind of personality that could make you laugh on your worst day. He was forever engaging in pranks and telling jokes. He was a good investigator and had no qualms with telling lazy people what time it was.

Diana answered the door. Detective Britt asked about

Bobby. She claimed she hadn't seen or heard from Bobby since he failed to appear in court. Detective Britt offered snitch money if she'd provide info on Bobby. The catch was, she'd only get the money once Bobby was in custody. She said she'd do some checking and give Detective Britt a call. I suggested to Detective Britt he should remind Diana about the Feds possibly opening a money laundering investigation on her and Bobby if she didn't help bring him in. There wasn't much chance of that happening, but she might not know it.

A few weeks later, Detective Britt wanted to make another run at talking to Diana. But before he could, Sandy called and said she received a motion filed with the court. Bobby hired an attorney named Kirk Kennedy, who asked the judge to quash Bobby's warrant and set a trial date. The motion was set to be heard the next morning. Bobby would have to appear in court if he wanted Judge Bell to consider the motion.

The motion included a long story claiming Bobby's grandfather had been ill and died in Alabama. According to the motion, Bobby "made the difficult choice" of failing to appear so he could go to Alabama and mourn.

I figured maybe Bobby's grandfather had died. But I was also betting Bobby hadn't been anywhere near Alabama.

The next morning, a team of detectives covertly set up watch on Mr. Kennedy's office. If Bobby showed up there, he would be surveilled to see if he was headed to court. If he went to court, things would happen as they should and the judge would make his ruling on the motion. But if Bobby got cold feet and didn't go to the courthouse, he'd be stopped and arrested on his warrant. I was positioned at the courthouse with a few detectives in case Bobby made it that far and decided to chicken out at the last second. I've actually seen wanted defendants show up in court only to leave before their case is called.

The courtroom was on the fifteenth floor. Bobby hadn't seen me in about a year and a half, so he probably wouldn't recognize me. Detectives were stationed in the hallway. Even more detectives were on the ground floor, so they could see Bobby enter the court building. If he somehow made it back downstairs, they'd be a safety net to stop him from leaving. I told the bailiff what we were doing and inconspicuously took a seat in the gallery.

Bobby never showed at his attorney's office. However, at about 8:20 a.m., he came into the courthouse and went through security screening. A few minutes later, he walked into the courtroom with Mr. Kennedy. I made eye contact with the bailiff, and he gave me a nod.

When Bobby's case was called, he and Mr. Kennedy approached the defense table. Sandy took her place by the prosecution table. The bailiff moved up behind Bobby, only a few feet away.

The bailiff was a heavily muscled young man who obviously spent a lot of time in the weight room. He was built like a tank, biceps bulging from his tight, khaki uniform shirt. There was no way for Bobby to leave unless Judge Bell astounded everyone by not remanding him. If Bobby tried to flee, he'd turn around and find himself facing an impenetrable, one-man human wall.

Bobby had to be nervous. He was there hoping Judge Bell would give him a break, yet common sense had to tell him the judge wouldn't be pleased with his antics. Bobby had to feel the ominous presence of the bailiff even though he didn't turn around to see him.

Mr. Kennedy started to explain the material claims contained in the motion.

Judge Bell cut him off. "I'm aware of the motion. I've read it and understand all the claims made. You may believe

what your client has told you, but I do not." He went on,
point by point, through his reasons for not believing Bobby.
He explained how Bobby tried to get his trial severed from
Daimon's and the request was denied. "So, your client
decided to do a 'self-help severance' on his own," the judge
said.

He looked at Bobby and said, "Your self-help severance
will end up costing taxpayers tens of thousands of dollars,
since you now get your own trial."

He continued, saying, "Mr. Kennedy, I understand you
don't know what the case looks like and don't have all of the
discovery materials. There were over 1000 exhibits in each
trial and over 80 witnesses, many from out of state. This is
the biggest criminal enterprise I've seen. And, by the way,
both of the other defendants were convicted on all counts.
So, I don't know if you're going to remain on the case, but
you have until August to decide if you are or I'm going to
appoint someone else to do it. And I'm not going to entertain
any delays."

The trial date was set in November, and it would be firm.
Bobby was remanded without bail and the bailiff handcuffed
him. The other detectives and I left the courthouse. Bobby
never even knew we were there.

A few days later, during the morning rush-hour, a
Las Vegas police detective was on his way to work in an
unmarked police car. He didn't know Donald Mason was
stalking him. Like Daimon Monroe, Mason was a criminal
with a long history. The detective had prior dealings with
Mason who decided he'd seek revenge. Mason found out
where the detective lived, followed him onto the freeway,
intentionally rammed him from behind, and forced the

detective's vehicle into oncoming traffic. Mason's vehicle flipped over at least once and landed on its wheels.

The detective hurried from his car to render aid, thinking it was an accident. Mason climbed out of his car and attacked the detective with a screwdriver. The detective and a motorist subdued Mason and took him into custody. Mason went to jail and the detective went to the hospital for treatment of minor injuries.

Mason was put into solitary confinement. Sometime the next day, he was found dead in his cell. The subsequent investigation showed Mason first tried to asphyxiate himself and failed. So, he turned to bashing his own head on the wall. He fell unconscious and bled to death before the C.O.'s knew what had happened. Video surveillance in the hallway showed nobody entered Mason's cell prior to him being found dead.

I figured the conspiracy theorists out there and the inmates in the jail, including Daimon, probably thought it was a cover-up. Word about things like this flow through the jail quicker than Budweiser at a NASCAR race. They likely figured the cops killed Mason and made it look like a suicide.

I pause to think how our society has come down to this. Criminals like Daimon Monroe and Donald Mason operate in the revolving doors of the justice system for years and finally, when authority takes special notice of them, they lash out. They're surprised when the system finally holds them accountable. I wonder the result if prison were made even more undesirable—not some kind of torture—but something harsher than the convict colleges, so many of them have become. If criminals really had more fear of going to prison, would it motivate them to change their lives? Or would their fear of prison hasten their fierce, maniacal resistance?

Not long ago, parents taught their kids if they were ever

in trouble or lost, to find a police officer. Now, some parents teach their kids to hate the police and never trust a cop. I don't know who Donald Mason was or if he had a family or kids. But I believe the world was probably a little bit better the day he ended his own life. Tragic, but real to the bone. <>

41

UNPREDICTABLE

Fear is pain arising from the anticipation of evil.
—ARISTOTLE

Jail Intel was still monitoring Daimon's incoming mail and who he was sending mail to. The FBI, Internal Affairs, the ACLU and other legal defense entities were being bombarded on a weekly basis. So I wasn't surprised to learn Daimon had filed a complaint against me with the Citizen's Review Board.

This body is authorized as an oversight committee to Internal Affairs for citizen complaints about officers. If citizens feel they're not getting satisfaction from Internal Affairs, the Citizen Review Board can review the matter and take further steps to investigate possible wrongdoing.

The notification consisted of a form letter from the board accompanied by a twelve-page copy of Daimon's handwritten complaint. The complaint rambled, claiming I'd coerced people to turn on him, and prevented other people from helping him. Same as in the federal complaint, he brought up that the tooth he had knocked out, and how he picked through his own feces for a few days without finding it. Apparently, Daimon swallowed the tooth when it jarred loose. He didn't specify how this involved me.

I called the Police Officer's Association and set up an appointment with the association's general counsel. A written response would be prepared for the ridiculous claims. I met with the association's attorney and provided a timeline, documenting every significant occurrence in my investigation of Daimon over the previous two years. After the meeting, I was relieved. It just seemed too implausible that reasonable people could believe Daimon's false claims.

Months later, when I received the findings from the Citizen's Review Board, a cookie-cutter letter from the Director of the Board notified me of the findings of their screening panel. The complaint was dismissed. The reason noted stated, "The Review Board does not have jurisdiction to consider the complaint or the complaint does not have sufficient merit to warrant further consideration by a hearing panel or LVMPD." I was thankful to know the Citizen's Review Board was objective and not on a witch-hunt.

The next day, I strapped on my pistol, grabbed an apple, and went out to my unmarked police car in the driveway. When I approached the car, I noticed someone had placed a book under one of the windshield wipers. I couldn't see anyone nearby, or anyone in a car down the street watching. The cover read: *Stripped: Uncensored Grace on the Streets of Vegas*, by Jud Wilhite. I'd never heard of the book, although its title made me uneasy. I inspected the book, looking for evidence of a device. Maybe wiring or something strange would reveal this wasn't just a book.

There had been a bombing about a year and a half before in Las Vegas where a small explosive device in a Styrofoam coffee cup was placed on the victim's car. When the victim picked up the cup, the bomb detonated, killing him. Not seeing anything weird, I didn't want to overreact. How would it look if I called the bomb squad to my house only to learn it was simply a book? I bent on my knees and made sure nothing looked strange under the car. I looked through the car windows for anything out of place.

I opened the trunk and grabbed an evidence bag and latex gloves. I released the book from the windshield wiper's grasp ever so carefully and picked it up as I prayed, "Lord, protect me today as you so often have done before." I could feel my heart beating in my chest. I handled the book in such a way that if there were fingerprints on it, I wouldn't smear them. The book had a place mark in it. I turned to the page apparently chosen for me.

This part of the book was about Las Vegas Police Sgt. Henry Prendes. Henry was killed in the line of duty on February 1, 2006. He was ambushed when he arrived on a violent domestic dispute by a man with a replica AK-47 rifle. I knew Henry. We worked together off and on several times back when I was in uniform. We played basketball together after work back then too.

When I saw these pages were what someone had intended for me to read, I looked around again. I put the book in the evidence bag and at that moment, my cell rang.

Dino, my old next door neighbor who moved recently, wished me a good morning.

"Hey Dino, what's happening?"

"Hey man, did you get that book I left for you?"

I paused and exhaled. I raised my voice a little and said,

"Dino, do you realize what you just put me through?"

He didn't understand. Dino had moved before this whole murder-for-hire spectacle started, and I never had the chance to tell him about it. After my pulse slowed and my blood pressure went down, we actually shared a pretty good laugh. He said the author, Jud Wilhite, was the Pastor of his church, Central Christian. When he read the part about Henry, he thought I might be interested in reading it.

We talked about Henry and how he became a Born Again Christian. By this time, I was on the freeway. When we ended the call, I looked over at the evidence bag in the seat and rolled my eyes.

I drove to the courthouse to testify in Daimon's gun case trial. I found Tammy walking down the hallway to the courtroom. As she approached, I had warm thoughts of how she'd gone from an unstable, dark, scary life to something promising a better future for her and her children. She had a glow, no longer depressed.

We exchanged greetings, and I asked how she was doing.

"Well, I'm six weeks pregnant," Tammy said.

That was the last thing I was expecting to hear. "I'm amazed at the poise you've shown though this. Are you ready to have another child?"

"Yeah, me and my husband are excited about it."

The courtroom door opened and the bailiff called Tammy to the stand. She testified that Daimon knew the gun was in the storage unit. She also said after Daimon was arrested, he desperately wanted someone to get the gun out of there as he thought the police might find it.

Tammy finished testifying and came out of the courtroom. We spoke about her kids and she said the girls were still in counseling. Tammy mentioned she was trying to get a job at their school. Right then, the bailiff called me to the stand. We quickly hugged and said our goodbyes. I told her to call if she ever needed anything.

She smiled, saying, "Thanks for everything. I don't know where I'd be right now."

"I know, I know, but give yourself some credit. You're a pretty brave woman."

The bailiff called my name again and I hurried into the courtroom. My main purpose at this trial was to introduce the phone call where Daimon was trying to get Bobby to, "Go clean out the spot" because of the "little thing."

The next day, after deliberating for an hour and a half, the jury found Daimon guilty of possession of stolen property, possessing a firearm with an obliterated serial number, and being an ex-felon in possession of a firearm. Sentencing was set a couple of months out.

Learning that Tammy was pregnant bothered me for a few days. Even though it had been nearly two years, it seemed way too soon for her to take the huge steps of marriage and bringing more young lives into the turmoil. I felt she needed time to sort things out and tend to the kids she already had; work to undo some of the horror they'd been through. But perhaps it would provide the kind of stability that Tammy and her children desperately needed for so long which Daimon was unwilling or incapable of providing. Still, could Tammy select a good man to spend her life with and be a loving father-figure to the kids? Answers that only time can provide, I presume. Besides, I'm just a cop. It's not my job to care, right? <>

42

////////////

JUSTICE

*A person often meets his identity on the road he took
to avoid it.*

—JEAN DE LA FORTAINE

When I went to the courthouse for Daimon and Bryan's
sentencing in the big property case, I met Sandy and
Shelly, and we went up to the fifteenth floor. Daimon was
already seated in the inmate area. He made eye contact with
me and smirked. His smirk was the same as before, like he
was trying to antagonize me into saying or doing something.

Wearing prison garb and belly chains, Bryan was brought
in from the holding area just outside the courtroom. He had
just arrived in the transport from the prison, and they sat him
next to Daimon.

Sandy was to make the sentencing arguments for the
state, but Shelly wanted to be there, too, since she helped
during the trials. Ms. Dustin was there, looking like she

wanted to scratch someone's eyes out. When Mr. Hart finally arrived, he was given a couple of minutes to settle in while he and Sandy exchanged paperwork.

Sandy presented several certified judgments of conviction for Daimon and Bryan's previous felony convictions. Judge Bell granted their admittance. Sandy spoke about the presentencing report on each defendant, provided by Parole and Probation. P&P recommended large habitual treatment on both Daimon and Bryan.

Three sentencing ranges exist for the large habitual in Nevada: ten years to life, ten to twenty-five years, or life without parole. Sandy requested life without parole for Daimon. She also asked for large habitual treatment on Bryan, leaving the range of the sentence to the judge's discretion.

Sandy first presented her arguments about Daimon and said, "This defendant keeps getting better and better at committing crimes. He gets caught, goes to prison, gets out, and he's a better criminal. Nothing has his name on it. No vehicle registrations, power bills, or storage unit rentals. Nothing with his name because that's how he got caught the last time. He got better at committing the crimes. He invented the Matthew tool. He would go around testing alarm systems and response times. He researched on the Internet how to defeat alarm systems and surveillance systems. He has never taken any responsibility. He has never shown remorse. He has never worked."

Judge Bell interjected, "Well, there was D&B Pressure Washing." He chuckled and said, "That's how they remembered the name of it, Daimon and Bryan Pressure Washing." He smiled real big at Daimon and there was a sense in the courtroom that the judge was calling Daimon out, letting him know he was no dummy. The judge was stalking the wolf.

Sandy said, "I have no doubt that if Mr. Monroe is ever let out of prison, he'll return to committing crimes and would be even better at it."

She intentionally didn't mention the murder-for-hire charges because she was a named victim in the case. Doing so could create the appearance of a conflict and bring about an appeal issue. Nonetheless, Sandy's argument was thorough and well done. Daimon's smug look and conceited body language brazenly displayed his pride in hearing people talk about him as though he were King of the Pirates.

Sandy made no further arguments about the sentence for Bryan. She had already told the judge what she was asking for and left it to his discretion. After all, Daimon was the main guy. If it weren't for Daimon, Bryan might not have been in this mess. Without Daimon, Bryan might've been leading some kind of semi-productive life that didn't include committing burglaries. Well, as productive a life as a convicted, hard-drug abuser might lead. But Daimon had indeed transformed Bryan into an accomplished thief.

Mr. Hart stood for his remarks. Pushing in his chair, he said, "These are *property crimes*," with a condescending tone. He asked the judge not to give Daimon a life sentence. He also asked for the sentence to run concurrent with the time Daimon received in the car-stop case. "This was all a continuation of that; it's all the same thing. Give him a chance at parole. I know you've thought about this, Your Honor. I've been in your courtroom enough times . . ."

Judge Bell cut Mr. Hart off and said, "I'll say this: I've thought about this case, and the sentencing more than any other case I've ever had here as a judge."

"Your Honor, I ask you to give my client the chance at parole. That's what I'm asking for. Nothing more, nothing less."

The judge asked Daimon if he wanted to say anything.

There was no way Daimon would miss the chance to take the stage. To this day, he thinks he can convince the world it's flat. His best move would've been to say nothing or feign remorse and hope the appellate process would work in his favor. But he couldn't pass on the chance to thumb his nose at authority again.

"It really don't matter," Daimon said." It's all about the appeal now. The van stop was no good and you should've granted the suppression hearing, but it's cool. It's all about the appeal. I'm cool with that."

Ms. Dustin stood to make her argument. She said she thought the recommendation on Bryan by P&P was unfair. She told the court about another client of hers who was convicted of six counts of sexual assault on a minor and how P&P recommended less time for that defendant than they did for Bryan. "These are convictions for possession of stolen property, not for taking it."

Judge Bell interrupted. "I understand what lies beneath this case. I was born at night, but not last night."

Ms. Dustin spoke quickly, "I'm not asking for a free ride. Don't give him a free ride. But consider only small habitual treatment and run it concurrent."

The judge gave Bryan the opportunity to speak. Bryan said, "I'd like to leave it with what Ms. Dustin said. But I'd like to ask for mercy from this court."

I wonder sometimes if Bryan ever thought about it—about what would've happened had he cooperated. That would've been the appropriate time to ask for mercy, to say, "I screwed up my life." Now was too late; the finish line had been crossed. Bryan's words weren't some form of remorse for what he'd done. The only regret either one of these guys had was in getting caught.

Judge Bell looked at Daimon and Bryan and said, "I've been around a long time—over forty years in this business.

This is the most prolific criminal enterprise I've ever seen. Mr. Monroe is the most prolific, resourceful criminal, and he's proud of it."

Incredible as it sounds, Daimon stood there nodding and said with a grin on his face, "It is what it is."

The judge continued, "This criminal enterprise has hurt many people. Some people lost their businesses. It's like a kick in the gut when people find out things they hold dear have been stolen. I believe these two men will repeat if they get out. We heard it on the tapes, talking about getting out and doing it again. They have zero remorse."

Even more incredibly, Daimon again was nodding his head up and down, affirming what the judge was saying.

"The public deserves protection. Habitual is a no brainer," Judge Bell said.

He sentenced Daimon to twenty-six terms of life without the possibility of parole. Two of the life sentences would run consecutive to each other while this case would run consecutive to the car-stop case. Daimon's face turned red. I couldn't tell whether he was amazed or furious. He'd be eligible for parole in the car-stop case after eight years. If he makes parole or when the sentence discharges, he'll start serving his first term of life without parole.

In some states, life without parole means an inmate can actually be paroled after twenty or twenty-five years. But in Nevada, life without parole means precisely that—life without parole. In effect, Daimon will never get out of prison unless he receives a pardon, his sentence is commuted, or his convictions are overturned.

Judge Bell sentenced Bryan to twenty-five terms of ten years to life. Two of the terms would run consecutive and this case would run consecutive to the car-stop case. For Bryan, this meant he'd have to serve about twenty-six years before he'd be eligible for parole to the streets.

I sat for a moment and thought about the gravity of the sentences. I was proud of the work I'd done. The hundreds of hours of follow-up investigation and testimony were worth it. The impact on the community was immeasurable. These criminals would never be able to wreak havoc in people's lives, ever again.

But I also went deeper. I thought about the humanity of the situation. I tried to imagine what it might've been like when Daimon and Bryan were kids. Someone somewhere must've entertained aspirations of greatness for them. Maybe it wasn't their parents—I don't know—maybe they didn't grow up like that. But someone—an uncle, a sister, or a grandparent—had to have dreams about these two when they were just boys. But their lives took a different path. Daimon and Bryan must've felt untouchable—kings of all they surveyed—when they were living high on the spoils of their crimes.

But their success plunged some of their victims into the depths of despair; some lost their businesses. All lost their sense of security and safety in their everyday lives; their equilibrium had been shredded and would never fully recover. Even though the victims weren't physically harmed and their homes were never violated, the effect on them was indeed no different.

The sentencing was over. Daimon was brought to the door leading to the inmate elevators. He made sure to flash his smirk again and laughed out loud. The laugh was bravado from a man whose twisted view of life skirted the edges of insanity, implying, "You haven't seen the last of me, not by a long shot."

Judge Bell spoke with Sandy. "With that over, do you see any sense in going forward with the other case?" He was referring to the sex-abuse case, which was also in his courtroom. "Do you really want to have those girls go through all of that?"

Sandy said, "I haven't spoken with Ms. Luzaich about it yet. May I approach the bench?" They spoke about it for a little while and then we left the courtroom.

As Sandy, Shelly, and I went to the elevator, there were happy exchanges between us, congratulating each other for a job well done. Happy about the successful prosecution of what was undoubtedly, the largest investigation of its kind in Nevada history.

However, I wasn't thrilled about human beings living locked away in iron cages. If any other way could be found to protect the public from people like Daimon and Bryan, it would be a monumental leap forward to a higher level of civilization. But the reality is, no better way exists currently. So, it wasn't about taking joy in someone's anguish, it was about taking joy in our successful triumph in protecting the innocent.

Sandy knew a defense attorney who was in the elevator with us. He had been in the courtroom for the sentencing. He looked at Sandy and sighed. "*That* was a little over the top," he said as he rolled his eyes, referring to the extensive punishment.

Knowing I wouldn't be able to change his mind, I didn't try. But he hadn't been in the courtroom for the trials. He hadn't met each and every one of the victims, and he had no idea about how many other unidentified victims were out there. He had probably never even been the victim of a serious crime. He saw a snapshot of this story and arrogantly thought he knew what he was talking about.

I turned away from him and commented to Sandy about the judge saying maybe the sex-abuse case didn't need to go forward. "If the judge is worried about the girls having to testify and be cross-examined, I think he's wrong. The girls testifying might actually be good for them—like medicine or a cathartic experience that would help them not live their lives as damaged people."

I wanted my interaction with Daimon to be over, but I wanted more for those girls to find some kind of closure.

Sandy agreed and said she would talk to Lisa Luzaich.

Some might've thought proceeding with Daimon's remaining court matters was overkill—Daimon was already doing life, two back-to-back lifes to be precise. However, trials aren't only about the defendants; they're also about the victims, something I think the system has lost sight of. Something that makes it easy for prosecutors to give up or offer weak plea deals, sometimes without even notifying the victims. If trying Daimon in the sex-abuse case might bring some form of closure for the girls, we owed them. And in the murder-for-hire case, the system as a whole must address instances where the very fabric of the system is challenged. When public officials are targeted for murder, it can't be whitewashed or minimized. Further, Daimon will be writing appeals to higher courts for a long, long time. It made sense for prosecutors to work on layering sentences on Daimon to ensure the days of The Joker preying on our community were over. But even life sentences aren't absolute guarantees. Appeals, sentence commutations, and pardons have happened in the past with horrendous results.

In 1990, Maurice Clemmons had been sentenced to a total of ninety-five years in prison in Arkansas. His convictions were for multiple felonies including stealing a gun and about $6,700 worth of other items from a state trooper's home, and for robbing a woman in front of a Little Rock hotel bar. In the robbery, he simulated a gun in his pocket, then beat the woman on the head while taking her purse. Clemmons was to be eligible for parole after twenty-five years, in 2015.

In 1999, with the support of an Arkansas Circuit Court judge, Clemmons filed a clemency petition with then

Arkansas Governor, Mike Huckabee. The petition was granted against the wishes of some of the victims and prosecutors in Clemmons' cases. Clemmons was paroled on August 1, 2000. In July of 2001, Clemmons, still on parole, was convicted of aggravated robbery and sentenced to ten years in prison.

Clemmons was again paroled in 2004 after serving only three years, and moved to Washington State. He stayed out of trouble for about five years while on parole, but trouble returned. In 2009, Clemmons was arrested several times, including charges of felony assault on a police officer, felony malicious mischief, and second degree rape of a child. His competency was questioned and after an evaluation was ruled competent to stand trial.

On November 29, 2009, Clemmons was out on bail. He and a friend drove past a coffee shop in Lakewood, Washington, where they spotted marked police cars in the parking lot. Clemmons and his friend parked nearby, and Clemmons went into the coffee shop. Clemmons shot four police officers in cold blood as they sat at a table, eating breakfast and working on laptop computers. Clemmons fled and after the largest two-day manhunt in the history of the Pacific Northwest, he was shot and killed while armed and resisting another officer.

To further ease criticism, it should be noted Daimon had the power to stop the remaining trials from being held. He could have pled guilty and probably received concurrent time—not that it mattered in view of his life sentences. However, I figured he would never plead guilty. The attention he was getting was better than anything he'd had before. This was narcissism on steroids. Get ready for the show of your life. <>

43

//////////

BUYER'S REMORSE

*Repentance is not so much remorse for what we have
done as the fear of the consequences.*
— FRANÇOIS DE LA ROCHEFOUCAULD

A few weeks later, D.A. Noreen Nyikos, the lead prosecutor
in Daimon's murder-for-hire case, called. Noreen was
a pretty, thirty-something, thin, redhead who looked like
she could be Kirsten Dunst's twin sister. Although she was
an emotional person who didn't hide her feelings, she was
smart, experienced, and loved her job.

Noreen said she received several motions from Daimon's
attorney, Ms. DiEdoardo. One was for the court to compel
Detective Kelley, me, and Johnny Marquez to provide
handwriting samples to a defense expert.

Obviously, the defense was going to claim Daimon's
own handwritten notes to Johnny could've been written by
Detective Kelley, me, or Johnny. It would be impossible

for an expert to say any of us wrote the notes—because we didn't. But if a defense handwriting expert said the findings were inconclusive, it would water down the evidence. I'd been waiting many months for the Mark Fuhrman defense to come out—and now here it was. I always figured I'd become the focus of a personal attack to discredit the police and take the jury's eyes off the ball. When a defendant can't dispute facts and evidence, one of the few options left is to create something unbelievable and put maximum effort into getting people to believe it.

Judge Herndon was the judge for the murder-for-hire case. He's always been known as a good, fair, yet, tough judge. He's a clean-cut looking man in his forties who's in good shape. He denied the request to compel the handwriting samples and said the court had no jurisdiction over parties who weren't defendants. He said Ms. DiEdoardo could *request* we provide the handwriting samples and if we refused, she could tell the jury.

I spoke with Noreen about the ruling, and she wanted to do the comparisons anyway without the defense requesting it. It would head-off their strategy. Ms. DiEdoardo probably would've been better off not tipping her hand. A few days later, we all provided the handwriting samples.

Chief Deputy D.A. Roy Nelson, Noreen's direct supervisor, signed on to work the murder-for-hire with her. He was experienced. Roy had bright eyes, and with his tanned skin and lean, muscular build, he looked like he could lead a men's beach volleyball team.

After a couple of weeks, Ms. DiEdoardo removed her handwriting expert from the defense witness list. I'm fairly sure her own expert believed Daimon wrote the incriminating notes.

November 4, 2008—Sandy ran for Justice of the Peace for Clark County in the Henderson Township. She ran against David Gibson, a veteran defense attorney of twenty-seven years. He was also the Henderson Mayor Jim Gibson's brother. The mayor was well liked and had a lot of influence in that city. The local newspapers endorsed David Gibson for the office, although one said in the endorsement, "DiGiacomo is a prosecutor and a good candidate. We wish she were in another race."

Sandy lost the election, forty-five to fifty-five percent. I was torn about it. Sandy would've been a great judge. Her motivations were pure, and she would've served the community well as a judge. At the same time, I was thankful in my own selfish way. I enjoyed working with Sandy on a day-to-day basis, and her shoes would be tough to fill if she left the ROP Unit. With all the time Sandy and I had spent working together on Daimon's and many other cases, Sandy's husband, prosecutor Marc DiGiacomo, nicknamed me "Sandy's work husband." I wasn't ready for a divorce.

On November 10, Bobby decided to take Sandy's latest offer. He agreed to plead guilty to two felony counts of possession of stolen property in the big property case and grand larceny in the Wynn Resort case. Sandy would argue for restitution and about the $75,000 from Tammy at Bobby's sentencing.

I heard Bobby on the jail phones talking himself into believing he might have a shot at probation. He wasn't eligible for a habitual sentence, so a huge prison term wasn't possible. But he must've been the only person in Las Vegas who thought he wasn't headed to prison.

When Bobby was sentenced, Sandy asked Judge Bell to

order Bobby to come up with the $75,000.

Judge Bell said, "And he's going to pay that how?"

Sandy said, "It doesn't matter, Your Honor. We would still like it in the Judgment of Conviction."

The judge gave Bobby a chance to speak. Bobby said, "Your Honor, I'm asking for mercy for me and my family. I'm a sinner, but now I have God in my life. I'm sorry for ever being friends with Mr. Monroe and the bad choices I've made."

Mr. Kennedy asked the judge to give Bobby probation and said, "He had it before, back in 1992. He could do it again now."

Judge Bell said, "Not a chance. He was an integral part of the most prolific criminal enterprise in the history of Clark County. Period. Without any doubt. Big part. It merits a severe sentence."

Mr. Kennedy asked for two to five years on the sentence. Judge Bell gave Bobby six to twenty years, but declined to order the return of the $75,000. Bobby later had another eighteen to forty-five months added on for the Wynn Resort case, and he was ordered to pay almost $20,000 in restitution to the Wynn since they completely reimbursed the victim. It was less than Bobby actually stole, as some of the money had been recovered.

Bobby fired Mr. Kennedy and brought in new counsel, who filed motions to withdraw his guilty pleas and go to trial. The probability of those motions being granted was extremely low. Once a guilty plea is accepted—and especially after a sentence is rendered—defendants have few options. Bobby would have to show he was mentally incompetent at the time he made the plea, or the plea was somehow made unwillingly—a tough row to hoe.

Bobby's motions were denied. One judge said she thought Bobby had buyer's remorse once he received the prison sentence. Bobby was shipped off to prison.

All this time, Lexie Mason had continued her research to locate more victims, trying to return property. She had found another dozen victims, including the owner of an Eric Clapton signed guitar, gold records signed by The Doors, and the owner of the large, framed Titanic artifact.

I called Lexie, and she said she was working on an authentic original handwritten letter from Abraham Lincoln, valued in the hundreds of thousands of dollars, but hadn't found the rightful owner. I told Lexie if she needed help to let me know.

On November 18, 2008, Daimon was brought to Judge Villani's court for sentencing on the gun case. Judge Villani said, "Sir, you have a terrible record. You're a bad thief; every time you get out of prison you commit new crimes. Hopefully I can protect our community here."

Judge Villani sentenced Daimon to three concurrent terms of life without parole. He ran this sentence consecutive to Daimon's other sentences. So, in the three cases Daimon had been sentenced on, he racked up eight to twenty years, three consecutive terms of life without parole, and twenty-six concurrent terms of life without parole.

Daimon was transferred to High Desert State Prison in Indian Springs, Nevada. This facility is about an hour or so north of Las Vegas and is the closest men's prison to the city. Normally, most prisoners sentenced to life without parole are sent to Nevada's maximum security facility in Ely, way up north. But since Daimon had pending court dates, they wanted him closer for ease and cost of travel arrangements.

But the High Desert Prison officials knew who they had in Daimon. I bet they didn't treat him like any ordinary bird. I'm sure they have special precautions in place for inmates like Daimon, who have nothing to lose in trying to escape.
<>

44

BELLAGIO

*Science has not yet taught us if madness is or is not
the sublimity of the intelligence.*

—EDGAR ALLAN POE

January 24, 2009, was a long night. I worked late on an unrelated case and arrived home as the sun was coming up. As I approached my house, I noticed something in my yard. Sticking out of the ground about every four or five inches were hundreds of plastic forks, like you'd use at a picnic. They were all over the place. There wasn't a spot in my yard without forks in the ground. Someone spent a great amount of time and effort to make sure these forks were stuck in the ground—they weren't just thrown or dropped. I've never seen anything like it before, but it sure seemed like a message.

I looked around. There wasn't a soul to be seen. When I was done picking up the forks, I went inside and fired up my computer. Maybe *Google* could help figure out the message. I stayed quiet. No one in my house was up yet and I didn't want to talk about the forks until I knew more. As I typed, "Stick a fork" into the search engine, it auto-populated possible search terms, bringing up "Stick a fork in it." According to the *Urban Dictionary*, it means 1) A state of completion or, 2) To be completely destroyed or defeated. My heart thumped for a moment.

I went back to *Google* and some of the other links gave some insight. Apparently, people like to stick forks in the yards of their targets, kind of like tee-peeing a house with toilet paper. The sort of harmless prank usually done by kids.

Just then, I heard a car engine out front. Looking out the window, I saw the van from our church pull up. I went outside and greeted some of the youth leaders and kids from the church. They were apparently out all night, sticking forks in the yards of friends from church. Funny for them. Funny for me, too, now that I understood. I was thankful this was a harmless prank and not a warning of some dark event on the horizon.

I spoke with Noreen about Daimon's upcoming murder-for-hire trial. She asked if I knew anything about a ROP detective interviewing Daimon about some bomb extortion investigation. I had no information about it, though I knew there was no way any ROP Detective had been to see Daimon.

Noreen said, "Yeah, his attorney said it had something to do with an extortion letter being sent to the Bellagio Hotel."

A light of understanding flashed in my head. Several weeks before, Robbery Detective Gordon Martinez had been handling an investigation where someone mailed an extortion letter to the Bellagio Hotel. The letter demanded a large sum of money and gave a time and location of where the drop was supposed to be made. The writer threatened that a bomb would go off at the Bellagio if the drop wasn't made. Detailed information in the letter aroused more than normal concern that it might be legit. I won't provide those details, as the investigation is still open. Needless to say, no money was ever dropped and the Bellagio is still standing.

"I have no idea why Detective Martinez would've talked to Daimon about it. But I'll get a hold of him and find out," I said.

When I called Detective Martinez, I asked if he knew the name Daimon Monroe or Daimon Hoyt.

"Yeah, that's a guy I spoke to at the jail a couple of months ago." Detective Martinez said Jan Seaman-Kelly in our forensic lab examined the extortion letter a while back. Mrs. Kelly was an expert in handwriting comparison, among other things.

"She compared my extortion letter to the handwriting of a suspect I'm looking at. She said it wasn't my guy but she thought the handwriting looked similar to someone else she had recently done handwriting on," Detective Martinez said.

Daimon's handwriting looked similar. Mrs. Kelly had previously examined the notes in the murder-for-hire case, so she was familiar with Daimon's handwriting. She later did a full, formal comparison between Daimon's handwriting and that on the Bellagio note. Her conclusion: Daimon couldn't be ruled out as the author of the extortion letter, yet couldn't be positively identified, either.

Detective Martinez said, "When I interviewed your guy, I thought he was weird, I mean he might be crazy. He kept talking about conspiracy theories and asked, 'Did Detective Nickell send you down here to talk to me?' I told him I didn't know what he was talking about."

Detective Martinez didn't think Daimon was involved in

the bomb extortion even though Mrs. Kelly thought Daimon was a possible suspect.

I said, "If you end up looking at him again and need any insight into who he is, what makes him tick, or who any of his friends are, give me a shout."

I spent a few minutes digesting the information. I wondered if Daimon could be the guy who sent the bomb letter. Could he be trying to raise money to hire a hit or two from jail? If he sent the letter, he would've needed outside help. Someone would have to re-mail the letter for him. Inmates have to put their name and ID number on the outside of the envelope before they hand their mail to the jail staff. Daimon couldn't send it to the Bellagio directly. My guess was Daimon didn't send the extortion letter. But I'd been wrong before.

Daimon's attorneys might be able to use this new information to make it look even more like the police were harassing him. I'm sure Daimon was bouncing off the jailhouse walls because I was "setting him up" on another case. <>

45
/////////

STOP
CORUPTION

Suspicion is not less an enemy to virtue than to happiness; he that is already corrupt is naturally suspicious, and he that becomes suspicious will quickly become corrupt.

—SAMUEL JOHNSON

Jury selection in the murder-for-hire case was completed on April 15, 2009, and the trial began. After opening remarks, the first witness called was Susan Young. Susan was a civilian who worked in Jail Intel. She explained how the inmate phone system operates and how investigators use the system to monitor inmate phone calls.

During Ms. Young's testimony, a local newspaper reporter and photographer were in the courtroom. Several times, Daimon scribbled notes and flashed them to the photographer. The notes read, "STOP CORUPTION" and, "DA + LVMPD = CORUPTION," and "REGIONAL CORUPTION CENTER." The last one played on the court building's name, Regional Justice Center.

Judge Michelle Leavitt was called to the witness stand. The tone in the courtroom became awkward. It's not every day a sitting judge is put under oath on the witness stand.

Michelle Leavitt was in her late thirties, had blondish hair to her shoulders and looked like your everyday soccer mom. After she was sworn in, Roy asked her to describe what her position as a judge entailed.

"As a criminal judge, I handle all aspects of a criminal case. From assignment, to pleas, to trial, pre-trial motions, to sentencings, as well as writs of habeas corpus."

Roy said, "You described one of the things you do as a criminal judge is sentencing, correct?"

"Yes, I handle sentencing for all the cases in Department 12."

"How do you consider yourself in terms of sentencing defendants coming in front of Your Honor?"

"I consider myself to be fair and impartial. I consider each case on its merits, based on facts and circumstances and the law and the sentencing guidelines."

"What might Mr. Monroe have been facing in your court if he had been convicted?"

"Well, he *could* face a sentence of life without the possibility of parole."

"Is that what you would sentence him to?"

"That would be the maximum."

"But you hadn't made any decision whatsoever with regard to his case. Is that fair to say?"

"Absolutely."

Roy asked Judge Leavitt about the threat made to her life. "Fair to say you took these threats seriously?"

"Yes. I have three children living at home."

"After hearing of these threats, did things in your life change?"

"Yes, things in my life changed. Obviously, I was most concerned about my children, so there were precautions taken as to my children, and where they were during the day, and where they were when I was at work. Precautions were taken when I was walking to and from my car and while I was in the courthouse. We took extra security measures to assure my safety as well as the safety of my family. My home was under surveillance for quite some time. I always had precautions in place to protect my family; they were just heightened during that time period."

"Including Metro setting up surveillance on your home?"

"Yes, they did set up surveillance on my home."

Ms. DiEdoardo cross-examined Judge Leavitt. "Did you ever receive any information from the Las Vegas Metropolitan Police Department about a threat to your children?"

"No. But obviously, I wanted my children protected. I didn't want them harmed because of what their mother does for a living."

"At the point when Metro advised you of what their allegations were, did they also advise you that everyone involved with it was in custody?"

"When they came to me in September of '07, yes, they did tell me Mr. Monroe was in custody, yes."

Ms. DiEdoardo said, "If these allegations had never been brought to light, and at some point during that case you were appointed to our state Supreme Court, what would happen to Mr. Monroe's case? In other words, would the case be dismissed?"

Judge Leavitt said, "By law, the governor would be required to fill my vacancy."

"So, is it fair to say if you could not serve, the state would find a new judge to handle the case? The state wouldn't be obligated to let Mr. Monroe go just because the judge—the judge the case had originally been assigned to—was no longer on it, correct?"

"Correct."

On re-direct, Roy said, "The information you received from Metro was not that Mr. Monroe himself was going to do this, right?"

"That is correct," Judge Leavitt said.

After Judge Leavitt's testimony, Judge Herndon put the jury on recess. The C.O.'s in the courtroom took Daimon's papers away from him. Roy informed Judge Herndon about the signs Daimon was flashing and how the jury may have seen them.

The judge told Ms. DiEdoardo, "Have a conversation with your client, please. Inform him there are spontaneous declarations defendants can make that can give rise to them being called to the stand to testify, if they're trying to put things in front of the jury without taking the stand. In addition, it's inappropriate to display things to the media, or to anybody else in the courtroom setting, during the trial. Have that conversation, if you would, please."

Ms. DiEdoardo said, "I apologize to the court. I didn't know what was going on. I would've stopped it if I had."

Daimon was sitting right next to her the whole the time, and she wanted people to believe she didn't know he was making signs and showing them around to people in the courtroom. Not very convincing.

After the break, the bailiff called me into the courtroom. Daimon was seated at the defense table with Ms. DiEdoardo. The smug look I was used to seeing was back. And his hair kept getting darker each time I saw him.

I testified about the burglary investigation, including a good portion of what I'd already testified about in the other trials. This was done so the jury could understand motive; so they could understand why Daimon was desperate; so they could understand why he wanted to kill public officials.

Noreen handled my direct examination. She asked about when I learned of the murder-for-hire plot. "Did you take the threat seriously?"

"Certainly," I said.

"Why?"

"I had spoken to Mr. Monroe in the past. I had listened to every conversation he had with his friends for over two years. Knowing so much about his background told me this was possibly true. It fit right into Daimon's personality to want to control everything around him."

"Did you have concerns about whether this was a legitimate possibility, something he could accomplish?"

"Yes. I knew through Joe Kelley's investigation and through what Johnny was saying on the phones that he was trying—Mr. Monroe was trying—to spend $10,000 to have each one of us killed, $10,000 a head. I knew $75,000 was still floating around out there somewhere. I knew Daimon had other associates who didn't go to jail. I knew there was a possibility my investigation hadn't uncovered all of the money out there. I knew from my investigation it was possible there were more storage units filled with hundreds of thousands of dollars worth of stolen property. The possibility of him being able to have something done was very real to me."

"Did your behavior change? Did you do anything different in your life in light of the information?"

I paused, not having expected this to happen. But at that moment, I realized I was uncomfortable testifying about this. It felt like a wave of heat across my body. Daimon was sitting there with his usual smug look, and I was about to admit he got to me. Even today, times crop up when I fear he may have figured out how to carry out his plan. But I didn't want Daimon to get pleasure out of what I had to say. I didn't want him to hear me say I felt vulnerable.

"I started changing my routes to and from work. And before this, I had probably started to get complacent and didn't always carry a gun with me when I was off duty. But now, I'm always carrying one again."

I thought about Colonel Grossman saying, "If you ever leave your house without your gun, you might as well stretch out your arms and let out a big 'Baaa,' as you aren't a sheepdog anymore. You've voluntarily become a sheep."

I described changes in my behavior and some of the steps I took to be more secure. But I didn't want to say too much. I didn't want to give Daimon a how-to lesson if he decided to lash out one day in the future. But I think the jury understood what was going on. I think they sensed my apprehension in letting my guard down.

When Ms. DiEdoardo cross-examined me, I'll admit, the experience was out of the ordinary. Ms. DiEdoardo, as I've previously explained, is a transgendered person. I'm not familiar with the specifics of medical procedures or other treatments she may have undergone, but from my perspective, she isn't very passable as a female. I don't say that to be disrespectful or to poke fun; it was simply my observation, and I had not worked with a transgender before now. So you can imagine I was distracted during her questioning.

Further, Daimon, an effeminate, vain man with homophobic tendencies, defended by an attorney who was built like a linebacker wearing a dress and a five o'clock shadow, was hunched at his table, smoothing back his hair. For sure, there was a strange mix of personalities in the courtroom.

Ms. DiEdoardo's direction with her questioning quickly took form. The police were being painted as people who had a serious problem with her client, going to extremes to pick on him. She implied Daimon was being framed. She'd only have to convince a single juror that the police entrapped him and made him do something he wouldn't otherwise, if not for being enticed by the police.

After a few minutes of questioning, Ms. DiEdoardo said, "Do you decide on your own or in consultation with the D.A.'s Office, who is and who is not a ROP target?"

I said, "We have a system in place which determines that. It's done according to a set of established criteria."

"What are those criteria?"

I looked at Noreen, which sparked her to rise from her seat. "Your Honor, may we approach?" she said. Noreen knew, just as I knew, the answer might cause a mistrial. My response might tell the jury about criminal history matters considered too prejudicial. The jury already knew Daimon was a felon. It was an essential part of the prosecution's case. They had to know Daimon was facing treatment as a habitual criminal in his previous trials, this was some of the impetus behind his desire to kill people. But they didn't know everything. They didn't know exactly how many convictions Daimon had or the details. They also didn't know about the charges Daimon faced in the sex-abuse case. The judge thought it would be too prejudicial.

The witness stand was right next to where Judge Herndon sat. I could hear the attorneys whispering, yet couldn't make out much. After a couple of moments, Ms. DiEdoardo walked over to Daimon, and they whispered to each other. Daimon nodded to what Ms. DiEdoardo was saying. She re-approached the bench. She said something to the judge and the attorneys returned to their places.

Ms. DiEdoardo continued, "Before we went to the sidebar, I asked you what the criteria is that your office uses to determine who is a ROP target or not a ROP target?"

"Yes."

"Go through those."

"It's a two pronged set of criteria. The first prong is the person's criminal history. They have to have three or more prior felony convictions. The second prong is basically the suitability of the case itself, the merits of the case. Is it a strong case, provable? Are there major deficiencies in the case? Are there witness problems? Do you have a victim who isn't credible? The provability of the case and the criminal history of the defendant enter into the decision."

Ms. DiEdoardo brought up information about when detectives were surveilling Daimon in Bobby's big truck and he was trying to do counter-surveillance. She said, "Did the detectives, who were following Mr. Monroe at this time, did they express aggravation to you because he was doing this?"

"They didn't express aggravation to me. It would be my assumption they weren't aggravated, because it's normal. They see that quite often."

"Fair enough," Ms. DiEdoardo said.

Ms. DiEdoardo asked about why we needed S.W.A.T. to serve the warrant at Daimon's house. She said, "Talking about the security cameras. It's not against any county ordinance to have cameras outside? Same thing with barred windows, nothing illegal with that?"

"Correct."

"So is it fair to say you made the assumption when you went into the house that the property in it was stolen because, as far as you could tell from jailhouse conversations, they had no visible means of support, other than Ms. Tremaine working part-time?"

"I didn't make an assumption when I walked into the house that anything was stolen. I suspected we would find stolen property there. I presented probable cause to a judge, and the judge authorized the search warrant. It was possible we would go to the house and find nothing. That wasn't the case. We started discovering stolen property, and that's when we knew we had stolen property."

"Is it standard practice for a Deputy District Attorney to be called out on a search warrant?"

"No, not standard," I said.

"So it would be considered unusual for Ms. DiGiacomo to be called out to the scene, as she was in this case, correct?"

"Yes."

"Was the reason that you called her out to the scene because there was some concern about the validity of the search warrant?"

"Absolutely not. The search was valid. It was signed by a judge."

Ms. DiEdoardo changed subjects and said, "Detective, let's talk about the money for a second. What you mentioned sounds like at some point in the investigation it transitioned into rather than searching for stuff, to searching for dollars, is that a correct statement?"

"Yes."

"All right. And as far as you know, Ms. Tremaine had no knowledge of your search warrant to seize the funds when she made the withdrawal you spoke of, correct?"

"I'm not sure. I mean it would be my guess she didn't. But I know there was a jail phone call where she had a discussion with Mr. Monroe about someone coming and doing a freeze, and she was referring to freezing the bank account. I think she suspected something was coming."

"Wouldn't it also be reasonable for anyone who just had a search warrant executed on their house and they were arrested to believe, perhaps, that their assets might be seized by law enforcement?"

"Maybe—if they believed their assets were profits from crime."

After Ms. DiEdoardo was done cross-examining me, Noreen stood for her re-direct. "Detective, Ms. DiEdoardo asked you what the justifications were for someone being a ROP target. You mentioned three prior felonies, recent criminal activity, things like that. Did Mr. Monroe fit those requirements?"

"Yes."

Noreen asked other questions about the search warrant, and I noticed, on the screen, the search warrant with the stamp from the District Court Clerk showing it was officially filed on November 15, 2006; nine days after we searched. During this time period of over two years, Daimon had been trying to convince people that I didn't have a search warrant for his house and I later forged the judge's signature on a doctored up warrant. Eventually, he even convinced himself of it, and I'm sure it's part of why he was acting so crazy and trying to hire people to kill public officials.

Daimon's false belief began many months before, when Sandy gave Mr. Hart a copy of the search warrant for Daimon's house. His copy didn't have the seal on it showing, "Filed with the Clerk of the Court." Sandy had made Mr. Hart's copy before she received the certified copy back from the court clerk. But if it were a big deal, Mr. Hart could've picked up a file-stamped copy from the court clerk at any time.

The stamp was a mere formality of course, but Daimon believed the warrant was invalid because the stamp wasn't on his copy. That morphed into a belief the warrants didn't exist and the judge's signature was forged. It morphed even further over time into Daimon believing Judge Bell indeed signed the search warrant—but ten months after we searched Daimon's house. Daimon believed the judge did this to help cover up his imagined police corruption.

Once the attorneys were done questioning, the bailiff

handed the judge several notes from the jury. Judge Herndon went through the notes and decided which questions would be admissible.

One question was, "Why do they call the tool Matthew?"

I felt my face blush a little. I didn't expect the question to come out in this trial where Matthew wasn't important. I turned to the jury and said, "Interesting question. Mr. Monroe had a friend, an associate from his past named Christopher Clayland. His nickname was Matthew. I don't know why his nickname was Matthew. But I've been told that Christopher Clayland has a bent penis. So they called the bent tool Matthew."

A couple of the women on the jury modestly covered their mouths in surprise while several others giggled.

Judge Herndon said sarcastically, "So glad I asked *that* question." He then asked the attorneys if they had follow-up questions.

Noreen said the state did not.

With a giggle, Ms. DiEdoardo said, "As much as I want to ask more about Matthew, no, Your Honor."

I never would've guessed that one day I'd be in a courtroom being cross-examined by a transgendered attorney who was joking about some guy with a bent penis. I couldn't have made it up if I tried. Court adjourned for the evening.
<>

46

EXPOSED

Human behavior flows from three main sources:
desire, emotion, and knowledge.

—PLATO

*F*BI Special Agent Rich Beasley was the first witness
called the next day. He testified about the phone calls
between him and Johnny and told the jury how Johnny had
been a reliable source of information in the past. He provided
an anchor of credibility to Johnny, where the defense would
insist he had none.

After Agent Beasley testified, Sandy was called to the
stand. This was probably the most awkward she had felt
walking into a courtroom since her first days as a young
prosecutor. It would be for any prosecutor, I imagine, being
in the box under oath. Roy handled the direct examination.

After Sandy identified Daimon for the jury, she explained
how she had been prosecuting Daimon on my cases.

"Why did you go to Mr. Monroe's house on the morning of the search warrants?" Roy said.

"Well, because the way the ROP team works, we handle being assigned to particular defendants or suspects by alphabet. And because it was Mr. Monroe, it was going to be my case because I cover M. So when I knew the warrant was being executed, and when Detective Nickell called and told me about the amount of property being found, I knew it was my case. I wanted to go there and see it for myself because I'd have to prosecute it."

Roy said, "What did you see when you went there?"

"I don't know how to describe it. Probably over four hundred crime scene photos were taken inside the residence, but they don't do justice to the amount of property there. It was unbelievable. The living room had vaulted ceilings. When you walk in, it was covered from floor to ceiling with art work, expensive furnishings and flat-screen TVs. I mean, the house was just packed. Even upstairs—there was some sort of storage space—it was packed. The rafters in the garage were also packed with costly looking artwork and other expensive stuff. In the garage, a fully stocked coke machine like you'd see in a restaurant was working. Multiple Viking refrigerator/freezers in the garage packed with food. It was unbelievable."

"On November 6, 2006, did you take any of the property home with you? Did you receive any of the property from the defendant's home?"

"Receive it personally? No, I had some of it photographed for evidence, but no."

"None of it would be contained in your home, right?"

"Correct."

Roy's line of questioning was to mount opposition to Daimon's claim that Sandy and I had "stolen his stuff and had a garage sale."

Sandy spoke about learning of the murder-for-hire plot. Originally, inmate James Mailer had told the police Danny Butcher wanted to kill Sandy. Sandy said she knew right away that Danny Butcher didn't want her dead. Although Sandy prosecuted Butcher, and he was serving a lengthy sentence, she knew he respected her and might even have had a crush on her.

"But want me dead? No way. If there was any one person I had to pick out who was behind it, it would be Daimon."

"After learning of the investigation, did certain things change in your life with regard to everyday life, both from being a prosecutor, and you also have children as well?" Roy said.

"Yes, I do."

"Please continue," Roy said.

"Well, personally, it was, I remember the date, August 9, 2007, when I got the call. I was asked where my kids were at that moment. I was asked where my husband was at that moment. They didn't know the time frame of the threat. So, we had to go get my kids out of school. We—since having kids, we didn't have our guns in the house—we got our guns back in the house. Two days later we were getting qualified for concealed weapons permits. I had special permission to carry a gun on county premises. I was told to never take the same route home, and I didn't for probably five or six months while this was going on. It affected our personal life. We kept our alarm on the house. We looked over our shoulders every time we backed out of the garage. Every time I took a walk to court—because my office is across the street—I'd look over my shoulder. But personally, I guess I was worried."

"In terms of the defendant, did you have any personal vendetta toward him whatsoever?"

"No."

Roy finished up his questioning. Ms. DiEdoardo began her cross-examination.

After asking Sandy about the functions of her office and how the cases get assigned, Ms. DiEdoardo brought up the issue of seizing monies from the attorneys. "So would it be fair to say, by your actions, you prevented Mr. Monroe from retaining counsel of his choice in the other case?"

"Yes. Well, I prevented him from obtaining counsel with stolen funds," Sandy said.

"Last year, were you a candidate during the last election cycle for Justice of the Peace?"

"Yes."

"Would it be fair to say in the course and scope of that campaign, it would require a certain amount of public appearances?"

"During the campaign, yes."

"And in general, Justice of the Peace candidates don't have a security detail, correct?"

"No, they don't have a security detail."

"So would it be fair to say during this period of time you were certainly—whatever your feelings about the allegations were—you were not in fear, you were not dissuaded from running for judge?"

"During the time I was out campaigning, this story broke in the news," Sandy said. "So it had already come to light. The investigation was over. So, actually, I felt *more* comfortable that nothing would happen because before I started campaigning it was out in public view."

"All right. So you don't have any fear currently, do you?"

"That's—no, I do."

"Why is that?"

"Because I think I'm going to look over my shoulder for the rest of my life. I think your client—the defendant—if he had the opportunity, would still do it."

"And you base this on what? You don't have the ability to see into our minds or souls, but what gives you the impression? What do you have other than the allegations in this case?"

"Well, actually it goes to my knowledge of the defendant, and what I have seen during the last two years of dealing with him. When I had the initial car-stop case, he spoke about taking out or trying to kill the victim in the case. They referred to him as "The Chinaman" on the jail calls and . . ."

"Objection, Your Honor," Ms. DiEdoardo said.

Judge Herndon said, "Ms. DiEdoardo, you asked the question. You can continue, Ms. DiGiacomo."

Sandy was getting upset. She wasn't used to feeling vulnerable in the courtroom setting. And she wasn't used to having someone antagonize her while she was only supposed to bite her lip. "What always stuck with me was he didn't go through with killing Mr. Chen. Not because he had any qualms about killing somebody—at the time, he didn't want to pay the money. He thought he had another scam to get me to give him the misdemeanor he was looking for. And, throughout the entire time, I have listened to hundreds of phone calls. I have seen the federal suit, which I didn't even know about until the news media brought it to my attention. I have seen all the letters to the FBI. I have seen the complaint written about Detective Nickell to the Citizen's Review Board. I have dealt with him. I have been in court with him. I have dealt with the smirking, like he's doing now."

Ms. DiEdoardo objected to the smirking reference.

Judge Herndon said, "I'll order the jury—it will be stricken. I order the jury to disregard it."

Sandy went on, "But it goes into everything I know about him. I know I'm going to deal with him for the rest of my life, legally. I know how much hatred he has for me and Detective Nickell."

Ms. DiEdoardo said, "You don't like him very much."

"Personally, I'd say I'm indifferent."

"From your comments there, it sounds like a relatively high level of distaste you just expressed."

"It's not distaste. I'm trying to—you asked why I'm going to look over my shoulder for the rest of my life—and I explained it. But to me, he's just a defendant, like any other defendant I've prosecuted. And so I'm going to deal with him just on the legal standpoint. I'm sure there will be more suits and appeals and whatnot. But personally, I'd say I was and am indifferent to him. He's no different than any other defendant. I don't know him on a personal level."

Ms. DiEdoardo asked a couple more questions and closed her cross-examination.

Roy stood up for re-direct and said, "What was said about the Chinaman?"

Ms. DiEdoardo objected saying, "This is getting beyond hearsay."

Judge Herndon said, "I'll give them limited leeway to explore what your questions opened up. Ms. DiGiacomo, you can answer."

Sandy said, "It's been a while since I listened to the calls. I know Mr. Monroe was on one of the calls talking to Mr. Fergason—who was still in custody—about the fact they were looking into having him taken out. It was going to cost $10,000. They spoke about him sleeping with the fishes. Other times, they spoke about trying to stop him from going to court because their game plan was, if he didn't show up for court, then I'd have no case, and I'd have to dismiss it or give him a deal. The calls spoke about the black man—which I believe would be Mr. Holmes—who went in, met Mr. Chen, and scouted the place as well."

"Thank you, Ms. DiGiacomo. Nothing further, Your Honor," Roy said.

Ms. DiEdoardo re-cross-examined Sandy and said, "Wouldn't it be fair to say your knowledge of the plot had no impact on your action as a prosecutor to stay or get off the case?"

"When the plot was first brought to my attention, I was urged to get off of the case. But I'm stubborn, so I refused. I wasn't going to let him pick his prosecutor or bully me out of the courtroom. So, no, I *chose* to stay on the case. Plus the case was so huge and was more than our office could handle, let alone one prosecutor. It wouldn't be fair to turn this case over to somebody else when it's not a small file someone can read in an afternoon and know everything. There was so much to it."

When Sandy was dismissed, the jury was given a break. Outside the presence of the jury, Roy requested permission to play the phone call where Daimon and Bryan spoke about killing George Chen. Judge Herndon ruled it had been explored enough and the phone call was excluded. <>

47

IIIIIIIIII

THE RIGHT
THING

Nobody can acquire honor by doing what is wrong.
—THOMAS JEFFERSON

FBI Special Agent Scott Bakken was sworn in. Agent
Bakken was being supervised by Agent Beasley when
the investigation into the murder-for-hire began. He was
assigned the duty of following up on Johnny's phone calls
and to work with Detective Kelley.

Agent Bakken described how they eventually went to the
jail and put the wire on Johnny. Afterward, Agent Bakken
and Detective Kelley watched the rec yard on closed circuit
television. Agent Bakken said the audio recording was about
thirty minutes long, and it was replete with background noise
from other inmates playing basketball. He watched Johnny
and Daimon on video, off to one side talking while another

inmate, Angel Garza, positioned himself a few feet away to stand guard.

Agent Bakken explained how they secretly retrieved the wire from Johnny and impounded it when the rec yard time was over. Not long after, the recording was sent to the FBI lab in Quantico, Virginia, for enhancement. Work was done to reduce the background noise and make the spoken dialogue easier to hear. Our own lab probably could've done the work, but having the Feds do it removed any appearance that the recording might've been tampered with. Agent Bakken was then excused.

The next witness called was Donald Ritenour, a distinguished looking man in his early sixties with gray hair and glasses. He looked comfortable in a suit, probably because he had been an FBI agent for many years before he retired from the bureau.

Roy handled the direct examination and said, "Mr. Ritenour, how are you currently employed?"

"I'm a Technical Consultant in the area of audio analysis and signal processing, currently under contract to the FBI."

"What's your experience in this field?"

"I've been working in this area since 1976 when, as a Special Agent of the FBI, I was assigned to what's now the Operational Technology Division and trained to conduct forensic examinations of audio recordings. I have testified ninety-four times, primarily in the continental United States and Hong Kong, China."

Mr. Ritenour continued to go through his impressive qualifications and professional history, which also included conducting forensic examinations of audio recordings in approximately four thousand cases.

Roy had Mr. Ritenour describe the processes he used to enhance the audio recording to provide better quality of sound. The recorded conversation had been transcribed, and the judge admitted it into evidence. The jury members were given audio headphones to use as the recording was played.

After the recording was played, Rebecca Balint, Ms. DiEdoardo's co-counsel, handled the cross-examination of Mr. Ritenour. Ms. Balint was a young, slender, comely brunette whose hair reached her shoulders. One trait stuck out about Ms. Balint: she never showed a hint of emotion.

Her cross-examination was brief, direct, and technical. The only question of real substance was whether Mr. Ritenour removed any sections of the recording when he enhanced the sound.

Mr. Ritenour said, "No, it's a continuous recording."

Mr. Ritenour finished and was excused.

Johnny Marquez was called to the stand in shackles and sworn in. He still looked like the perfect fit for a TV show about the Mexican Mafia. Johnny had been brought down from High Desert State Prison and a couple of the prison guards stayed in the courtroom.

Noreen made sure the jury knew Johnny was no angel. She spoke about his felony convictions and about how he'd be in prison for a long time.

Johnny testified that Daimon introduced himself, and how he went by the nickname Dinkie. He said Daimon claimed he had a lot of guitars and Play Station-3 game systems he wanted to sell. "He said he had over $100,000 of the stuff stored in a warehouse." Johnny spoke about when Daimon told him Sandra DiGiacomo was prosecuting him, and how I had investigated him.

Noreen said, "How did he describe Bradley Nickell to you?"

"As a motherfucking asshole, basically. Daimon hated him."

"How did he say he felt about Sandra DiGiacomo?"

"He said she's a bitch. She came out and paraded around

his house and helped take inventory of the property and haul it out with Detective Nickell."

"Did he indicate any specifics to you about this property?"

"Daimon said it was—the property taken from him was worth somewhere in excess of $2 million dollars."

"Did he seem upset with them?"

"He was very angry."

"Did there come a time where he started talking about the judge on his case?"

"He did. He came in pretty upset because he got put in lockdown in his cell. Apparently he had mouthed off to Judge Leavitt. I don't think Judge Leavitt locked him down, I think Metro did it. He was throwing things around. He was angry. He said he believed if he was found guilty he would possibly get life in prison."

"And after he was done being locked down, did he begin to talk to you about something he wanted you to do for him?"

Johnny said, "I mean, once we struck up conversation, we started talking. He felt me out as we say and we spoke for days. And he just—it wasn't a conversation, he just kept saying, I'd like to kill that son of a bitch, or I'd like to kill this asshole or bitch.' He said, 'I'm looking for somebody on the outside to go do this deed. I want somebody to whack this bitch.' That's what he told me. He showed me some paperwork where he had over $300,000 taken from him. And he said he had assets and money on the outside."

"Did he describe how he had money on the outside?"

"He said it was proceeds from robberies and burglaries."

"Did he mention any persons who may have money of his?"

"The immediate person he said he kept in contact was a Hispanic man by the name of Carlos. He also mentioned a black guy and a white guy. Each held between $75,000 and $100,000 for him. He said the white guy worked at the Crazy

Horse as a pit boss."

Noreen said, "Now when he's talking to you about wanting to find somebody to get this done, what's going through your mind?"

Johnny said, "Accessory before the fact, for not reporting the crime."

"You're afraid you're going to get in trouble?"

"I'm already in trouble."

"What else is going through your mind?"

"That he's for real. He's got the money. He just can't get out there. He's being monitored. He knows he is. He's very, very cautious," Johnny said. "He needs to get the word out. His burglary crew has left him alone. Nobody wants to talk to him anymore."

"Did he specifically tell you who he wanted killed?"

"He said Judge Leavitt, District Attorney DiGiacomo, and Detective Nickell of the ROP team." Johnny went on to explain how he called Agent Beasley because of his past experiences with him.

Noreen said, "How often would you and the defendant talk about wanting to get these people killed?"

"Every day."

"Did he put a price on it?"

"Yes, the total price was half a million dollars. The initial price for the street people to do it was $10,000 apiece."

"Were you yourself supposed to be the one to do it?"

"No, I have associates on the outside. Either Cartel members or Mexican Mafia would do it."

"Did he ever tell you how he envisioned these killings to go down?"

"Yeah, he and I had extensive talks. He'd come to me and talk about ballistics. I'm versed in firearms. He decided a nine-millimeter would be the best caliber. He also decided that a motorcycle would be the best access in and out of the location. He wanted it to be a city block from where the judge or the district attorney lived. No more than a city block. Pop them in the head, take off."

"Did he tell you where the judge lived?" Noreen said.

"At one point I did see addresses Daimon had pulled from the county assessor's web page."

"How did he get those?"

"He had Mexican Nationals in the unit making three-way calls and taking notes to the outside. So he had some communication with the outside."

Daimon teaching himself to speak Spanish ended up coming in very handy.

"How else would you guys communicate?"

"Through notes slipped through the opening of doors. If I had been warned not to reach the door, then Garza would reach."

Noreen showed Johnny the series of handwritten notes and asked if he recognized them.

"I remember those," Johnny said.

"Are these the notes given to you by the defendant?"

"Yes."

"Were you and Mr. Monroe trying to be careful?"

"He was extremely careful. I was careful for him not to find out I was giving information to Metro. This is a man who wants a judge and a detective and a district attorney killed. He could easily have me killed. Matter of fact, I just recently turned in a note to High Desert Intelligence about the Aryan Warriors having a hit on me by him."

Noreen asked Johnny to read one of the notes out loud. Johnny looked at the note she handed him and said, "It says, 'Go with killing levit, nicols, hold digiccamo.'"

"Is there a reason why he was telling you to hold off on DiGiacomo?"

"He apparently had somebody else he was looking at to

contract for killing DiGiacomo."

Johnny explained how he gave Daimon the phone number to the undercover detective posing as Johnny's girlfriend.

Noreen said, "Did he tell you the number wasn't working?"

"Yeah."

"Did the defendant tell you why he wanted D.A. DiGiacomo and Judge Leavitt and Bradley Nickell dead?"

"Initially it was Detective Nickell and District Attorney DiGiacomo because they were the ones who went into his property and disrespected him. Daimon was a gangster and he needed to keep that image. What Nickell and DiGiacomo did was very disrespectful. He needed to prove a point: he was not to be messed with."

"Did he tell you what was going to happen once these people were dead, what was he expecting?"

"He wanted to create shock and awe, so the spotlight would go away from him. Because every time he tried to bail out in cash or through attorneys, they'd go to the attorney and seize the money, large quantities of money."

Noreen passed Johnny to Ms. DiEdoardo. She did her best to impeach Johnny's credibility by talking about his criminal past and the convictions for which he was currently in prison. She also tried to make it appear as though Johnny received a deal in exchange for his testimony.

Johnny "reaped" two things for helping: first, less ability to negotiate his case. The D.A.'s Office didn't want his testimony to appear bought. Second, he'd been labeled a snitch and was moved into protective custody for twenty-three hours a day—a sentence within a sentence.

When the attorneys were done with their questioning, a question from the jury was asked.

Judge Herndon said, "How would you have set up the Cartel or Mexican Mafia to execute the hits for the defendant?"

"The defendant *believed* I was connected."

Noreen said, "Did you cause him to have that belief?"

"No. Other Mexican Nationals did, based on conversations we had of cartel activity in Mexico."

"Now, the question about why you cooperated with Metro and the FBI; your answer was, you didn't want to be an accessory. Was there another reason?" Noreen said.

"It's morally right to stymie his plans to murder three people."

When Johnny was done testifying, the judge recessed the court for the evening. <>

48

THE SMOKING
GUN

*The demand for certainty is one which is natural to
man, but nevertheless an intellectual vice.*
—BERTRAND RUSSELL

When the trial resumed, Angel Garza was called to the
stand. He was in prison garb and belly chains. Angel
is a big, Hispanic guy, about six foot two and more than
two hundred thirty pounds. He has full sleeve tattoos on
his arms and a tattoo in Spanish on his neck. After Angel
was sworn in, Roy asked about his prior felony convictions.
They were for possession of a stolen vehicle, felony reckless
driving, voluntary manslaughter with a deadly weapon, and
conspiracy to commit kidnapping.

"It's fair to say you don't want to be here today, but the
state issued you a subpoena to be here?" Roy said.

"Objection, leading," Ms. DiEdoardo said.

Judge Herndon sustained the objection.

Roy started again and said, "Do you want to be here today?"

"No, sir."

"We issued you a subpoena, which is a court order for you to be here today?"

"Yes, sir."

Roy had Angel describe how he met Johnny in jail, and how he came to be acquainted with Dinkie. Angel only knew Daimon as Dinkie in the tank.

"I direct your attention to September 10, 2007. Did you hear Johnny and the defendant talking that day?"

"Yes, in the rec yard."

"Do you recall what was said?"

"He wanted Johnny to do things for him."

"When you say do things, what were those things?"

"He wanted to pay him to do some murders for him," Angel said.

"When you say he wanted to pay him, you are talking about Mr. Monroe wanting to pay Mr. Marquez to do some murders for him, right?"

"Yes, sir."

"And did he say who he wanted to be murdered?"

"Yes."

"Who are those people, sir?"

"He wanted Judge Leavitt, D.A. DiGiacomo, and Detective Nickell."

"Were you employed as a look-out to keep other people away?"

"Not employed, just asked to."

"Would Mr. Marquez do the same for you? How did that work, sir?" Roy said.

"No, not the same thing for me. I was just there, you

know what I'm saying?"

"I want to direct your attention to September 15, 2007. Do you recall another conversation between Mr. Monroe, who used the alias Hoyt, and Mr. Marquez?"

"Yes, sir."

"What was said in that conversation?"

"He wanted—Detective Nickell was a son of a bitch."

Roy said, "Do you recall him using the word motherfucker?"

"Yes."

"In fact, you wrote a statement, is that correct?"

"Yes, sir."

"Hoyt said he wanted those motherfuckers killed?"

"Yes, sir."

"He said especially Detective Nickell first, is that right?"

"Yes, sir."

Roy directed Angel to recall a conversation on September 18. "Do you recall Mr. Hoyt's answers to certain questions?"

"Johnny kept asking, 'Are you sure you want this done? Are you sure you want this done?' numerous times."

"Did Mr. Marquez ever ask Defendant Monroe how the murders were going to be accomplished?"

"Yes, sir. Johnny was supposed to have one of his cartel buddies have the murders done."

"How did Mr. Monroe say he was going to pay Mr. Marquez?"

"He was going to pay $10,000 for each head initially and half a million when it was done—all through."

"Do you ever recall him saying he had over a million dollars in property?"

"Yes, sir."

Roy added, "Mr. Hoyt—that is, Mr. Monroe said that, correct?"

"Yes, sir."

Roy went through a line of questioning where Angel explained he hadn't received anything from the state in exchange for his testimony. Angel said it had turned out bad for him to testify. Like Johnny, he had been labeled a snitch and was in protective custody. Angel explained how he can't take classes or be involved in programs to knock time off his sentence because of the lockdown.

Roy passed Angel to Ms. DiEdoardo.

"Sir, are you affiliated with a gang?" Ms. DiEdoardo said.

"I'm a crossed-out Southsider. It means I was a Sureño but I'm no longer in the gang life."

"All right. Why did you decide to act as a lookout for Mr. Marquez?"

"I had his back."

"Why was that?"

"Because he trusted me, I trusted him."

"Do you recall Detective Kelley telling you if the information you provided proved to be one hundred percent accurate and of substantial assistance to his investigation, he'd recommend the D.A.'s Office issue you a letter documenting your assistance?"

"Yes."

"Did you understand the letter could be useful to you when you came up for parole?"

Angel said, "Parole? Letters don't mean nothing to the parole board. They don't have to look at it. They don't want to pay attention to such stuff."

"But did he communicate to you it could be useful if they chose to look at it?"

"He just said, 'I'll get you the letter.'"

"Did you know when you were acting as a lookout that Mr. Marquez was wired?"

"No, Ma'am."

"Did you know Mr. Marquez was working as an informant for the FBI as well?"

"No."

Ms. DiEdoardo passed Angel back to Roy.

Roy said, "In the meeting in the rec yard, did you ever hear the defendant mention anything about an individual named Carlos?"

"Yes, sir."

"What was said about Carlos?"

"Carlos—I can't get a hold of him. Hoyt was very paranoid. His phone calls were being monitored."

Angel explained how he passed notes several times between Daimon and Johnny. When Angel was done testifying, the prison guards took him out of the courtroom.

Later in the day, Detective Kelley was called to the stand. He testified about when the information about the murder-for-hire plot first came to him. It had to do with James Mailer pointing the finger at Danny Butcher. He went on to describe his interview of Butcher on August 9, 2007.

Roy said, "Without telling us what was said, did you confront him about the potential of him being a suspect in the solicitation of murder?"

"Yes. Sat him down and went right at him."

"What was his reaction?"

"Absolute shock. Just absolute shock. You could see it in the expression on his face. It was like somebody kicked him in the gut. He had no concept of what we were trying to say. It was outside his realm of reality. Gave me a clear indication he had no idea of what we were speaking of."

"Did you name the individuals who were the subject of your investigation?"

"I did not. But he actually guessed who the target of the investigation was."

"That was your initial conversation or interview with

Danny Butcher, correct?"

"Correct. During the course of the interview with Mr. Butcher, it was clear he didn't have any direct knowledge of what we were referring to, and he certainly wasn't what we believed to be a suspect. He took a piece of paper he had with him and wrote a name on it. He laid it face down and said, 'Tell me who you're talking about, and we'll see if it matches my name.' Of course, we didn't do that. But he eventually turned it over; his paper had the name Daimon."

"Daimon Monroe?" Roy said.

"Exactly. And as we went forward, he identified him by his full name, Daimon Monroe."

Roy had Detective Kelley explain the plan to wire Johnny for a meeting with Daimon.

Detective Kelley said, "On the 14th, I went to the jail just so I could get my mind around this whole thing. I physically walked the route they were going to walk. I went to their housing module and saw where they were housed and the hallway they'd go down. I went out into the rec area. I got to observe the entire area where they were standing. I then went up to the control area which houses the cameras, so that we could find out how much we could view and see of the rec area itself. When I was there, I also learned while we could view it, we couldn't record it. That camera didn't have recording capabilities, but we could see what was going on. While I was there, I went to the bank of phones the inmates used. You have to keep in mind they're not free to move around all the time. Some areas might be locked down. So when they're in their housing area, I have free rein and can walk around. I went to the bank of phones there. We attempted to establish an account with the phone service provider to allow a telephone call to go from the jail to one of our detectives. I attempted a telephone call from there, and it appeared to me to be working fine. It looked like the call was going to go right through without an issue, so I was happy to learn that."

Roy said, "You mentioned an undercover detective on the outside of the detention center, correct?"

"During the contact I had with Johnny, he said the defendant, Daimon, was having trouble getting a call out. Daimon didn't feel he could make any phone calls that wouldn't be listened to. He knew Detective Nickell was listening to calls. He suspected his mail was being checked. He was trying to make three-way calls through other people. But in doing that, there would be someone on the other end listening. So he was trying to find someone on the outside he could contact who could facilitate the movement of money. What we were attempting to do was use our undercover female detective as his point of contact. So I met with Johnny Marquez and gave him our undercover's cover name and the telephone number. He was then to pass it on to Mr. Monroe, who would then contact her. Our hope was he'd say, 'Go see this person and you'll find the money under a rock,' or something."

Detective Kelley testified about the dozen incomplete calls made to the undercover detective's cell. He said on some of the calls, Daimon's voice could be heard on the recorded line, although the calls were never actually connected to the undercover cell because of the glitch with the service provider.

Roy asked about Johnny being wired in the rec yard.

Detective Kelley said, "Mr. Marquez was concerned about the wire. 'Daimon is going to check me. He's going to make me raise my shirt. He'll hug me. He's going to check me.' We decided to put the wire down in his upper thigh or crotch area because most guys are reluctant to reach down there to check it out."

Detective Kelley also explained how he obtained writing

samples from Johnny and Angel and collected several pages of Daimon's writing from jail personnel. Daimon had been filing papers and documents for months, and those served as great material for forensic comparison with the notes.

On cross-examination, Ms. DiEdoardo asked a lot of questions about Danny Butcher. She was trying to paint Butcher as being the person behind the plot, how Detective Kelley went after the wrong guy. "Would it be fair to characterize Mr. Butcher as a fairly experienced criminal?" she said.

"That would be a fair summation, yes," Detective Kelley said.

"Would it be fair to characterize Mr. Butcher as a member of a criminal association?"

"There are allegations, yes."

"Would those allegations be the Aryan Warriors?"

"Allegations I've heard, correct."

"Have you verified those allegations?"

"No, I have not."

"Just explain for the jury what the Aryan Warriors are," Ms. DiEdoardo said.

"I know very little about them other than they're an alleged prison gang, I don't work that type of investigation so I can't tell you what their function is."

"Are they known for assassinations?"

"I don't have any background or knowledge of how the Aryan Warriors function."

During re-direct, Roy asked Detective Kelley about why he figured Butcher wasn't the person behind the plot.

Detective Kelley said, "The first source of information leading us to Danny Butcher was James Mailer. When I spoke with Jail Intel, it was real clear to me his information might be a little suspect. The reason being, Mailer was a current ROP target in custody on a number of serious charges. His sentence could put him in prison for the rest of his life. I was also receiving information that not only did Mailer give this information, but he alleged he had information on narcotics and on a possible homicide. What I believed Mailer was doing was picking up information out of the module and trying to do the Velcro thing—throw it against the wall and see if something sticks. So, by the time I got to Butcher, Mailer's information was so convoluted, I didn't feel Mailer was a credible source."

"Mr. Mailer wanted out of custody, didn't he?" Roy said.

"Exactly. He wanted somebody who would get him out of jail right now and, 'I'll go do all of this wonderful stuff for you.' In my experience, if you do that, they take off and the chase is on."

The attorneys finished up, and the jury presented their questions through the judge.

Judge Herndon said, "What initially led you to interview Johnny Marquez after the Butcher interview?"

Detective Kelley said, "I received, I believe on August 29th, a call from Special Agent Bakken. Scott Bakken indicated he had been in touch with Mr. Marquez and Mr. Marquez had information about a Judge Leavitt. So based on that, he suggested the two of us go to interview him, so both of us could have a better background of his information and try to determine whether or not we were looking at our Judge Leavitt or his Judge Leavitt. The call from Special Agent Bakken is what led me to interview Johnny Marquez."

Judge Herndon said, "Did you or Detective Nickell coach Johnny as to what to say or what information you were looking for with regard to the taped conversation between him and the defendant?"

"I never gave him any coaching, only to go over the things he was telling me were occurring. I never said, 'Say this, say this, say this.' It was just, 'You go meet and discuss what you've been talking about. Do what you've been doing.' "

Judge Herndon said, "This is kind of part and parcel. Did you instruct Johnny to solicit specific information from the defendant?"

"Quite the contrary. You run into a situation where I could be involved in entrapment. I have to be really careful. I cannot try to coax the person to say something he normally wouldn't say, so I have to be really careful not to get into such an area. We have to make sure we keep it within the frame of what he's already told us."

"Thank you," Judge Herndon said. He unfolded another note and asked about Johnny and Angel, "Why do you think they cooperated?"

"In this particular case, Johnny Marquez made it real clear that, number one, he was concerned for the safety of these victims. Number two, he felt it was a moral obligation on his part to report this. He was concerned if he didn't get involved, this might occur outside of his scope. This was like an open hit; it was just put out there for whoever could get it done. And the third thing is, it's kind of maybe honor among criminals. He believed this was over the line. There are certain things you do and certain things you don't. This was just over the top. You don't do this."

Ms. DiEdoardo had follow-up questions. She said, "Detective, you testified in response to the juror's question whether you coached Mr. Marquez to say particular words when he was meeting with Mr. Monroe. You testified you didn't do that?"

"Correct. I did not."

"As part of your training and experience, are you familiar with the elements of criminal offenses—particularly the elements of solicitation?"

"Yes, I am."

"So you would know what Mr. Marquez would need to

say in order to have enough evidence to proceed and have a case you could refer to the D.A., would that be a fair statement?"

"I'd know the things in the letters he was providing me was evidence of the solicitation, so if he could just continue to do what he'd been doing and cover the same information, I'd know I was fine."

"But you felt—you didn't think you had enough to go forward with just the letters, correct?"

"That's not true," Detective Kelley said, shaking his head.

"It isn't? Then why did you feel the need to create this undercover situation?"

"I was looking for the smoking gun."

"What do you think the potential consequences would've been if Mr. Marquez was discovered wearing a wire?"

"Objection, speculation," Roy said.

Ms. DiEdoardo withdrew the question and said, "With regard to—fair to say the only reason you put Mr. Marquez in this position with cameras, recordings, a wire, was because you needed it in order—you felt you needed it in order to make your case. Fair to say?"

"No, not fair."

"So you put Mr. Marquez in that danger just as a maraschino cherry or you felt you needed it?"

"First, he's the one who volunteered to do it. Second, it would've furthered my investigation. I didn't doubt it was the thing to do."

"So it was necessary, in your mind?"

"It wasn't necessary, but desirable."

On re-direct, Roy said, "In terms of the danger to Mr. Marquez, when you placed the recording device, fair to say while they were in the rec yard there were multiple eyes on Mr. Marquez as well as Mr. Monroe, right?"

"Everyone involved with this, including the C.O.'s in the module, knew what we were doing. If something had gone wrong, we would've been there in seconds."

"Thank you, detective. The state has no further questions for this witness."

This concluded Detective Kelley's testimony. The next witness coming up was an expert scientist from the crime lab, Jan Seaman-Kelly. Her testimony was paramount to the case. <>

49

CONVINCING SCIENCE

Science may have found a cure for most evils, but it has found no remedy for the worst of them all— apathy of human beings.

—HELLEN KELLER

After the lunch break, the jury took their places in the jury box. Mrs. Kelly was called to the stand. Jan Kelly was in her forties, had light brown hair, light skin, and a soft smile. She always looked professional, and when she spoke, she clearly had a very high intellect, with just a touch of southern drawl.

Noreen said, "How are you employed?"

"I'm a Forensic Document Examiner with the Las Vegas Metropolitan Police Department."

"How long have you been there?"

"Here in Las Vegas for a little over eleven years."

"Prior to that, what was your employment?"

"I was employed by the Oklahoma County District Attorney's Office in Oklahoma City, Oklahoma. For eleven of the sixteen years, I was there as a document examiner."

"Can you briefly describe your duties as a Forensic Document Examiner?"

"A Forensic Document Examiner compares questioned or disputed writing or printing processes—in this case, writing—to known writing to determine if both were prepared by the same writer or different writers."

"Have you had any formal education?"

"I have a Bachelor's Degree in Criminal Justice from the University of Central Oklahoma."

"What about specialized training in the field of forensic document examination?"

"To be a Forensic Document Examiner, you have to be trained with a minimum of two years from a recognized Forensic Document Examiner. I was trained by the U.S. Postal Crime Laboratory in San Bruno, California, by George Lucas and Cecil Morton."

"Are you board certified?"

"Yes."

"What board certifies you?"

"It's the American Board of Forensic Document Examiners." Mrs. Kelly went on to explain the certification process, some of the training, and how often she has to be recertified. She continued by telling of how she had won several awards in her field, and how she had published several papers in the Journal of Forensic Sciences and the American Society of Questioned Document Examiner Journal.

Noreen said, "About how many questioned documents do you examine each year?"

"From the time I started over twenty years ago, I've

averaged one hundred cases a year."

"Have you previously testified in state and federal courts as an expert?"

"Yes."

"Do you only conduct examinations when asked by the state or police?"

"No. Metro has an open door policy. We will do examinations for the defense, if the defense attorney would like it. I've done quite a few for the Public Defender's Office."

"Do you charge a fee, if you were to do it for someone other than the state?"

"No, ma'am."

"What makes handwriting identifiable?"

"Handwriting is identifiable because it's comprised of a combination of characteristics that are within your set of writing. When *you* look at writing, you pick up a lot of pictorial habits, which I don't pay attention to. But there are certain things I pick up on. The combination of habits tends to be more in the internal structure. And those are habits you are not aware of, which people don't tend to change."

"Is one letter characteristic enough to identify somebody?"

"No, ma'am. You have to look at the whole combination of what's in the writing. The identification or elimination—I do both of course—is based on the combination within the range of variation the writer has."

"What are you talking about when you say variation?"

"Range of variation refers to—we're not machines. So every time you write, it's going to look different and that's normal. People always tell me, 'I never write my signature the same way twice.' Well, I would hope not. You're not a machine. There will be a range you will fall in but it's still a pretty well-defined boundary. So, I'll examine a lot of signatures to determine what's your range of variation or a great deal of writing to determine that range. It's an integral part of comparison."

Mrs. Kelly went on to explain some of the process in how she conducts her examinations.

Noreen said, "So, any doubt in your mind that the defendant, Daimon Monroe, wrote these notes?"

"No, ma'am."

Mrs. Kelly used a chart to show the jury, in detail, the numerous similarities in Daimon's known handwriting when compared to the handwriting on the notes. She explained how she was able to view the obliterated text on the blacked out note by using a Video Spectrum Comparator (VSC). The top line of text on the note read: "Go with killing levit, nicols, hold digiccamo."

Noreen said, "Once you completed your comparison, were you able to make an identification?"

"Yes."

"Who did you make an identification to?"

"Daimon Monroe is the writer of this note."

"Nothing further," Noreen said.

Ms. Balint stood and said, "What title do you prefer? Detective? Officer?"

"Mrs. Kelly."

"Are you related to Detective Joe Kelley by chance?"

"No, he doesn't spell his name right. He has an extra E."

"So, you've always worked for the police department, correct?"

"Police department and D.A.'s Office. I do a lot of work for the public defender, as well."

"You consider what you do to be one tool in the police investigator's bag, correct?"

"It's a resource for them to determine if someone wrote something or did not."

"So you are part of the investigative team?" Ms. Balint said.

Mrs. Kelly answered with a shrewd tone, "No, ma'am, I'm not."

"Handwriting analysis, is this something I could go to a four-year college and get a degree in?"

"Forensic document examination is a field covering a variety of aspects of documents. You cannot get a four-year degree. You can take some college courses covering it, and there is also at Oklahoma State University, a master's certification. You don't get a Master's Degree but you get a certificate after you complete the courses."

Ms. Balint said, "Do you have laws in your field?"

"Yes."

"Do you use the scientific method?"

"Yes."

"What is the scientific method?"

"The scientific method has to do with developing a hypothesis and testing it to determine whether your hypothesis is true or not. In forensic document examination, part of our tenets are, no two people write exactly alike and you do not write the same way twice. This is based on a great deal of research over the years, from all the document examiners in the field who conduct and do the work. For the science basis, when a detective or a public defender or a defense attorney or prosecutor comes to me, I have no idea if I'm going to identify the individual or not. I tend to eliminate far more than I identify. So if a detective brings me a case and wants to know about—like in this case—did this individual write a document? I'll then begin an exam to determine whether they did or not."

Ms. Balint said, "Is there like a text or doctrine where all of your laws are found? A text or doctrine in handwriting analysis that everyone follows?"

"Yes."

"Do you know what the name of that is?"

"Well, I co-authored the most recent one. Its title is, *The Scientific Examination of Questioned Documents*. It's a revision of a book that Ordway Hilton originally wrote back in 1952, then again in the early 1970s. A lot has changed in forensic document examination, so I wasn't able to just add a couple pages. It's a total rewrite of the previous work. It's a textbook. We also have a textbook that's old, done by Albert Osborne in 1901 that goes through the tenets of handwriting and principles of handwriting identification. It tends to cover lead pens because that's what they had in 1900. A database I have access to has well over 10,000 papers on document examination published since the mid-1940s."

Ms. Balint seemed to shrink while listening to Mrs. Kelly's response. She had no idea she was questioning one of the world's foremost experts in forensic document examination—until now.

"Would you say that everybody who passes the certification for document examiner is equally good at analyzing documents?"

"The purpose of the certification test is to establish minimum competency. That's all it establishes. Taking the proficiency tests each year will reveal if somebody is having a problem they need to be taken off the certification for. One of the things we have in our lab is one hundred percent peer review. When I finish each report, the other document examiner, Jimmy Smith, totally peer reviews my work to make sure he's in agreement. If he didn't agree, he wouldn't sign off."

"So he signed off on all your work?"

"After he reviewed it, yes, ma'am."

"He also worked for the police department?"

"Yes."

"You said that you had no doubt in your mind about your identification in this case, correct?"

"Yes."

"So, you are saying you are one hundred percent sure?"

"When I identify somebody, yes, they are the writer of that note, yes ma'am."

"Have you ever gotten an analysis wrong?"

"No."

Ms. Balint asked questions about the examination using the VSC technology and Adobe Photo Shop digital imaging software. "Earlier, you said you played around with Photo Shop with the colors. Is that what you do, play around until you get the answer you're looking for?"

"I don't play around. I did play around in the context of trying different colors because Photo Shop has a lot of different tools. I don't change what the document is, but until I find the correct setting that helps where I can see something, yes."

"So there's no methodology to it. You play with the settings?"

"You adjust the settings," Mrs. Kelly said with a touch of asperity.

"Do you go word-by-word when you do your analysis?"

"I go word-by-word. I go down letter-to-letter. I go down to individual little construction for the minute details within the letter. But I read every page that was submitted."

"That was a great deal of writing to go through," Ms. Balint said.

"Yes, ma'am."

On re-direct, Noreen said, "Is it your job to tell the Metro Police detectives and myself and other members of my office what we want to hear?"

"No. I usually *don't* tell you what you want to hear because I usually eliminate a suspect writer."

"So if you were unable somehow to identify Daimon Monroe as the writer, would you have any problem telling Detective Kelley or myself or members of the jury that?"

"No, absolutely not. If he were to be eliminated, I would've eliminated him."

"You said that Jimmy Smith signed off on your exams, right?"

"I don't like the term 'signed off.' He does a peer review. I do my work. He takes it and he goes through it and he does it. And, if he's in agreement, then he signs the peer review so stating."

"Was he in agreement with all of your reports associated with this case?"

"Yes."

"So sitting here today, are you one hundred percent sure that Daimon Monroe is the writer you identified?"

"Yes, he is the writer of the notes."

When Mrs. Kelly's testimony was complete, she was excused and the jury was sent home for the weekend. <>

50

DISTRACTIONS

*The truth is incontrovertible, malice may attack it,
ignorance may deride it, but in the end; there it is.*
—WINSTON CHURCHILL

On April 20, 2009, the jury was called back into court and
Judge Herndon said, "On the record in 241570, state
of Nevada versus Daimon Monroe. Mr. Monroe is present
with his attorneys. State's attorneys are present. We're in the
presence of our jurors. When we ended last week, I believe
the state was prepared to rest their case, correct?"

Roy said, "We are. And we do rest. Thank you."

"All right, Ms. DiEdoardo, does the defense wish to call
a witness?"

Ms. DiEdoardo called James Mailer to the stand. Mailer
was in a prison uniform and shackles. His dark hair was
greasy and his demeanor was shifty. Ms. DiEdoardo wanted
him to testify about how he thought Danny Butcher was the

343

person behind the murder-for-hire plot. But Mailer didn't want to testify. It would likely expose his story as false and potentially subject him to criminal liability for obstructing justice or perjury, since he received a deal in his own case for providing information to the police. He got his plea agreement on bogus information. But the judge had already ruled Mailer had a Fifth Amendment right not to testify about that, as he might incriminate himself.

So plan B was for Ms. DiEdoardo to use Mailer to diminish Johnny's credibility. After several questions to form foundation, Ms. DiEdoardo said, "During the period you were living with Johnny in the jail, did you form an opinion as to his truthfulness?"

"Yes, he was known for fibbing a little."

"Did he lie about big things or small things or all kinds of things?"

"All kinds of things. He was always telling stories."

Ms. DiEdoardo passed Mailer to Noreen.

Noreen said, "When you were being held with Mr. Marquez, Mr. Monroe was in that same housing unit, correct?"

"Yes."

"Would you observe Mr. Marquez and Mr. Monroe passing notes and talking a lot?"

Ms. DiEdoardo objected. "Goes beyond the scope of the cross."

Judge Herndon said, "State?"

Noreen said, "Well, Your Honor, this goes to—I mean, he's being put up here just to paint Johnny Marquez as a liar."

"All right. The objection is overruled."

"No, I never saw them pass notes," Mailer said. "I saw them talk from time to time. Everybody spoke in the unit."

Mailer was dismissed and taken out of the courtroom.

His impact vanished with him.

Ms. DiEdoardo called Danny Butcher to the witness stand. He was brought in from the inmate waiting room wearing prison garb like the others we'd seen. He was a rough looking kind of guy. He carried some size and wasn't the kind of man you'd want to make mad if you were alone together. Butcher had been to prison several times before, and he knew how to survive in the gladiator academy. When he spoke, he sounded like he'd smoked two packs of cigarettes everyday for twenty years.

After Butcher was sworn in, Ms. DiEdoardo said, "Mr. Butcher, would it be a fair statement to say that you're not thrilled about being compelled to testify in court today?"

"Yeah, that's for sure."

"Why is that?"

"Because I don't really know nothing about the case. I don't know why I'm up here in the first place."

Ms. DiEdoardo had Butcher identify Daimon in the courtroom and tell about how they'd been housed together in the same module. She then said, "Do you recall at some point getting into a physical altercation with Mr. Monroe?"

"No."

"So, you don't remember swinging a bat at his head?"

With a condescending look and tone in his voice, Butcher said, "A bat at his head? In Clark County Detention?"

"Yes, sir."

"Where are you going to find a bat in a detention center?"

"Just answer the question."

"I never hit him with a bat or tried to."

"You were prosecuted at one point by Sandra DiGiacomo, correct?"

"Yes, ma'am."

"In fact, Sandra DiGiacomo is one reason you're serving a fairly substantial sentence, true?"

"I don't know if she was a reason, but she was the prosecutor who prosecuted me."

"Do you remember having a meeting with Detective Kelley and another detective?"

"No," Butcher said.

Butcher was being difficult. Ms. DiEdoardo pressed harder and was able to help him remember the meeting.

"Do you remember Detective Kelley telling you he heard you were involved in an alleged plot to kill Deputy D.A. DiGiacomo?"

"I remember the rumor, yes."

"What was your reaction when you heard that?"

"I don't think you want the answer."

"I do sir, or I wouldn't have asked."

"I think Detective Kelley is crazy. I didn't find it believable," Butcher said.

"You didn't find the story or the detective believable?"

"Both."

"Mr. Butcher, are you involved with an organization called the Aryan Warriors?"

"Absolutely not."

"So, you're not an A-dub prospect?"

Butcher appeared hostile, on the edge of his seat. He raised his voice and said, "No. Why would you ask something like that? What does it have to do with this case?"

"Sir, I get to ask the questions. You get to answer them. You testified originally you didn't recall a meeting with Detective Kelley. I pressed you on it and you said it did take place?"

"What I said was I don't remember talking to a couple of detectives. I don't know Detective Kelley."

"All right, but you recall having this meeting?"

"Yes."

"And is some of the reason you're a little hesitant about

confirming you had this meeting with the detective . . ."

Butcher raised his voice again and said, "I ain't got nothing to hide."

"Are individuals in prison who talk to cops generally thought well of by their peers?"

"Depends on what you're talking about, being rats, of course not."

"All right, do you think . . .?"

Butcher raised his voice yet again, "Why don't you just ask the question instead of beating around the bush?"

"Hold on," Judge Herndon said, trying to get Butcher to calm down.

Ms. DiEdoardo continued, "Do you consider yourself a rat in your conversation with Detective Kelley?"

"Absolutely not."

Ms. DiEdoardo passed Butcher to Noreen who said, "Mr. Butcher, did you at any time ever solicit anyone to kill Deputy D.A. Sandra DiGiacomo?"

Butcher said, "No. No way."

"Nothing further," Noreen said.

Judge Herndon asked a question from the jury. "Did you tell any detectives that Defendant Monroe put hits on any of the victims?"

"Never ever said that. Ever."

Ms. DiEdoardo said, "Mr. Butcher, is it fair to say there's bad blood between you and Mr. Monroe?"

"Other than me sitting here, I'm not mad at that dude. Why I'm involved with this is the only reason I'm mad. I shouldn't be sitting here. I'm not mad at that dude, no."

Butcher was led out of the courtroom. As he walked past Ms. DiEdoardo, he looked like a predator surveying his prey.

Butcher's testimony, although dramatic, had no purpose other than an attempt to distract the jury. Perhaps the theatre would distract them. It worked for O.J. Simpson.

Ms. DiEdoardo called Steve Fulmer to the stand. Visibly uncomfortable in a courtroom setting, he was sworn in and sat down. Answering the question, Steve explained how long he'd known Daimon.

Ms. DiEdoardo asked said, "If you had to state how well—how close is your relationship?"

"I know him fairly well."

"Close friends?"

"Sure."

Ms. DiEdoardo wanted Steve to testify about his conversations with Daimon on the jail phones. She wanted the jury to hear that Daimon told Steve he was innocent, and the police had set him up. But the judge had put her on notice earlier, outside the presence of the jury. He wouldn't allow her to ask Steve questions about the phone calls to elicit specific comments Daimon had said. It would be self-serving hearsay and akin to Daimon testifying without the state being able to cross-examine him.

Ms. DiEdoardo said, "Mr. Fulmer, do you recall having a conversation with Mr. Monroe while he was in custody at CCDC?"

"I spoke to him on the phone several times."

"All right. And during any of those conversations, did you hear anything that would cause you to be concerned about harm to another person?"

Noreen said, "Objection, hearsay."

Judge Herndon sustained the objection.

Ms. DiEdoardo was frustrated. But even though Steve didn't answer the question, the jury knew what he would've said. Something to the effect of, "No, he's a harmless guy." Even though the result was miniscule, Ms. DiEdoardo still got what she wanted.

There were no further questions from either side. Steve's testimony was a waste of time. Daimon's testimony—coming next—promised to be much more interesting. <>

51

////////

THE BIG SHOW

A sociopath is one who sees others as impersonal objects to be manipulated to fulfill their own narcissistic needs without any regard for the hurtful consequences of their selfish actions.

—R. ALAN WOODS

*M*s. DiEdoardo called Daimon to the stand. Months before, I'd forewarned Noreen and Roy to expect this. Daimon believed he could convince anyone of anything. He was the most flamboyant criminal I've ever encountered. Weeks earlier, I told Sandy, "You're going to be pretty upset if Daimon testifies."

"Why's that?" Sandy said.

"After all the work you put into these trials, and everything before this, and some other prosecutor gets the chance to question Daimon under oath?"

Sandy paused and I could see the gears turning in her

head. "You're right, I will be mad."

Ms. DiEdoardo asked Daimon, "How are you today?"

"Nervous."

"Speak up, you have a soft voice."

"Nervous."

With Ms. DiEdoardo asking questions, Daimon said he was born in Los Angeles, moving to Las Vegas sometime in the 1980s with his Mom and Dad. He said when he was fourteen, his family lived in a vacant house and he worked in a calendar factory to help make ends meet. Ms. DiEdoardo was trying to humanize Daimon, make him empathetic to the jury. But my research showed it was all fantasy, stuff he had made up years ago in order to remake his identity, as his mother had put it.

Ms. DiEdoardo asked Daimon to describe the module he was housed in when he first made it through booking and processing.

"Well, like, at first, they had me in South Tower. There's South Tower and North Tower. South Tower is for non-violent offenders. North Tower is violent offenders. I was in South Tower. It's dormitories. They got like sixty-four beds. At the time, they had, like, cots laying on one side of the wall for extra people."

"Would it be—I'm imagining something like when you see military barracks in movies?"

"Kind of, yeah."

"Did your cell mate say anything strange to you?"

"No," Daimon said. "But Danny Butcher asked a lot of weird questions about my case, and questions about the search warrants. He was asking for the names of the cops who arrested me and who my D.A. was. I was uncomfortable. It wasn't like a friendly kind of asking you questions. The questions were really weird. Like uncomfortable questions."

"Did you feel like you were being interrogated by Mr.

Butcher?"

"I felt like I was being manipulated."

Daimon said he told Mr. Hart about what Butcher was doing—asking a lot of weird questions. Mr. Hart told him to stay away from Butcher. "I didn't have much ability to stay away from Butcher; we were housed in the same module. And Butcher was on the cots, so he was never locked in a cell. Anytime I was out of my cell, he could come right up to me. But after a while, he was moved off the cots and into a cell, which gave me some time away."

"At some point thereafter, did Mr. Butcher do anything to you?"

"He had a room like five doors down from mine, and I was walking from the showers and he had a guy holding his door open. He had like a mop bucket. He had a broom and tried to hit me in the head. Two days later, Butcher was shipped off to prison."

Daimon testified about a guy named Braden Moran. He wore glasses and the inmates nicknamed him "Squints." Daimon explained how he and Squints had been cellmates and, after a few days, Squints admitted to working for the police as a snitch. "He went into stuff, saying he signed paperwork that would make it a felony for him to—do you want me to tell you what he told me?"

"Go ahead," Ms. DiEdoardo said.

"I said, 'Well, I don't understand why people are being sent in here for me. I don't understand,' and he kept saying . . ."

"Objection, hearsay," Roy interjected.

Ms. DiEdoardo said, "Mr. Monroe, it's probably safe instead of saying what people said to you, just say what you said to them."

Later, Daimon testified about how he met Johnny Marquez and James Mailer, nicknamed "Wal-Mart James" because he liked to steal from Wal-Mart. "They were, like, walking and they both fell over each other. I swear to God. They tripped over each other and got up and came toddling over to me. I was like, 'What the hell?' you know?"

Daimon said they had a conversation and afterwards, Mailer and Johnny hung out by his bunk, trying to go through his paperwork. "I knew what they were trying to do. I knew they were trying to set me up on something."

Daimon spoke about his conversations with Johnny, saying, "What weirded me out about Johnny is this conversation never happened. When he was trying to set me up, he never spoke about—murder was never what he was talking about, ever. He always spoke about property. He always spoke about the money frozen in the bank, and how his lawyer could get the money out. He never spoke about anything, like, not remotely close to this."

Ms. DiEdoardo said, "At some point, did Mr. Marquez do anything you would consider unusual?"

"Well, Mr. Marquez is unusual. Everything about him is weird. The guy is strange. Some days he'd say he was with the Cartel. Some days he'd say he's with MRU (an acronym for a prison gang named Mi Reza Unidos or *My Race United*), sometimes he'd say he was a preacher—Hebrew. It was always some weird stuff. But at the same time, he came up to me and said . . ."

Roy objected, "Hearsay." The objection was sustained.

Many of Daimon's answers rambled, and the judge admonished him to answer only the questions asked.

Ms. DiEdoardo said, "Do you recall having a meeting with Detective Kelley?"

"I went into this room, and there was Kelley and a weird looking guy beside him. And I sat down and said, 'What did I do?' Detective Kelley said, 'Well, we have information that you are trying to kill a cop, a judge, and a D.A.'"

"What was your reaction to that?"

"Crazy, dude," Daimon said.

"Why do you think it was crazy?"

"I never said nothing like that. I wasn't trying to do that. I told him, I said, 'Bro, I'll take a lie detector test. I'll jump through whatever hoop you want me to right now. Let's go do it.' But Kelley didn't want no part of that."

"With regard to the meeting with Detective Kelley, do you remember making any assertions to him, anything you said to him?"

"If somebody killed the judge, they'll just put you in front of another judge. I don't understand what the point would be. Then the weird guy was, like, a really weird looking guy started . . ."

Noreen objected for hearsay, which was sustained.

Ms. DiEdoardo continued, "Go back to what you said. You hit the point I was hoping you would bring out. You said the charges were—you were pretty clear saying you weren't diminishing the significance of the charges, but you felt they were stupid, right?"

"The whole thing is ridiculous."

"Your statement was, if a judge is killed they'll just put another judge in that person's place?"

"And you would potentially face murder charges," Daimon said.

Ms. DiEdoardo asked about the civil rights complaint Daimon had filed.

Daimon said, "Like at first, the whole thing was kind of weird. They brought everything out and started giving it away on the lawn. If you want to argue about something, I think I got some due process here. So I filed the civil thing and asked to see the warrant. We didn't get to see the warrant until a year later. It wasn't file-stamped, there were a bunch of weird things with the warrant. You've got to understand, there wasn't a warrant on November 6. That makes them responsible for the property they gave away. And who would be responsible except the directing officer? That would maybe be a career-altering situation."

"When you say the directing officer, would that have been Detective Nickell?"

"Yes, ma'am."

After several minutes of other questions, Ms. DiEdoardo said, "Mr. Monroe, do you bear ill-will toward Judge Leavitt?"

"No."

"What about Sandra DiGiacomo?"

"No."

"Detective Nickell?"

"No."

"Do you think they were out to get you by any means?"

"Yes."

"Have you ever solicited anyone to kill Judge Leavitt, D.A. DiGiacomo, or Detective Nickell?"

"No," Daimon said.

"Would it be fair to say, that the reason you didn't do any of those things is because you had your pending federal civil case going, among other reasons?"

Daimon said, "I'm not violent. It's not in my nature. It doesn't make sense. I mean the civil thing—I'm going to do it legally. I'm going to report to the Citizen's Review Board and Internal Affairs. I'm not trying to hurt nobody."

Ms. DiEdoardo had a pained expression—you could almost hear her thinking, "Oh, crap!" She knew Daimon may have just paved the way for the prosecution to eviscerate whatever believability she had hoped to create for him.

Ms. DiEdoardo finished her questioning and passed Daimon to Roy.

Before beginning, Roy approached the bench and was

met there by Ms. DiEdoardo. A brief discussion was held with Judge Herndon who then said, "We need to take a recess."

The jury members were given the usual admonishment to not talk about the case and were escorted out of the courtroom.

When a defendant takes the stand, on cross-examination, the prosecutor can usually introduce a lot of their criminal history to impeach the defendant's credibility. The judge already ruled during pretrial motions that thirty-three of Daimon's now fifty-one felony convictions would be fair game to the prosecution since they were within the past ten years. But any reference to the pending sex-abuse case had been ruled out.

Judge Herndon said, "The issue raised at the bench by Mr. Nelson was Mr. Monroe's statement toward the end of his testimony, 'I'm not violent.' This raised the state's eyes to other evidence that should be gone into at this time."

Roy said, "We will have two minors testifying in case number 07F15166, I believe that's Ms. Luzaich's case. Both of the minors testified that the defendant used a Taser or stun-gun on them before committing sexual acts against them. The state's position is the sexual events are not only violent, but using a Taser or stun-gun against the minors, as well, would go into the realm of violence."

Ms. DiEdoardo said, "As the court is well aware, those are merely unproven allegations. That case hasn't gone to trial. My understanding from speaking with Ms. Browning is that the trial in that matter is not expected to take place for several months. Judge Herndon, as you are well aware, this was one of the very first issues taken up when I was appointed on this case. The state's motion was filed when Mr. Waterman was Mr. Monroe's counsel as to prior bad-act evidence. At that time, the state sought to introduce the evidence of the property case and also at least in theory with regard to the sex case. I didn't think it was appropriate to bring in the property case, and so stated. But the part that all parties seemed to agree upon was the probability that the sex case would be highly more prejudicial than probative."

Judge Herndon said, "Absolutely."

Ms. DiEdoardo continued, "I understand counsel's position and the argument that Mr. Monroe has quote-unquote opened the door because he said, 'I'm not violent.' But I think, Judge Herndon, they have more than enough evidence to attempt to impeach him based on his prior record, without getting into an area that's going to lead us all to a realm of perdition down the road."

Judge Herndon said, "It's not a 'more than enough' standard though. Here's the thing: to begin with, when Mr. Fulmer was on the stand, you sought to elicit character evidence from him about an opinion that Mr. Monroe was non-violent. The state said, 'Hey, can we approach the bench?' At the bench I told you if you try and elicit the character evidence, then pretty much everything would be fair game to come in and challenge the credibility of that opinion, which would include the sex case."

Ms. DiEdoardo said, "Understood."

The judge continued, "That was a while ago. So certainly the defense was on notice if some issue of non-violence started to come up, if somebody wanted to come up and portray him in that light, these other things may become relevant."

"I understand," Ms. DiEdoardo said.

"Second, Mr. Monroe, despite my earlier admonitions, wants to add to his answers. When you take the stand, you run the risk if you're not going to answer the question, you are going to open the door to something bad coming in. You tried to lead him. They didn't object and I know why they didn't object, because your question was, 'Is one of the reasons—is it fair to state that the reason you wouldn't have wanted to solicit the murder of these three people because you have this federal lawsuit pending?' You tried to coax him on that. And he wanted to get more in. He wanted to go around that and say, 'No, no, I'm a non-violent person. I wouldn't hurt anyone.' I tend to think it's admissible at this time because he wants to portray himself in a certain light, beyond what the scope of the question is. They're entitled to challenge that portrayal by him on the stand."

Ms. DiEdoardo said, "With regard to that, I keep saying, these are unproven allegations not yet gone to trial. I think unless the state is planning on putting these two minors on the stand and eliciting that testimony from them, they should be precluded from going into that."

Roy said, "Not only did they open the door now, but they opened the door this morning with Mr. Fulmer. And we were polite enough to approach and warn Your Honor what we were going to elicit from Mr. Fulmer, if he was going to suggest an answer to the question. We did them a favor earlier this morning. We're not going to continue to do that after he testified he's a non-violent person. Especially with his prior record, and what he did to those two young ladies."

Ms. DiEdoardo looked at Roy and said, "Allegedly."

Judge Herndon asked Roy, "What's your intention?"

"Judge, quite honestly I didn't think they were going to go there because of the prejudicial nature of it and the fact that we'd given them so many warnings. My intention is to ask Mr. Monroe if he was present during a preliminary hearing in which two girls testified he used a Taser against them. If he says he was and gives an affirmative response to that, we'll leave it be."

Judge Herndon said, "The state is entitled to cross-examine him on that, by making the statement he did. I agree.

I don't think you were trying to elicit that. Nonetheless, he chose to answer it in the way he did, opening the door up to what followed. I'll allow the state to cross-examine him about that—to a limited extent, obviously."

The jury was brought back into the courtroom and Daimon was reminded that he was still under oath.

Roy said, "Sir, do I refer to you as Mr. Hoyt or Mr. Monroe?"

"Daimon."

"You took a job as what, sir, at fourteen years old?"

"Yes."

"In what?"

"In a calendar factory."

"How long did you work there?"

"I don't really remember. Maybe a year."

"Say within the last ten years, have you had any employment whatsoever?"

"Yes."

"What do you do for a living, sir?"

"What time? I've had different jobs."

"What did you do in 2006 for a living?" Roy said.

"We pressure washed and we gambled. I gambled with a friend of mine."

"Where did you gamble?"

"Everywhere."

"Were you making in the millions per year?"

"No."

"Showing you what's previously marked as state's proposed exhibits 50 and 51, do you recognize those?"

"Yes."

"What are they?"

"Flyers that were hung up around town," Daimon said.

"Did you put them up?"

"Yes."

Judge Herndon admitted the flyers into evidence.

Roy said, "It says, "WARNING! FELONS" at the top, correct? And in it you list ROP detectives, correct?"

"Yes."

"You tell other felons these detectives are waiting, waiting to set you up or catch you committing a crime?"

"That's what they do."

"They set people up?"

"Yes."

Roy presented questions to Daimon about his prior felonies, so the jury would hear about his jaded past. Afterward, Roy questioned Daimon about the things said between him and Johnny on the recording.

Daimon said, "The best information is disinformation."

"What does that mean?"

"If he's going to try to elicit responses from me, the best thing to do is let him run around like a crazy man—just tell him what he wants to hear."

"So, you were just agreeing with him because he was bringing these things to your attention?"

"Well, no. He was more like a Danny Butcher to me. I had a broom swung at my head. I didn't want no problems. At the same time, I knew he was working with them. I figured the best thing to do was listen to what he's got to say and see if he tells me anything. At the same time, you know, tell him whatever he wants to hear, but there were never no conversations about murder."

"On the covert recording, doesn't he ask you, 'Do you want these people murdered or not?'—and you say yes?"

"I swear to God, I don't remember him saying that. I remember I had just woken up. I remember him talking. But he was always talking about getting an attorney. He was never talking about getting anybody murdered. He was always talking about trying to get me an attorney and trying to get my money unbroken."

"In terms of Mr. Nickell, you understood that Detective Nickell was watching your mail as well as your phone calls, correct?"

"Well, I knew the jail was. They were watching everything I was doing."

Roy said, "Did you send out letters through other inmates?"

"Absolutely."

"Did you make three-way calls to call other people?"

"Absolutely."

"Did you also hear Ms. DiGiacomo talk about an attempted solicitation or a solicitation?"

Ms. DiEdoardo objected and the attorneys approached the bench. After a brief discussion, the judge overruled the objection.

Roy continued, "In regard to the owner of the Anku Crystal Palace, did you ever talk to anyone including Bryan Fergason about having him killed?"

"No."

"If we had a jailhouse recording, that would be false?"

"The one with the swimming part?"

"Yes."

Daimon said, "Absolutely."

"You were talking about him swimming somewhere?"

"More hyperbole, yeah."

"You acknowledge you had a conversation with Mr. Fergason about Mr. Chen?"

"I don't know if it was about Mr. Chen."

"No?—did you have a conversation about someone swimming with Mr. Fergason?"

"Yes."

"What was said, sir?" Roy said, getting impatient.

"I don't remember precisely. It was a joke. Right after

that we both say, 'Yeah, right,' you know what I mean?"

"Did you make mention of how much someone would pay to have Mr. Chen killed?"

"Yes."

"What was said about that, sir?"

"$10,000."

"$10,000 to have Mr. Chen killed?"

"No."

"What was it?"

"I said for $10,000 somebody could go swimming."

"Someone could go swimming?"

"It was a joke, man."

"That was a joke too?"

"Absolutely," Daimon said.

"And so are these charges?"

"I said the charges are ridiculous."

Roy changed gears and paused for a moment. "Now, on direct examination from Ms. DiEdoardo, you told me and the ladies and gentlemen of the jury that you're a non-violent individual, correct?"

"Yes."

"Were you at a preliminary hearing where two girls testified?"

"Yes."

"How were those girls related to you, sir?"

Daimon said, "My children."

"Did you hear your seven-year-old testify you would spank her with a board?"

"No."

"You never heard her say that?"

"No."

"Did you ever hear her say you used a Taser against her?"

"Yes."

"Did you hear her say that you performed sexual activities

towards her?"

"Yes."

Roy related some of the sexual things his daughter had testified about and Daimon acknowledged hearing his daughter testify about it. Roy said, "Did you use a shocker on her more than once?"

"I never used one on her."

"She just testified to that, correct?"

"Same thing going on with all of that. Like Tammy moved to Kansas and changed her name. The name isn't changed. She's scared. They're scared." Daimon's posture had slumped and he didn't look so confident anymore. The over-sized suit jacket he wore rode up on his shoulders. His voice cracked, and he seemed to feign tears at one point. Roy asked if Daimon had seen his eleven-year-old daughter testify.

"Yes."

"She testified you sexually assaulted her over the course of years. Isn't that what she testified to?"

"Yes."

"In the Jacuzzi when she was six?"

"We didn't have a Jacuzzi."

"Did she testify to that?"

"She said that but we didn't have a Jacuzzi."

"She also testified that your sexual abuse of her stopped when she was finally ten, correct?"

"I don't remember."

"She also testified you would electrocute her. Do you recall that?"

"Yes."

Roy moved away from talking about what Daimon did to the girls and asked questions about the burglaries. He put a photograph of the burglary tools from Tammy's car up on the video screen.

"What are those?" Roy said.

"Screwdrivers and pry bars."

"Do they have a specific name?"

"No."

"What's called Matthew? Is there something called Matthew?"

Daimon used the touch-screen at the witness stand and said, "That one there," as he circled one of the screwdrivers.

"You had a couple of Matthews, didn't you?"

"Yes."

"Some smaller, some bigger?"

Daimon indicated with the touch-screen and said, "You can see one here and one here."

"What was the purpose of using those, sir?"

"I'm not going to answer that."

"You're not going to answer that? Do you break into commercial estates with that?"

"No. Absolutely not."

Roy pressed harder, "Were these the tools you used to commit your burglaries?"

"When you pressure wash, when you do the kitchens—you are cleaning the kitchens—we clean the Excalibur, and each kitchen has got a vent that sucks in the grease and heat and all that, they have hoods. That's what we would do. You take the hoods down. You separate them and clean the traps."

"Would there be some reason you wouldn't want Metro to figure out what Matthew was if you were using it as a burglary tool?"

"Not Metro as a whole, but ROP, yes."

"Because they might charge you with it?"

"No, because they might set me up. That's what they've done to my family and the rest of us, yes."

Roy showed Daimon one of the notes he wrote to Johnny and said, "Is this something you wrote?"

"No—I can't tell. Part of this, this part here, I can't see where it stopped. There's a part of it—most of this I wrote here. Somebody added that."

Daimon was pointing to the top line that read, "Go with killing levit, nicols, hold digiccamo."

"Somebody else added the first line?"

"Somebody added the top. The go part, somebody added that. This part where it says someone came up to me the other day, that's my handwriting down. But this right here, I didn't write that."

"You wrote the entire rest of the document but not the first line?"

"Absolutely."

When Roy finished his questioning, he passed Daimon back to Ms. DiEdoardo who said, "Daimon, you heard Mr. Nelson mention you have been convicted of several felonies, correct?"

"Yes."

"Have you been sentenced on those?"

"Yes."

"And of your most recent felonies, what sentence was imposed?"

"Life." Daimon went on to explain he had been sentenced to three consecutive terms of life without parole.

Ms. DiEdoardo continued, "Would it be fair to say the reason you went to trial on those cases is because you were innocent in your mind?"

"Yeah. I mean the property case, I always said we can argue that. But it was like—like this weird thing going on with them."

"Are you appealing the convictions in those cases?"

"Yes."

"So do you have any incentive—if you did the things Mr. Nelson is saying you did—would you have any incentive to lie about them?"

"No, I didn't do this," Daimon said.

"You recall the flyers? Mr. Nelson showed you some individual's names on them? Those flyers didn't list anyone's personal addresses did they?"

"No."

"And when you were posting those flyers, as you have testified, nobody came up to you and said, 'You are not allowed to post those bills?' "

"No. I knew they were following me. I wanted them to leave me alone."

Daimon's answer to this question makes me chuckle to this day. We weren't following him, but he was convinced we were. Like I said before, they always think we're there.

Ms. DiEdoardo brought attention to the sex-abuse case. "You haven't been convicted in that case, correct?"

"No."

"In fact, you've pled not guilty in that case, correct?"

"Right," Daimon said as he wiped his eyes.

Ms. DiEdoardo said, "I know this is difficult."

"It's disgusting."

"Is that because you believe it's such a variance with your love for your children?"

"It's disgusting."

"In fact, you're doing three consecutive lifes. Absent any change in those sentences, you have no motive to lie in that case or in this one, correct?"

"I wouldn't hurt my kids."

"Daimon, with regard to everything the jury has heard so far, did you solicit the murder of anyone?"

"I did not. I swear to God I didn't. I never spoke to them about it. I didn't talk to nobody about it. Never came out of my mouth."

"Fair to say any comments that seem somewhat

ambiguous were attributable to you trying to get information out of Mr. Marquez?"

"I feel stupid, because it's like I thought I was trying to get him to tell me things. And look at all of this now. You know, maybe it would've been better to have him swing something at my head. I didn't know what to do. I didn't think the guy was a rocket scientist or anybody would believe him. He's a weird dude."

Ms. DiEdoardo passed Daimon back to Roy who referred him to 1996 when Daimon took ROP detectives on a car chase that resulted in a wreck. "Do you remember telling Detective Brady that you apologize for running into the other officer and stated you were scared and just didn't want to go back to prison?"

"No, absolutely not."

"Do you want to see the document?"

"I don't care."

"You never said that?"

"No."

"According to Detective Brady, you stated you were really sorry. You didn't want to go back to prison?"

"Never spoke to Brady."

"Never said that?"

"Never."

Roy referred Daimon to the sex charges and said, "Ms. DiEdoardo also asked if you had any reason whatsoever to lie about those charges?"

"I didn't do them. I'm not going to lie," Daimon said.

"That's not my question. Did she ask you a question regarding that?"

"I don't remember."

Roy sighed and continued, "She asked if you had any incentive whatsoever to lie about the charges?"

"Yes."

"You don't have any incentive to say you didn't sexually assault your two young daughters?" Roy said as he gestured doubtingly.

"That's disgusting. I'd never touch my kids."

"You testified you never had a gun with regard to this last conviction, correct, in 2008?"

"No."

"It was in a storage unit?" Roy said.

"In a garbage can full of shampoo," Daimon said.

"Did you ever make any incriminating statements whatsoever via phone call about that weapon?"

"No."

When Daimon finished testifying, Judge Herndon asked some of the questions from the jury members. The first question was about Tammy. "Are you and her still together?"

"She's scared."

Judge Herndon added, "That's no."

Daimon went on, "We are, but she doesn't want to say it. She's scared of these people."

The next question was, "Did you ever exchange letters with Mr. Marquez?"

"Did I get notes or give notes? Yeah, I gave him notes."

Judge Herndon asked another question, "Why do you think all of these different people were trying to get information from you? Why do you think they were trying to set you up?"

"Good question. Because I believe on November 6, 2006, when the man asked me to take him and show him what was stolen in my home, he would need a warrant if I took him in. So when he asked, 'Take me in the house and show me what's stolen, they'd broken my door down. It would invalidate the illegal entry by me consenting to take him in. Since I didn't do that, he was stuck. There is no search warrant. He gave the property away. He's in trouble. He needs to do something to keep—because I had been in jail for a year—do something to cover up for the time I'd been in jail. So the first thing he does is go after my children."

Judge Herndon asked the next jury question, "What types of threats are or were made against your family—your girlfriend and kids?"

"Good question. She moved to Kansas, and they were calling her regularly, threatening to take her kids if she spoke to me. She was going to go to jail. Carlos, the same thing. They took his papers and threatened to seize his home if he spoke with me. They raided his home. Anybody I knew—they listened to all my calls. Why was I so important? I mean, now I understand. But at the time, I didn't understand."

Ms. DiEdoardo had a follow-up question from the jury questions. She said, "Do you think you were an easy target for all of this in your own view?"

"I think I was the only target."

"Why?"

"I think a bad search and this guy's career is on the line. I was the only one asking to see the search warrant out of everybody. They had to shut me up. Started with my kids. They try to set me up for Chris Trickle. Tried to set me up for this. Four months ago they tried to set me up that I was going to blow up the Bellagio for some money. The detective pulled me out and says they have some information . . ."

Roy objected, "Hearsay, relevance."

Ms. DiEdoardo said, "Nothing further."

Roy asked a few follow-up questions. "You're aware that Tammy has remarried, is that right?"

"She did not."

"So, if she said that, she would be incorrect?"

Ms. DiEdoardo objected, "Calls for speculation."

Daimon said, "I don't mind answering that."

Judge Herndon said, "Overruled. You may answer the

question."

Roy restated, "If she said that, that's incorrect?"

"Incorrect."

Roy showed Daimon the main note on the screen that said "Go with killing levit, nicols, hold digiccamo." Roy said, "You recognize that?"

Daimon said, "No."

"You don't recognize that?"

"No."

"You heard Mrs. Kelly testify that it's your handwriting?"

"She said it's my handwriting?" Daimon shrugged his shoulders and made a vacillating face.

Roy said to the judge, "Please direct the witness to answer the question."

Judge Herndon said, "Answer the question. Don't shrug your shoulders. You know to answer the questions."

Roy continued, "Is that your handwriting?"

"No, sir."

"It's not your handwriting?"

"No."

When Daimon's testimony was complete he stepped down, adjusted his suit jacket and tightened his pony tail. Judge Herndon sent the jury home for the evening. <>

52

///////////

THE GOOD GUY

Lawyers hold that there are two kinds of particularly bad witnesses—a reluctant witness and a too-willing witness.

—CHARLES DICKENS

The next day, Ms. DiEdoardo called Corrections Officer Nagler to the stand in his tan uniform. As he walked into the courtroom, he looked confident but nervous. Nagler was well over six feet tall and very thin. His pointy nose and buzzed hair made him stick out in the room.

Nagler was the source of the leak to a snitch about the whole Chris Trickle murder thing. In fact, a few months before the trial, I had to testify at an Internal Affairs hearing about the matter, and I heard Nagler was disciplined and booted out of Jail Intel for his actions.

I'd been hearing for some time on the jail phones how Daimon supposedly made friends with a C.O. Daimon nicknamed "the good guy." Every now and then, Daimon would talk about how "the good guy" came by his cell and told him this or that and how "the good guy" was going to testify for him.

I wondered if "the good guy" had an axe to grind because he got into trouble and was booted out of a nice assignment. He had mishandled informants, letting confidential information get into the wrong hands. It was speculation on my part, but it sure seemed the defense was unusually eager to call on Nagler, as if he would save the day.

All hat and no cattle—Nagler's testimony didn't amount to much, other than Nagler boasting and exaggerating his credentials and reputation. When he described his qualifications, he made it sound like he invented Jail Intel and was the best informant manager ever. There certainly was no lack of ego there. Narcissists can be in law enforcement too.

Ms. DiEdoardo wanted to use Nagler to say Johnny wasn't reliable and Detective Kelley wasn't a good investigator. She said, "Did you come to form an opinion regarding Mr. Marquez's credibility?"

Noreen objected, "Lack of foundation."

Judge Herndon sustained the objection.

No foundation had been laid to show how Nagler would know anything at all about Johnny. Nagler had no significant contact with Johnny. Ms. DiEdoardo tried to resurrect the foundation, but there was none. Nagler had met Johnny twice, spending only an hour or two with him. He wasn't allowed to say whether or not he thought Johnny was credible.

Ms. DiEdoardo said, "Officer, given your training and experience, did you form an opinion about Detective Kelley's investigative work on this case?"

Noreen objected, "Relevance."

The judge sustained the objection. Ms. DiEdoardo wasn't allowed to create a courtroom gossip session to distract the jury. But I'd like to know what Nagler would've said. The truth is, Joe Kelley had forgotten more about investigating than Nagler ever knew. Nagler would've looked foolish tooting his own horn. Ms. DiEdoardo passed the witness.

Noreen said, "No questions, Your Honor." She didn't want to extend the time that an irrelevant witness was on the stand.

Ms. DiEdoardo rested the defense case. Next up was the state's rebuttal.

I was called back to the stand as the first rebuttal witness.

Noreen said, "Detective Nickell, we've heard testimony regarding a series—well, from you—regarding your monitoring of the defendant's phone calls. I want to direct your attention to late September and early October of 2006. You were monitoring calls at that time?"

"Yes."

"During one of those phone calls you listened to, was there ever a call that caused you concern for the safety of another person?"

"Yes."

The "take a swim" phone call wasn't allowed in the prosecution's case-in-chief. But since Daimon opened the door wide with his self-portrayal of not being violent, Judge Herndon allowed the call in the prosecution's rebuttal case.

Noreen played the call and said, "After hearing this conversation, did you take action with respect to who you think they were talking about?"

"Yes, I did."

"Who did you think they were talking about?"

"George Chen, the owner of the Anku Crystal shop."

Noreen said, "What made you think that?"

"They were talking about him showing up to court, whether or not he'd come and testify and be a victim in court. And talking about spending $10,000 to make somebody go "bye" and make them go swimming. It alarmed me."

"What did you do?"

"I contacted Mr. Chen. I already knew who Bobby was—Robert Holmes, Mr. Monroe's associate. I showed Mr. Chen a picture of Mr. Holmes to find out if he recognized him. From the phone call I assumed Mr. Holmes had gone—or told Daimon he had gone—to the shop. Maybe Bobby had posed as a customer and had talked to Mr. Chen. I think the phone conversation said that Bobby had gone by there and tried to feel him out or something like that. Mr. Chen had no memory of Mr. Holmes ever being to his shop, but he said he couldn't be certain."

"Did you just basically give him a 'be on the lookout?' "

"Yeah. I told him to be on the lookout. He was quite alarmed as I think anyone would be."

Ms. DiEdoardo objected, "Speculation."

Judge Herndon sustained the objection.

I continued my response, "I told Mr. Chen to be careful going to and from home and not to answer the phone if he didn't recognize the number on his caller ID. I basically gave him pointers on how to be safe."

"Did you also discuss this phone call with Deputy District Attorney Sandra DiGiacomo?"

"I did."

"Did you make a determination as to whether or not to file charges on this?"

"I did not make a determination. The investigation really didn't go farther, other than what these two men spoke about on the phone. If Mr. Chen had remembered Bobby being there, maybe it would've gone farther. But there really was nowhere to go with it."

Noreen played several of the phone calls that made up the basis for my search warrant affidavit. She showed me a copy of my search warrant for Daimon's house and said,

"Showing you what's marked as state's 54, do you recognize it?"

"I do."

"Is that a certified, file-stamped copy of a search warrant affidavit and search warrant return?"

"It is."

"Now I don't know if you can see it on the screen, I'll zoom in. Is this the file-stamp of November 15, 2006?"

"Yes."

Noreen later said, "We heard testimony that Mr. Monroe asked to see a copy of the search warrant. Did he make such a request to you?"

"That was nearly three years ago. I'm not sure if he made that request to me or not."

Ms. DiEdoardo objected, "Foundation. There hasn't been a statement that Detective Nickell was present with Mr. Monroe at the time. Mr. Monroe's testimony was that he was escorted out by S.W.A.T. I thought he asked S.W.A.T. for that."

Judge Herndon said, "No, the detective earlier said he was present when the warrant was served, although he waited outside until S.W.A.T. was done. He did take control of Mr. Monroe. Go ahead."

Noreen said, "Was it brought to your attention that anybody said, 'This dude wants to see a copy of the warrant?' "

"What I do recall is that Mr. Monroe and I did have some discussion at the scene. Mr. Monroe asked me why we were there. I told him we were serving a search warrant. He asked what we were looking for. I told him we were looking for burglary tools and stolen property. I don't recall him specifically saying he wanted to see a copy of the search warrant."

Noreen said, "Did you leave a copy at the residence?"

"Yes."

"Why did you do that?"

"It's normal procedure. We leave a copy at the residence. A copy of the seal, the warrant, and a copy of the return at the residence."

"But you didn't leave your affidavit, which stated all the facts?"

"I didn't leave the affidavit because it had been sealed."

"Did you document that in some fashion?"

"They were photographed being left on a table in the living room."

Noreen concluded and passed me to Ms. DiEdoardo.

Ms. DiEdoardo asked a series of questions about the "take a swim" jail phone call. "You've known about this tape for, goodness, two and a half years, would that be about right?"

"Yes."

"In fact, until it became tactically interesting in this case, nothing more was being done with it—it's not currently under investigation or anything like that?"

"As far as the criminal investigation, no."

"Just so we're clear, no one has ever charged Mr. Holmes with soliciting the murder of anyone, including Mr. Chen?"

"Correct."

"As I recall, your words were, the reason you did not refer charges is, 'There was nowhere to go with that investigation?' "

"Yes. We didn't have notes with anybody's handwriting on it. We didn't have any further evidence other than a phone conversation."

Right after I answered, I thought, "Be careful of what questions you ask, counselor."

This concluded my testimony. I was pleased with how things went. I had a lot of eye contact with the jury, and it seemed they were getting it.

Roy called Sandy back to the stand. He presented her a copy of the search warrant for Daimon's house and said, "What is this?"

"That's the search warrant for Daimon's house that was executed on November 6, 2006."

"There is also a return attached to it?"

"There is a handwritten return."

"Has the validity of the search warrant ever been litigated?"

Sandy said, "There were multiple motions and multiple judges—two different judges."

"What were the results of the motions?"

"The motions to suppress the evidence—I believe it was Judge Bell and Judge Villani—both denied the motions to suppress."

Roy thanked Sandy for her testimony and passed her to Ms. DiEdoardo.

"Good morning, how are you?"

"Good," Sandy said.

"You've testified in response to Mr. Nelson's question that there was some litigation in the property case with regard to the warrants?"

"There was in that case."

"And in your ten years of experience as a Chief Deputy, is it uncommon for warrants to be challenged by criminal defendants?"

"It's not uncommon."

"In fact, wouldn't it be fair to say that it's also not uncommon for a trial judge—for whatever reason—to hold the warrant valid and it is occasionally reversed on appeal?"

"Sorry, that was . . ."

"I'll rephrase the question. In your experience, given your decade of experience with the law, are you familiar with any situation where a trial judge has decided, 'This seems like a valid warrant,' and that judge is later reversed on appeal? Has that occurred in your experience?"

"I'm sure it has occurred but, offhand, I can't think of a time."

Ms. DiEdoardo asked questions about the seizure of monies from the attorney-client trust account. "All right, can you recall a single case in the past ten years, besides Mr. Monroe's case, where that procedure was followed? In other words, where a warrant was sought to take money out of an attorney-client trust account?"

Sandy said, "That I've been involved in?"

"Yes, ma'am."

"I've never been involved in any other case like this in ten years."

Ms. DiEdoardo said, "Fair enough."

When Sandy's testimony was complete, she was excused, and Noreen rested the state's case. Closing arguments were next. <>

53

////////

CLOSING
ARGUMENTS

*There may be some incorrigible human beings who
cannot be changed except by God's mercy to that one
person.*

—WARREN E. BURGER

Judge Herndon said, "That closes the presentation of
evidence. We're going to take our lunch recess and finish
getting the jury instructions settled for you. When you come
back, we'll move into closing arguments."

When the jury was brought back into the courtroom. Roy
began his closing remarks. Part-way into the argument, Roy
said, "What I would ask you to take into consideration is not
only the way the defendant testified on the stand yesterday,
but as you listened to the phone calls we played and you
look at his demeanor from September 2006 until November

of 2006, the difference in the demeanor of the defendant. As you heard him laugh and talk over the phone, 'This is no big deal.' On November 6, that life comes to an end as he knows it. And he knows who is involved. He knows Detective Nickell is involved. He knows Ms. DiGiacomo is involved. And the defendant will not be released from custody at that time."

Roy spoke about Daimon's criminal pedigree. "There's a number I'd also ask you to remember—thirty-three. Thirty-three is the number of convictions that were introduced—felony convictions for the defendant yesterday. As you look at the defendant's background and as he testified yesterday, you recall from their own witness, Mr. Fulmer. He and the defendant met each other in 1994 while they were both serving prison time. And you heard him at the end of his testimony yesterday tell you, 'I'm not violent.' Then you heard about a case in which his two young girls testified. They won't feel safe until he's not going to be allowed out of jail."

Roy went into the handwritten notes and reminded the jury about Mrs. Kelly's testimony. "There should be no issue in your mind whether the defendant wrote those notes."

Roy spoke about motive. "Motive is what prompts a person to act. And while the state of Nevada isn't required to prove a motive to you, if we do provide evidence of a motive, you can certainly take that into consideration. That's where life after November 6, 2006, begins for the defendant. He's pissed off. And he's angry not only with Detective Nickell, but with Sandra DiGiacomo. He attempts to bail out—the money is seized. He attempts to hire an attorney—the money is seized. He says he can't make any moves because his mail and his phones are watched. One of the things that angered the defendant so much was Sandra DiGiacomo being at his residence. He thought she held a yard sale on his front lawn.

She went to the home and according to him, stole his stuff—gave the property away on the front lawn."

Roy discussed the covert recording in the rec yard. "Johnny Marquez says, 'Do you want to get these people murdered or not?' And the defendant's response was, 'Yeah. But how are we going to do it? That's what I've been trying to figure out. How do you do it, though? I can't make the move. I can't call. I can't do shit. I can't make the call.' But he wants to get the murders done. He'll have you believe yesterday from the stand that he didn't hear Johnny say the murders. The audio recording speaks for itself. And that's exactly what the defendant said in response to Johnny Marquez.

"The defendant made that statement with zero prodding from the Las Vegas Metropolitan Police Department. And with zero prodding from Johnny Marquez. When you read the note saying "Go with killing levit, nicols, hold digiccamo," this was the defendant's own handwriting.

This wasn't something Johnny sent to him saying, 'Do you want these people dead?' This is his handwriting."

Roy closed his argument with, "Ms. DiEdoardo told you that Metro would freely admit the defendant didn't have the money to do this. And of course you heard from Detective Nickell on the stand that there is $75,000 still outstanding. Ms. DiGiacomo testified to the same thing. And then on the recording, Johnny saying, 'Listen, why are you only giving me $10,000 if you have this much more money on the outside?' The defendant replied, 'Yeah, I just need to get a hold of Rob.' That's the way the recording ends. At the close of evidence and at the close of argument, ladies and gentlemen, we're going to ask you to return verdicts of guilty for all three counts. Thank you very much."

Roy sat down and Ms. DiEdoardo began her closing. Ms. DiEdoardo attacked Johnny's credibility. "The reality, of course, is all of their accusations stem from one man, Mr. Marquez. We remember him, don't we?" She brought up a photo on the screen of Austin Powers, played by Mike Meyers. She was trying to be funny while saying Johnny wasn't credible. "We would say that, given some of Mr. Marquez's comments on the stand, the comparison is apt."

Nobody in the courtroom laughed or smiled—except Daimon.

Ms. DiEdoardo continued, "Is Johnny Marquez a gang affiliate? That's what he told the grand jury. Or is he not? That's what he told you. Is he a former private investigator as he told you? Is he a paid FBI snitch, or is he not a paid FBI snitch as he said he was? Can any of you truly trust a man who has lied at least twice under oath?"

Noreen objected, "Objection as to the character relation to lying under oath."

Ms. DiEdoardo said, "It's supported by the evidence."

Judge Herndon said, "What the evidence supports is up to the jury. I don't want any speaking objections or answers. I'll sustain the objection to the use of the word lying." The judge reminded the attorneys if there were objections, he wanted them to approach the bench rather than argue for the jury to hear. He didn't want the attorneys to interrupt the other's Grand Finale.

Ms. DiEdoardo brought up how Detective Kelley eliminated Danny Butcher from being involved with the murder-for-hire plot. "Ladies and gentlemen, listen to Detective Kelley and after watching and meeting Mr. Butcher in person a couple of days later, all I can think of is the classic scene in the movie *Casablanca* where Claude Rains is playing the French Chief of Police. As they're coming into Humphrey Bogart's bar, Claude Rains says, 'I'm shocked. Shocked there's gambling going on in a Good Samaritan Café.' Then his assistant comes up and says, 'Here's your winnings, sir.' Without missing a beat, Claude Rains says, 'Thank you very much,' and we keep going. Was that the kind of shock Mr. Butcher displayed?"

Ms. DiEdoardo's argument was so convoluted that it never hit its mark. I know I stopped listening to it mid-sentence, not understanding the comparison she was trying to make—maybe because I've never seen *Casablanca*.

"We promised you we would show that Mr. Monroe had no means to harm anyone. It's undisputed that Mr. Monroe was and has been indigent since he was incarcerated in 2006. In fact, so broke that the court had to appoint counsel for him in this case and his underlying property cases. He testified in direct examination that he couldn't even afford shampoo and Ramen noodles because there was no money on his books. Yet somehow, he's supposed to—as the state would have you believe—that he intended to solicit the murder of three very high profile individuals, members of our community. And he would pay the people doing this with what?

"Ladies and gentlemen, there are only two conclusions and only two of them are supported by the evidence here. The first conclusion is that Metro, along with the D.A.'s Office, along with Judge Leavitt, along with Ms. DiGiacomo, and Mr. Nickell are all victims. The reason they're all victims is because Detective Kelley placed confidence in a man who is wholly incredible: Johnny Marquez, the international man of mystery. They believed the jailhouse chatter. They believed the comments of Mr. Butcher and Mr. Marquez, and the allegations grew like gossip.

"Remember the contempt that Mr. Butcher showed you and showed me when being asked those questions? Do you remember how he claimed he knew nothing? It was a struggle to get him to admit his own name. And he knows nothing about Mr. Monroe. He never swung a bat or a broom stick at Mr. Monroe. Ladies and gentlemen, I think it's fair to say that Detective Kelley, Detective Nickell or any of the ROP detectives wouldn't qualify as charter members of the Daimon Monroe fan club."

Little did Ms. DiEdoardo know, in some ways I was a fan of Daimon Monroe. I thought he was smart, funny, gifted musically, and had the panache to be successful with many things. I'd learned that Daimon and I had many likes in common; he loved the Denver Broncos, UFC fights, rock and roll, and several other things I enjoy. Our personalities mirrored each other's in a strange way. We were both driven and obsessive, although to different degrees, and confident that nothing could stop us from achieving whatever goal set before us. We both endured difficult upbringings, though I suspect his was much harsher than my own. Mine was tough because my mother died when I was young, which cast a shadow upon my maturation for many years. The cause of Daimon's difficulty is something I may never know. But that is where the resemblance ends. For the most part, I overcame my struggles, while I believe Daimon's carry on and have multiplied. Whatever likeness we share could never motivate me to protect our community any differently.

Daimon and I are polar opposites when it comes to morality. We're on opposite sides of trying to do right and trying to do wrong, and he took it to the extreme, much like he did everything else in his life. I don't hate the man, indeed, I think it's sad that he never tried to live as an upright, honest man. I wish the thirteen-year-old boy had been given more of a chance. I wish he hadn't passed on his poisonous legacy to his children. The horrors to which he exposed his family were unimaginable.

Ms. DiEdoardo went on, "There is a second conclusion and this is it: Detective Kelley operated Mr. Marquez as an informant to entrap Mr. Monroe. And he did this because the ROP detectives were, despite all denials, aggravated and annoyed at Daimon for a variety of reasons. Ironically, the state has given you some rationale for that. Apparently the ROP detectives don't like their names on flyers, but they're not aggravated by those flyers. I suggest to you they were aggravated—they being Ms. DiGiacomo and Detective Nickell—by being named as defendants in Mr. Monroe's federal civil suit.

"What I suspect—submit to you—look at the reaction from Ms. DiGiacomo when I asked her—Do you remember when she was on the stand and I said, 'You really don't like Mr. Monroe, do you?' She immediately said, 'It's nothing personal.' Well, ladies and gentlemen, I think it's fair to say it would be personal. And it was personal. And you can certainly read from her demeanor and her attitude and things she said right before I asked her that question, far more than what her response to it was.

"You may be asking, 'What motive would Detective Nickell have to do this?' We would submit to you the motive was simple. Mr. Monroe testified there were issues both with the car stop and with the warrants that were ultimately executed on his home. Now as much as the state would like to have you believe that Mr. Monroe is one crazy outlier in the wilderness who believes such things, Ms. DiGiacomo admitted on the stand that Mr. Monroe's attorney filed eighteen motions over those issues. In terms of what their motive was for this, they may have been concerned at some point that those warrants would be ruled bogus. If the searches were ultimately ruled bad, there is a danger of it entirely going the way of the dodo, and the state would be forced to retry the case.

"A quote from Henry Kissinger reads, 'Just because you are paranoid, doesn't mean they're not out to get you.' Now to a certain extent, you also heard the state talk about how Mr. Monroe thought everyone was out to get him. Can you blame him? As it turned out, there really were people out to get him. Johnny Marquez was wired for sound. Johnny is the person the state chooses to talk to Daimon to inveigle him into this conversation. Would it have been better and easier perhaps if Mr. Monroe had run away from this conversation and never met Johnny?

Sure. But a conversation does not a solicitation make.

"Ladies and gentlemen, the instructions require you to focus on the evidence before you and you are not to be swayed by the fear of public opinion or by whether or not you like Mr. Monroe. The only thing to be concerned about is this: has the state met their burden beyond a reasonable doubt. The only person who's got no motive to lie in this case is this gentleman," Ms. DiEdoardo said as she pointed at Daimon.

"And you know where he's going to be tomorrow, next week and the next week. And as I asked him there, why are you on trial today?—'Because I'm innocent.' Ladies and gentlemen, we just ask that you find him so. Thank you for your time."

During the past several days, talk rippled through the courthouse about how Ms. DiEdoardo was ineffective. So much that if the jury came back with guilty, the case might be sent back on appeal for ineffective assistance from counsel. But after Ms. DiEdoardo's closing, those arguments may have been silenced. Things people were seeing as ineffective were indeed strategic moves purposefully made to create the conspiracy theory defense and entrapment theory.

I think they wanted his criminal history in. I think they didn't mind much about having knowledge of the sex-abuse case in. They wanted the jury to know why we supposedly hated Daimon so much. Ms. DiEdoardo's closing was very competent. Yes, it was peppered with awkward metaphors, but competent enough to make me think she may have succeeded in manufacturing reasonable doubt. Some of the experienced attorneys in the room thought so as well.

Noreen stood to present the state's rebuttal to the defense closing. Her demeanor was clear. She was incensed. The jury needed to see that someone was seriously upset. They needed to have their impressions laced with emotion by someone who cared. But for Noreen, it wasn't an act. It wasn't a show for the jury. She was offended by Daimon's crimes and wanted to provoke the same response from the jury.

"The very most important thing to point out to you right now is statements, arguments, and opinions of counsel are not evidence in this case. Mr. Monroe had the intent. And he tells it to you, in his own words, in his own writings. 'Set it up with the hits.' Jan Seaman-Kelly testified it's his handwriting. The defendant took the stand and said, 'No, no, no, I didn't write that one. I didn't write that one.' And we're supposed to believe him because he has no motive to lie? He's the one person who has no motive to lie in this case because his other cases are resolved? Really?

"So what does he do when he takes the stand? He follows the old rule: admit what you can't deny, deny what you can't admit. He can't deny he was talking to Johnny. He's on the tapes. He can't deny he wrote a good portion of the notes. I say 'good portion' because remember, he's got to deny what he can't admit. But he can't admit he wrote those notes. They make him guilty. That's him asking for it. Him saying to do it. Not entrapment. He can't deny Jan Seaman-Kelly testified that this is his handwriting, but he can't admit he wrote it. He can't admit it because it makes him guilty. It's him asking for it. Him wanting it done. Him without government inducement, without—'come on, come on, give me an answer'—he just wrote it." Noreen pointed at the note on the screen.

"We need to believe him because he has no motive to lie? This man took the witness stand and said, 'This is Matthew, yes. But Matthew is a tool to power wash to get up inside the vent.' He can't admit it's a burglary tool. But he convicts himself on the jail calls. 'There's no damage to the doors, dude. They can't figure it out. You think they're going to figure out Matthew? What is this? I can make me a whole bunch of new Matthews.' But he can't take the stand and admit to it. That messes everything up."

Noreen did her best to resurrect Johnny's credibility. "Ms. DiEdoardo spent a lot of time and energy discrediting Johnny. A lot of time and energy. That was most of her argument. She said the state relies solely on Johnny. Now, no one in this room is going to stand here and tell you that Johnny Marquez is the Pope, is a hero. No one is going to try and tell you that."

I thought, but Johnny did the right thing. He probably saved me, Sandy, and the judge from being killed. If Daimon had figured out that Johnny wasn't getting the job done, he might've found someone else who would. He might've figured out how to get Bobby or someone to get the money together. Johnny did do the right thing. He snitched on Daimon and, in Johnny's own words, 'stymied Daimon's plans to murder three people.'

Noreen continued, "Johnny Marquez is doing significant time for a real ugly crime. And Johnny himself looked straight at you guys and said, 'I feel like I got railroaded because of this case.' He doesn't think he got a deal. You heard what Joe Kelley said, 'Twenty-three hours a day in the cell.' That's a deal? Think of what this case gets people: twenty-three hours a day all alone. You don't see a soul except for one hour. Angel Garza, same thing: twenty-three hours a day in. Would it be ideal if there was a nun in the Clark County Detention Center we could've used instead?

Yeah. But when the crime occurs in hell, you're not going to have angels as witnesses. This crime occurred in the Clark County Detention Center. We're stuck with it—Angel and Johnny. I've got to tell you, it's not such a bad thing to be stuck with.

"There's a covert recording that the defendant will have you believe he has no clue they were ever talking about murder. The defendant would have you believe he didn't hear Johnny say, 'Do you want these people murdered or not?' Because the defendant's response isn't, 'Huh?' It's, 'Yeah, but I don't know how. How do we get it done?' He had the motive, he had the means. Bobby Holmes had that money. Listen to that recording again, because the very last thing on the recording is about money—the defendant saying, 'I just gotta figure out how to get a hold of Rob.' Who is the only person Rob could be? Holmes, who has $75,000 of never found money.

"What would Daimon Monroe also have you believe? That Detective Nickell went on this cover-up rampage because a search warrant was never filed. You saw the filed search warrant. It's there in evidence. Flip through it. It's there. But what would be the point? Think about what he wants you to believe Detective Nickell has done. Gone to Tammy, told her what to say. Got her to change her name so Mr. Monroe would think she married somebody in Kansas. But, 'No, no, they didn't fool me.' Gone to the kids and got them to say, forced them to say—*threatened* them to say what Detective Nickell wanted. Think about that when you are thinking about credibility."

Noreen drew her summation to a close. "Yes, Daimon Monroe does have means. He does have motive. He thought with Johnny Marquez he had the opportunity—and he put it in writing." Noreen again pointed at the note on the video screen. "Go with killing levit, nicols, hold digiccamo," she said. "Ladies and gentlemen, he's telling you he's guilty."

Judge Herndon had the bailiff take the jury to the deliberation room. They began deliberations and later ended for the day.

If the jury thinks someone isn't believable, they can disregard that person's testimony in whole or in part. I thought, for argument's sake, let's throw out Johnny and Angel's testimony. Let's consider them both to be completely unreliable. How does the case fare then? The answer brings about another question: how do you get past the notes? "Go with killing levit, nicols, hold digiccamo." How could that be rationalized? How do you get past Daimon's own voice on the covert recording where he spoke about wanting us dead? The answer? You don't. <>

54

//////////

VERDICTS

It is what a man thinks of himself that really determines his fate.

—HENRY DAVID THOREAU

The next day, with the jury deliberating, the day seemed to grow longer. The other juries had only taken an hour or two to come back. It was nerve racking, but I wasn't sitting around, waiting at the courthouse. I was busy taking care of the many other cases I had on my desk. At the end of the day, Judge Herndon sent the jury members home.

On the following day, the jury sent a note to the judge with a question. The attorneys were called to the courtroom and Daimon was brought from the jail. We waited as Judge Herndon finished up a hearing in an unrelated murder case coming up for trial soon.

One of the defense attorneys for that hearing had a boy

and a girl around seven or eight years old with him for "take your child to work day." The kids were sitting in the gallery, just a couple of chairs away from Sandy and me. The attorney kept his kids there, so they could see what goes on in a courtroom.

The jury was brought in and back on the record; the jury question was revealed. They wanted a read-back of testimony from Angel Garza. They wanted to know if Angel heard Daimon talking about having the killings done, or if Johnny was doing the talking.

The judge quietly asked the attorney with the kids to leave the courtroom. The testimony read-back likely had language or information in it the kids shouldn't hear. The attorney took the kids and scampered out of the room.

The court reporter read back the pertinent portions of the testimony. Angel clearly testified he heard Daimon talking about having the killings done. It wasn't Daimon responding to a question—it was Daimon's idea.

At the conclusion of the read back, the jury was taken back to the deliberation room and the court went back into recess. Sandy and I were still in the courtroom. "What do you think about this, from your experienced point of view?" I asked her.

"I don't know what to think. Juries are so hard to predict," Sandy said.

"Well, from my point of view, I think it's pretty good. I think it's an indicator that they're getting it and they want to be sure. I think the read-back can't hurt. They must not think Angel's a liar or they wouldn't care what he said at all."

Sandy gave the shut up look again. "Don't talk like that, you might jinx the jury."

"You can blame me if the jury acquits or is hung," I said.

About ninety minutes after the read-back, the jury had a verdict. Everyone was called back to the courtroom again.

This time, Judge Leavitt also came to the courtroom to hear the verdicts read. When the jury was filing in, none of them made eye contact with Daimon. Their solemn march into the courtroom, right past Daimon, seemed like something out of a movie.

Everyone was silent. One juror looked at me a couple of times. I can't explain the look on his face. He didn't overtly make a sign or expression; he was simply looking at me. But it seemed like he was saying, "We got your back." Maybe I was imagining it. Maybe wishful thinking was clouding my mind. I adhered to my thoughts as we waited.

Judge Herndon called for Daimon to rise from his chair and asked the jury foreman if verdicts had been reached. The jury foreman said verdicts were reached and handed the verdict forms to the court clerk who read them aloud: guilty on all three counts of soliciting murder.

I detected a strange tension from the jury box. A couple of the female jurors started crying—silently, but visibly.

Judge Herndon asked Ms. DiEdoardo if she wanted the jury polled. She did. The clerk went one-by-one through the jury members calling them by number. One of the female jurors who was crying nearly sobbed as she confirmed her verdict. The mood in the courtroom was peculiar and tense.

I saw no reaction from Daimon. No smirk, no bravado; just a little man with long hair, standing expressionless.

The judge thanked the jury for their service and asked them to go back to the deliberation room. He wanted to talk with them about their experience and thank them again personally.

A sentencing date was given, and Daimon was taken out of the courtroom to the holding area. Sandy had to leave and go to another courtroom while I went with Roy and Noreen to meet with the jury downstairs. Only one of the jurors was there—one of the female jurors who cried. She had left the deliberation room by herself while the rest of the jurors were still upstairs with the judge. She was now sitting in a side room with Ms. DiEdoardo and Ms. Balint, talking privately.

This scene was uncomfortable. Some defense attorneys might see an emotionally charged juror after a guilty verdict and try to use that person's vulnerability to their benefit. Maybe try and change the juror's mind about their verdict, or create some kind of argument suggesting juror misconduct or something to benefit their client who was just convicted.

The rest of the jury came downstairs, so we made ourselves available to them. One of them asked if this now meant they should worry about Daimon coming after them, too.

I said, "I don't think so. If Daimon were ever to try and lash out or could figure out a way to do it, he would probably target Sandy or me."

One of the jurors said she saw Daimon make an obscene hand gesture toward a police officer in the courtroom. That's precisely what The Joker would do, I thought.

Roy asked the jurors why they were crying when the verdict was read. The other juror who had been crying said, "We saw the two kids in the courtroom when the testimony was read back. We thought the kids were Ms. DiGiacomo's, and it was just emotional."

The gravity of the events had indeed affected some of them. Seeing the kids and thinking they were Sandy's put the emotional tension over the top.

The juror who was talking with Ms. DiEdoardo and Ms. Balint came out of the side room and joined the rest of us. When I had a moment to speak with her, I thanked her for her service and told her I was personally thankful to her for what she'd been through.

She said, "I left before the others because I just had to get out of there. I just want to be done with the whole thing. I'm ready to move on."

I said, "I'm not sure what the defense attorneys spoke to you about, but I think it's not cool if they were trying to take advantage of you being emotional and possibly trying to use that to somehow benefit their client."

"No, that wasn't it at all," she said. "They just wanted to know what made us convict him and if there was anything they could've done better."

Her words and tone assured the interaction had been above board. They were looking for a critique of how they did. I didn't have a problem with that. If someone or something can help them do their jobs better, and in a way that's ethical and righteous, I'm all for it. I absolutely would rather see a guilty man go free than an innocent man go to prison.

Two weeks after the trial, Sandy received a call from a local defense attorney. The attorney had a client he wouldn't identify.

The attorney said, "I have some artwork that my client wants to turn in."

Apparently this client had seen the story about Daimon's convictions for solicitation of murder on TV and decided there was too much heat in the kitchen. Whoever this person was, they seemingly wanted to rid themselves of anything Daimon. I'm fairly certain of the person's identity, but that's for another day.

The attorney brought the stuff to Sandy's office and turned it over. I had the chore of identifying to whom the items belonged and attempt to get them returned. When I picked the items up, it wasn't hard to figure out. They were original oil paintings signed by the artists, several of the pieces were the remainder of the missing Annie Lee collection. The rest belonged to an associate of Annie Lee who had exhibits in Annie's studio at the time of the break-in.

I photographed the artwork and contacted Annie Lee, who had moved to Florida. One of her associates came to my office, and the artwork was released to him. I wondered if the Daimon Monroe saga would ever be over. Every time I thought it had been put to bed, it reared up and showed how wrong I was. <>

55

CHICKEN ON
THE BONE

*Reality is the number one cause of insanity among
those who are in contact with it.*

—UNKNOWN

*P*aperwork about Daimon's civil rights complaint arrived
at my office. I was notified that the department would
provide legal representation for me in the case. I called
Sandy and told her about the notice. She received one from
the D.A. Civil Division as well.

The next day brought word from the Citizen's Review
Board: Daimon had filed yet another complaint. Most of it
rehashed the same old tired things Daimon was claiming;
claims the board had already rejected.

I wrote a response to the Citizen's Review Board and
delivered it to the police association's secretary. In the

response, I wrote, "Mr. Monroe has also filed a federal civil rights lawsuit against me, the LVMPD, and the District Attorney who prosecuted his cases. The LVMPD and the District Attorney's Office are now responsible for having to use taxpayer money to provide legal representation for their members against frivolous claims made to frustrate the system. The mechanisms in place with the Citizen's Review Board and in the federal court system are to protect citizens from wrongdoing by public officials. Mr. Monroe is manipulating those processes and has taken them away from their proper use. I hope these bodies will develop methods to ensure that only complaints with merit are allowed to consume valuable public resources."

A day or so later I had time to reflect. I was disgusted by how criminals and lawyers have turned the criminal justice system on its head. It seems in so many ways our laws have been shredded by decades of circus acts like this one. The courts are supposed to protect crime victims—not empower thieves, murderers, robbers, and rapists to escape responsibility for their criminal actions. Here we have a man who had spent his entire adult life taking from people and destroying the lives of others. Yet our society gives him access to mechanisms that make life tough on people trying to serve their communities.

What's needed is a legislative cap on the number of frivolous motions and lawsuits a convicted felon can file from prison. And while they're at it, legislators should institute monetary sanctions for attorneys who file indiscriminate suit after suit. That's the language they speak—hit them in the wallet, and they'll stop the nonsense. Right now, civil attorneys base their practices on the probability of winning and how profitable it might be. It should be balanced with the prospect of failure and how many dollars they stand to lose. Make them put some skin in the game.

I imagined the faces of all of the people Daimon had victimized over the years. I thought about Tammy and her kids and what he put them through. I wondered what might've happened to Sandy, Judge Leavitt, and me if we'd never found Daimon's money. And Daimon wanted to convince people he had been wronged?

Over the next few weeks, it seemed Ms. Browning had contrived a new strategy. I'm certain Daimon didn't like it, yet went along as he thought it would give the FBI time to complete his imagined corruption investigation.

On July 21, the new strategy was revealed in court. The defense challenged Daimon's mental competency, claiming he couldn't effectively assist in his own defense. In the grand scheme of things, this motion had the potential to delay everything for so long that the remaining matters would be difficult to resolve. When mental incompetence is claimed, all other proceedings grind to a halt until psychological examinations are performed and a determination can be made.

Incompetence as used here does not mean legally insane and therefore not responsible. It simply means not mentally capable of assisting in his defense. It's a different legal standard. I've seen defendants in the past found incompetent and sent off to the state mental facility, not to come back for well over a year. I've seen others go there for just a few months and come back.

Oftentimes, as cases suffer lengthy delays, witnesses become hard to find or uncooperative, have their memories fade, or I've even had some victims die before the broken wheels of justice attempt to deliver satisfaction. Long delays are almost always exclusively beneficial to the defense.

How many months or years would Tammy continue to help? How old would her daughters be before they received the opportunity to testify in front of a jury? How long would their memories stay intact? If enough time went by, would their memories differ enough from their original testimony to make their credibility come into question? Would they simply give up on the abject justice system and want to move forward with their lives?

Ms. Browning must've realized Daimon wouldn't let her keep him off the stand in the sex-abuse trial. He'd had a taste of that attention and reveled in it. He wanted the eyes on him. The prospect of having Daimon deemed incompetent was probably better for her than having him get on the stand and blow any chance of her winning an acquittal. That's what it's all about for some attorneys. It's not so much a pursuit of truth and justice. It's a contest, a sporting event you try to win. Many defense attorneys try to come across as ethical and benevolent. But behind closed doors, many of them scheme and plot to trample the very ethical ideals they've sworn to uphold. I'm sure some prosecutors are the same way.

During this period, I learned that the Citizen Review Board denied Daimon's latest complaint. It didn't mean much except the relief knowing the review board was able to see Daimon for what he was.

I also learned Daimon had withdrawn his federal complaint. No, he didn't have an epiphany, it was legal posturing. The Federal Magistrate told Daimon his lawsuit was premature in light of his state appeals not being ruled upon. If Daimon didn't withdraw the complaint, he'd face certain time constraints that might bar him from ever proceeding. I'm quite certain, however, Daimon will file the federal complaint again once the Nevada Supreme

Court makes all of their rulings. It's part of the whole paper terrorism playbook.

On September 29, Daimon's competency hearing was held. Earlier, a psychiatrist visited and evaluated him he in the jail. The doctor's report essentially said Daimon was delusional and not competent to assist in his defense. For the court to accept this finding, a second mental health professional would have to concur. If the second doctor did not concur, a third doctor would be brought in as a tie-breaker.

The second doctor tried to visit Daimon for an evaluation, but Daimon refused to see him. Yes, it's true; our system has granted inmates the power to decide, at times, if they'll participate in exams, or refuse to go to court when they don't feel well and other patently absurd excuses.

The second doctor wrote a report anyway, which was merely based on his evaluation of the first doctor's findings. The second doctor concurred with the first without ever having seen or spoken to Daimon.

The hands of the court were tied. If the court made a ruling against the defense or ordered another evaluation, it would create a prolonged and messy appeal issue. The judge did what had to be done and ordered Daimon transferred to the state mental facility, Lakes Crossing Center, near Reno for evaluation and treatment.

I wasn't too torn up about it. The staff at Lakes Crossing know it's not in their best interests to have people there who don't belong. Such people consume the limited time and resources needed to treat people there for good reason. I trusted it wouldn't take long for them to figure out Daimon was competent. People can fake their way through a psyche interview. But it's an entirely different matter to go to a mental facility and act like a crazy person for any length of time when you're under constant supervision by trained specialists making evaluations.

Sure, Daimon has serious issues—probably antisocial personality disorder and even maybe clinical paranoia. But I don't think any of it amounted to being incompetent in the legal sense. The sentencing in the murder-for-hire case and the trial in the sex-abuse case were put on hold.

Several weeks later, a secretary gave me copies of letters Daimon had been writing from the mental facility to his inmate friends in his old housing unit. Daimon was bragging about how good the food was compared to the "crap" they get in the jail. He got to eat chicken "on the bone" and would get ice cream if he sang karaoke. He also wrote about being allowed to play a guitar from time to time. His letters made him seem pretty clear of mind, and he even told his old cell mates he'd be back with them pretty soon.

I was glad to learn Daimon had put on some weight and was able to exercise his mind and play the guitar. I was reminded of his mother saying he had suffered anorexia when he was a teenager and wondered what brought that about. Was it abuse in the home? Perhaps some abusive behavior at school before he dropped out? Probably something he'll never reveal to anyone.

One thing is certain: I'm not interested in Daimon living out a tortured life devoid of comforts. But limiting what dangerous inmates have access to serves a necessary purpose in prisons, so there are a lot of things Daimon would never be able to acquire.

One day, I had occasion to speak to Lexie Mason on an

unrelated case. At the end of the conversation, I said, "Hey, tell me you've done all you can with all of that property from the Daimon Monroe case and you don't have to mess with it anymore."

"I'm just about done with it," Lexie said. "I've found a bunch more victims, and they've had their stuff released to them. Oh, and guess what? I found the owner of the Abraham Lincoln letter."

Lexie had discovered the letter was stolen in 2003 from an auction house belonging to an attorney. When the burglary report was taken, the letter was listed as "antique letter" on the police report. That made it nearly impossible for Lexie to cross-reference when she was querying thousands upon thousands of reports looking for anything to do with Abraham Lincoln. But her diligence paid off, and the letter was reunited with its owner.

On January 7, 2010, Daimon was transferred back to the jail from Lakes Crossing. The doctors there found him competent. Ms. Browning immediately filed a motion to contest the findings of the state mental facility. This dragged matters out for several more months, but little did anyone know, another unexpected and unimaginable twist to the story was about to hit. <>

56

///////////

POISONED
MINDS

When we forgive evil, we do not excuse it, we do not tolerate it, we do not smother it. We look the evil full in the face, call it what it is, let its horror shock and stun and enrage us, and only then do we forgive it.
                              —LEWIS B. SMEDES

*O*ctober 13, 2010—a bombshell hit: officials at the jail discovered that Tracy Browning was having sexual contact with an inmate client while she visited him. Corrections personnel found several nude photographs of the attorney in the inmate's cell, along with racy love notes she had apparently written to him.

The inmate Tracy involved herself with was being held on an extremely brutal kidnapping and hours-long rape of a young woman. How in the world Tracy could get herself tangled in that, I'll never understand. What could've made her think a monster should be the object of her desires? Even more puzzling when knowing she had a husband and kids.

During a recorded interview, Tracy confessed to a detective about the sexual relationship and said her boss, the head of the Public Defender's Office, told her to resign before it became a problem for him. The local newspaper broke the story, and Tracy was put on administrative leave. The head public defender refused to comment, but within a few weeks, the buzz at the courthouse was Tracy had resigned and abruptly moved out of state.

The investigating detective submitted the felony charge of voluntary sexual conduct with an inmate to the District Attorney's Office and the case was denied. The screening D.A. felt the case couldn't be proven independent of the confession. The courts have consistently ruled that confessions must be corroborated. I think the photos and love letters provided sufficient corroboration—but I'm not a prosecutor.

Tracy's resignation brought the matter to a close. I don't think she even had a bar complaint filed over it. In fact, I think she went on to practice law in Arkansas without a mark on her record. If it had been a cop or a prosecutor or almost anyone else having sex with an inmate, it would've been a prison sentence, for sure—and rightfully so. Should a member of the defense bar be treated differently? But they routinely are.

Of course, Daimon thought this was another branch of the conspiracy at work. Since Tracy and the FBI would be getting him out of jail soon, the cops had to do something drastic to get her off the case. ROP must've planted evidence and wrongly accused her. Somehow, the cops scared her so badly that she up and quit her nineteen-year career and ran off to hide in some other state.

With Tracy no longer serving as Daimon's attorney, her co-counsel, Jennifer Schwartz took over the reins. This led to another delay, so Ms. Schwartz could get up to speed on the competency issue.

December 28, 2010—the final hearing was held in Daimon's competency matters. There had been many hours of testimony given over a period of several months and stacks of reports from psychiatrists and psychologists were reviewed. Some of the psychiatric reports were later made available on the Nevada Supreme Court website in response to one of Daimon's appeals.

The reports stated Daimon is a classic example of someone with antisocial personality disorder, common with most career criminals. One report stated, "He is extremely narcissistic and obsessive with an enormous sense of self-importance."

Furthermore, the reports cited Daimon's thoughts of a corrupt conspiracy of public officials out to get him wasn't delusional; these were simply very strongly held beliefs in false things. They noted the conspiracy theory was based on actual facts contorted to fit Daimon's false beliefs. In other words, he'd take a small piece of factual information, like a copy of a search warrant not having a stamp on it, and blow it up to mean the warrant was a forgery. Or the fact that Tammy wanted no contact from him, so he created the belief that the police were threatening her.

The report said Daimon was able to consider alternatives to his false beliefs. He was able to consider consequences that might result from the false beliefs, which, in their professional opinions, show he was competent—but wrong.

One of the doctors testified, "I asked him what he would do if the police officers involved were given lie detector tests and the results indicated the officers were telling the truth and there was no conspiracy. He responded, 'I'd have to accept it. Anything's possible.' "

This was convincing evidence that Daimon was competent.

The defense had a couple of doctors who held fast to their belief Daimon was delusional and incompetent. I thought maybe they were hired guns.

The competency judge ruled Daimon was sufficiently able to assist in his own defense. The prolonged ordeal was finished. Unfortunately, at just about any time in the future, the defense could raise the issue of competence again, and it might have to start all over. Ms. Schwartz quickly announced she'd request an emergency stay from the Nevada Supreme Court and ask the justices to examine the competency issue.

After hearing this, Judge Herndon set the sentencing in the murder-for-hire case out three months, to give the Supreme Court a chance to decide if they should intervene. I didn't think they would.

Three months later, Daimon's day for sentencing in the murder-for-hire case arrived. The Nevada Supreme Court did not grant Ms. Schwartz's request for an emergency stay. Daimon refused to be transported from the jail, same as he had done several times over the previous months. Before Judge Herndon took the bench, I heard Ms. DiEdoardo talking with Noreen. She was going to argue a motion for retrial based on juror misconduct.

Ms. DiEdoardo said, "If he denies my motion, I'm going to ask the judge if Daimon can be sentenced in absentia. I don't want people to use force on him to bring him here."

Noreen said, "I'm not sure if it's okay to do that, but I'll defer to the judge's discretion."

The judge came into the courtroom and everyone stood up. The bailiff called the courtroom to order and we took our seats. The clerk informed the judge that Daimon refused to be transported.

"Let's get him here. He needs to be here for this hearing," Judge Herndon said.

The rest of the court calendar continued, and we waited about an hour. Sandy arrived in the courtroom a few minutes before Daimon was brought in. She wanted to see the outcome if the sentencing was to go down.

When Daimon was brought in, he was in jail garb and belly chains. He looked thinner and worn, almost haggard. His face was gaunt. He looked like he'd aged twenty years since the cases began in 2006.

Daimon spotted Sandy and I seated together in the front row on the prosecution side. When he saw us, the smile on his face vanished. He looked confused. I'm sure he couldn't understand why Sandy and I were there. When he found out the judge had ordered him to court, which had not happened before, he must've figured, "This is it! This must be the day I'll be freed and learn DiGiacomo and Nickell have been arrested by the Feds."

Judge Herndon said, "Today is potentially your sentencing date. I had the officers bring you over even though you didn't want to come. If you don't want to stay, I'll have them take you back to the detention center."

Daimon said, "I don't know what's going on. I haven't talked to my attorney. I see no point in being here because this whole thing has been a charade. I'll ask my attorney to come see me after the hearing. I'm going to go ahead and go back."

Daimon pointed at me and Sandy with his shackled hand and said, "I've seen the emails that Nickell and them went through. I know that Nyikos sat with the officers and went through the emails. In the emails, they talk about how they were setting me up and all of this drama. I'm kind of curious . . ."

Judge Herndon cut Daimon off and said, "Hold on.

You're going to get a chance to talk if you want to stay. But first we'll deal with the motion for a new trial."

I leaned over to Sandy and whispered, "What emails is he talking about?"

Sandy shrugged and said, "I have no idea."

Daimon said, "It's not that, Your Honor. I'm tired of standing here like some goof. I'm telling you what happened. It doesn't matter. They knew they could get away with this. They knew all of you guys would play along with it. I'm trying to be respectful. I don't want to be dragged out of the courtroom, but I'm angry."

Judge Herndon said, "You'll get your chance to speak if we get to the sentencing phase. Basically, it's a yes or no question."

"I'm cool," Daimon said. "I want to go back."

Daimon was escorted out of the courtroom and taken back to the jail.

Judge Herndon said he reviewed the brief for a new trial and asked Ms. DiEdoardo if she had anything to add.

Ms. DiEdoardo said after the trial, five jurors told her investigator they were afraid of Daimon during the trial. She said the jurors should've revealed this to the judge, and he should've held a hearing to decide if they could be impartial.

Noreen said, "You can't expect them not to have a reaction when they learn the case they're hearing has a judge, a prosecutor, and a detective as victims."

The judge ruled nothing brought up in the motion for retrial rose to the level of misconduct by the jurors. He denied the motion and moved forward to the issue of sentencing.

Noreen spoke first on behalf of the state. She reminded the judge how the documents supporting habitual treatment were filed back in 2009. Judge Herndon went through the numerous prior felony convictions Daimon had amassed.

Noreen said, "Throughout his entire life, he made a

day-to-day career out of burglaries. And his home and several storage containers were literally 'Aladdin's Cave,' as Detective Nickell described them. Burglaries were his job. Crime is what he did, over and over and over again. And what you can see from his judgments of conviction and as you can see by what we're here for today, his criminal behavior has escalated."

Noreen described how Daimon's criminal behavior escalated into acts of violence. She spoke about him trying to run over a detective in 1996 and talking about possibly killing George Chen. "This man is violent. The pre-sentence investigation report got it right. He needs to be sentenced under the large habitual. He needs to be given life without the possibility of parole for each count, consecutive to each other and consecutive to the cases he's in for now."

Ms. DiEdoardo stood to present her arguments on Daimon's behalf. I wished he had stayed for the hearing. I wanted to see if there would be a glimmer of remorse when he was given the chance to speak. Even something disguised to look like remorse would be a beginning. I hoped to see Daimon capable of moving forward with his life in some productive way, even if it was to be in prison forever. Would he be forever stuck in this cycle of trying to prove an untruth? Would he get shipped off to prison and forever have false hope of being exonerated? That would surely give birth to insanity.

Ms. DiEdoardo said Daimon was never charged with trying to kill Mr. Chen and the state must've felt they didn't have enough evidence to support it. She then said, "Which case are we here for? We're not here for a bunch of burglaries. There needs to be a bigger picture here. Mr. Monroe is already doing life without parole. He's looking at more potential life sentences in the sex case. He's not going anywhere. He'll never see the light of day. What does one more habitual do?

This should be about justice, not vengeance. Giving three more life sentences is vengeance."

Judge Herndon said, "Your client has at least forty-eight prior felony convictions. Those were about the wholesale pillaging of businesses, so I cannot disagree at all with the prior sentencing judges saying, 'Enough is enough. You have demonstrated you have no ability whatsoever to comply with the rules and regulations of an honest society so I'll sentence you to life without parole.' Now, Mr. Monroe is being sentenced for trying to have people killed. Call it vengeance—you can call it anything you want. You attack the fabric and integrity of the justice system by contracting to kill prosecutors, judges, detectives, and defense attorneys who work in the system."

Judge Herndon sentenced Daimon to three additional terms of life without parole. He ordered each term to run consecutively to each other and consecutive to Daimon's other sentences.

Court was adjourned. This hearing had been a long time coming, although I didn't think anyone was surprised with the outcome. Except maybe for Daimon, who seemed to never stop hoping this would be the day of his release.

Of course, I'm proud of the role I had in taking Daimon permanently off the streets. It meant the countless hours and hard work Sandy and I put in was worth it. I still sometimes try to imagine the magnitude of Daimon's lifelong crime-wave and the benefit our community received with it being halted. But the ordeal isn't over yet. It probably won't ever be over. Daimon will likely file motions and lawsuits and complaints until the sun doesn't shine.

On a more personal level, Daimon introduced fear into

my family, a new kind of uncertainty born from the plot to kill me. It changed how my kids think about the world; it changed how my wife thinks about our safety. It challenged me in ways I had never been before and haven't been since. Even now, the first thought with any unexpected knock at our door is expectance of danger. I've considered leaving Las Vegas when I retire and taking further steps to become anonymous, but that's a rabbit hole with no end. Security won't come from those things. It will only come from knowing who lays out my path. Daimon Monroe came home with me in September of 2006 and hasn't left my house yet. But that doesn't make him the architect of my future.

I'm also beleaguered about some things—how our justice system has been turned upside down by farcical motions and paper terrorism. Attorneys have eroded the ideas that uphold justice. In many law schools, one of the first things they teach is, there is no black and white—no perfectly defined difference between right and wrong; there are simply shades of gray. And lawyers become judges and lawmakers—a dangerous cycle that's brought us to having a flimsy imitation of the original fabric of the justice system.

The lack of deterrence with slap-on-the-wrist plea deals, never-ending lists of excuses accepted for criminal behavior, and weak sentences to institutions where the inmates are treated better than our military folks represent a disgusting new reality. It's rational for society to want justice in some form for crimes committed against the innocent. But decades of drip-drip diminution has transformed our system into something much different. Yes, something where victims are overlooked, criminals are coddled and attorneys engage in sporting-event-like contests in the courtrooms. Much of the deterrence in our system has been stripped away by wolves who pretend to care about people. They don't care about people; they care about abstract arguments and paydays.

They care about winning.

Other large issues added to the difficulties here as well. I'm no advocate for releasing criminals back to the streets to repeat their crimes on new victims. It's my life's work to stop it where I can. But in this age of space exploration, microprocessors, and mapping the human genome, the best way we have to cope with criminals is to cage them like animals? Over two million men and women are warehoused in American jails and prisons—at a staggering expense to the public. Including those on probation and in other justice system programs, more than *seven million* people are being controlled or supervised by America's justice system. The taxpayer cost already exceeds $75 billion dollars annually and is steadily rising. Is there another way without putting our communities at risk? Unfortunately, I see no evidence of it.

Maybe it comes down to the disintegration of the American family. Tons of kids being raised in broken homes. Kids sending themselves off to school early in the mornings and packaged into safe-key after-school programs until dark while their divorced parents work long hours or two jobs to pay the bills. Kids being raised by people who have no vested interest in the fabric of who they have become. Or worse, being raised by the modern-day babysitter, the television. If they get a daycare worker or a teacher who really cares, they're the lucky ones.

Perhaps all of this is part of what's brought about the epidemic of damaged people who turn to drug-ridden lifestyles, and those who cannot or will not conform to the idea of living a crime-free life. Maybe if we, as a people, focus on raising our young properly, not simply providing sustenance to them, it will have an effect on how society as a whole evolves. Maybe if our children become less of a burden to us and more of a treasure, we will nurture them into changing the future immeasurably.

Perhaps we can undo the decades of justice favoring the criminal over the victim by raising new generations of people who have a genuine respect for themselves, each other, and the law. Perhaps our society needs to experience a revival in the values our country was founded upon and a renewed interest in God, our Creator.

As the years passed, Daimon's, Bryan's, and Bobby's appeals were reviewed by the Nevada Supreme Court. All were denied except for one: Daimon was granted a new trial in the car-stop case because of an overblown legal technicality. In late 2013, the District Attorney's Office offered Daimon a plea in the car-stop case: plead guilty to one count of burglary and the state would stipulate to a sentence of three to eight years. The sentence was meaningless since Daimon was serving life without parole on his other cases, but the deal would save the state time and money required for an inconsequential trial.

Surprisingly, Daimon accepted the offer. When he entered his plea, the judge canvassed him to ensure the plea was voluntary and that he understood it. During Daimon's allocution, he told the judge, "I stole some Asian shit."

Initially, it didn't make sense why Daimon would plead to anything. This was his greatest form of entertainment now. Why would he end his pursuit of exoneration? I hoped he had come to accept his fate and perhaps find a way to become a productive person from within the prison system. Maybe he could counsel other criminals on the perils of continuing their nefarious pursuits. Or he might find a spiritual calling and help other inmates seek the same. But I learned he thought it was a delay tactic, so the Feds could finish up their investigation and bring the ROP team and Sandy DiGiacomo down. The same old hopeless song.

Daimon's oldest daughter called out of the blue one day and asked if I could help her contact her dad. Curios, I asked, "Why would you want to do that?"

"Because I want him to see that he couldn't destroy me," she said. "I've moved on, but I want some closure. I've forgiven him because I don't want to carry this around with me all of my life. He's pretty messed up for what he's done, but in a weird way, I still love him. He's my dad."

The District Attorney's Office tried to facilitate the contact but Daimon thought it was some kind of trick and refused.

Daimon was transferred to Nevada's maximum security prison, Ely State Prison, in 2014. The trial in the sex-abuse case had been pushed back into 2015 and, at the time of this writing, still hadn't been concluded.

His oldest daughter called in July of 2014 and renewed her request to contact him. "I'm turning eighteen tomorrow, and I know I can pretty much do what I want now," she said. "You're the only one I trust and like there in Nevada, so I'm hoping you can help me talk to him."

I said, "Like always, I'm not going to put up any road blocks for you. I think it could be healthy for you to have contact with him and, besides that, nobody can stop you. Maybe if he will communicate with you, it might even be healthy for him."

I'm not interested in Daimon suffering all of his life, not any more than he brings upon himself. I hope at some point, he'll see that everyone's not out to get him.

"You're a strong young woman," I said, "and I'm proud

of how you've conquered this thing. You're a warrior."

I provided information about how she could get in contact with Daimon through an online service the prison system uses. "You can send email and they'll print it out at the prison and give it to him. You can even attach pictures, if you want," I said. Daimon doesn't have any pictures of anyone.

"I don't think I'll send him pictures," she said. "Not until I see how it goes and how he responds to me contacting him."

"I think that's a pretty solid approach. If he chooses to respond, he can use old-fashioned mail or give a call if you want to give him your phone number."

When our conversation was over, I called Lisa Luzaich to let her know what was going on. She concurred that we should support whatever Daimon's daughter wanted to do and just let it take its own course. My hope is, if they communicate, his daughter will be able to continue growing through her experience and keep on the healing path. I also hope it gives rise to a breakthrough that ends Daimon's endless, hopeless pursuit of conspiracy theories and gives him a jump-off to escape the merry-go-round from hell. Even though he'll never get out of prison, I'd like him to find a way to be free inside. I'd like that for everyone who's incarcerated and who can become remorseful and repentant. Forgiveness is a gift you give not only to the forgiven, but to yourself as well. Daimon's daughter gets it. I wish more people would reach that understanding. She has freed herself from the bondage that only forgiveness can give. At the time of this writing, Daimon's daughter has not yet reached out to him. Maybe she never will. Maybe she just needed to spread her wings and show the world she was now in control of her destiny.

In August of 2014, I received notification Robert Holmes had filed a civil rights complaint in federal court, naming the police department, me, and several other people involved in the investigation as defendants. The heart of the complaint claimed I had stolen $70,000 and other detectives stole property from Bobby under color of authority. The handwritten complaint rambled for forty-eight pages and spelled out his request for $290,200 in compensatory damages and unspecified punitive damages. So much for thoughts of Bobby having come to Jesus and fully accepting responsibility for his actions.

I won't say more since it still has to be litigated, but the attorneys appointed to represent us against the false claims are confident the case will be dismissed. I've said my peace about our court system allowing this sort of nonsense to continue, and I have faith that the light of truth can light up the darkest of untruth. The scary part is, sometimes, the courts get it wrong.

I've stayed in contact off and on with Tammy over the years, mostly to keep her apprised of the delays in the court cases. But sometimes, it's just an excuse, so I can check in on her and the kids to see how they are doing. This case that consumed me for a couple of years became so much more than just an investigation. For me, it became a journey where I uncovered evidence of how God can turn bondage into freedom, transform destruction into redemption, and give repentant people something magnificent to live for. There were a lot of times where we just spoke about life, and Tammy spoke about her girls from time to time and, from what I could tell on the outside, they're doing just fine. They're on the road to becoming successful, wonderful, young women.

Tammy has spoken about the different jobs she has had and the different states she has lived in. She hasn't returned to teaching, yet, and life has been tough at times, especially where money is concerned. But I think she'll always say she's thankful to live the rest of her life chasing what's right rather than hiding what's wrong. It's something money can't buy.

At times, Tammy and I have talked about spiritual faith, and I have told her of my love for Jesus Christ. I've offered advice when she sought it and gave an ear when needed. I remain proud of her and especially admire her for how she climbed out of the pit of destruction and forged a new life for herself and her kids.

==<>==

ACKNOWLEDGMENTS

First and foremost, I would like to thank my Lord and Savior, Jesus Christ for his sacrifice. I have seen how God's plan for humanity trickles all the way down to my own life. Without God's grace in my life, this book would never have been written. I praise him for loving me!

My deepest thanks are to my beautiful and loving wife. Punkin, this has been a long journey and you've been my biggest cheerleader. You tolerated all the times I had to withdraw to my writing while you took care of everything else. Your support and understanding is a treasure to me. Your love has always been steady and true. You are the love of my life.

My children deserve special recognition for the times I didn't pull away from my writing to be the Dad I should be. Kenzie, Curly, Shabbadoo and Ryno, your sacrifices have not gone unnoticed. I adore all of you and am proud to be your Dad. I'm thankful each one of you are smart, loving and destined for great things!

Special thanks to my co-author, Warren Jamison. To me, you were a writing coach, an editor, a co-author, a writing industry teacher, a mentor and a friend. I believe our meeting was no coincidence and I am thankful you stuck with me. You've helped bring the best out of me and I now chuckle at the writer I was when we first met. I'm thankful you were able to see Repeat Offender have a release date, I only wish you had made it to that day. My thanks are passed on through your lovely wife, who I know did such a great job in supporting you.

Thank you to literary agent Chip MacGregor. You prompted me to push my writing to a new level. You motivated me to be brutally honest with myself and it brought out a new writer in me.

Thanks to Scott Morales. I don't believe our meeting was just by chance. You introduced me to Chip and encouraged me to press on. The rest is history and you helped make it happen!

Huge thanks to Andy Meisenheimer and Holly Lorincz, both great writers and professional editors. The both of you individually taught me more about writing than I could have learned on my own. I hope to be as great as you one day.

Enormous thanks go unnamed family, friends, writers and co-workers who have supported me, lent an ear, provided advice, given me hope, pushed me forward and waited patiently for this work to be completed.

To the thousands of great folks who subscribed to my newsletter or are connected with me at the social media sites such as Facebook, Twitter and others—thank you! You've been there for me when at times I felt I might not finish. Whether you are writing industry professionals or writing fans, you often gave me purpose in continuing. Thank you for cheering me on and for helping spread the word about my work.

My final thanks go to Steve Jackson and Michael Cordova of WildBlue Press. You've given me the ability to make my dream come true by telling this story to people. I'm humbled and thankful that I will continue to grow under your guidance.

For More *Repeat Offender* Photos
http://wildbluepress.com/ropg

Use this link to sign up for advance notice
of Bradley Nickell's Next Book:
http://wildbluepress.com/AdvanceNotice

Word-of-mouth is critical to an author's long-term success.
If you appreciated this book please leave a review on the
Amazon sales page:
http://wildbluepress.com/roa

NOW FOR THE FIRST TIME
AS AN EBOOK AND AUDIO BOOK!

NO STONE UNTURNED: The True Story Of The World's Premiere Forensics Investigators

"A fascinating journey into the trenches of crime [investigation]"
--Lowell Cauffiel, New York Times bestselling author of House of Secrets

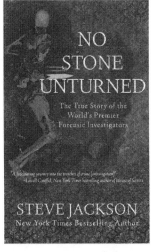

Pre-Order Your Updated Copy of NO STONE UNTURNED at **wildbluepress.com/ NSU-BM**

NO STONE UNTURNED recreates the genesis of NecroSearch International as a small eclectic group of scientists and law enforcement officer who volunteer their services to help locate the clandestine graves of murder victims and recover the remains and evidence to assist with the apprehension and conviction of the killers. Known early on as "The Pig People" because of their experiments in locating graves using the carcasses of pigs (because of their similarities to human bodies), NecroSearch has evolved and expanded into one of the most respected forensic investigation teams in the world. In NO STONE UNTURNED, New York Times bestselling author Steve Jackson, the author of **BOGEYMAN** and MONSTER, vividly tells the story of this incredible group and recounts some of their most memorable early cases that if taken separately would each make great true crime books.

See the Next Page for More about No Stone Unturned

"The book covers the group's quirky beginnings and digs into its most important cases suspensefully; Jackson's sharp eye misses nothing in the painstakingly rendered details. A must-have for true crime fans, it should also be of great interest to anyone fascinated with the practical applications of science."

—Publisher's Weekly (Starred Review)

"A fascinating account of a group of extraordinary people who volunteer their time and expertise to locate hidden murder victims for the police and prosecutors. ... Recommended for public and academic libraries."

—Library Journal

"No Stone Unturned" delves into cases that would make good novels, but they're real. Furthermore, he describes a group of uncommon people performing uncommon tasks, and he does it with respect, accuracy and genuine style."

—Ron Franscell, bestselling author
of The Darkest Night.

Pre-Order Your Updated Copy
of NO STONE UNTURNED at
wildbluepress.com/NSU-BM

WILDBLUE
P R E S S

Check out more True CRIME and Crime Fiction from WildBlue Press

www.WildBluePress.com

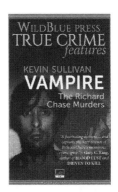

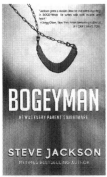

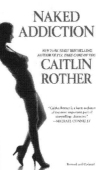

SUBSCRIBE TO OUR NEWSLETTER FOR ADVANCE NOTICE OF NEW RELEASES.

http://wildbluepress.com/newsletter-sign-up/

By subscribing to our newsletter you'll get *advance notice* of all new releases as well as notifications of all special offers. And you'll be registered for our monthly chance to win a **FREE collection of our eBooks and/or audio books** to some lucky fan who has posted an honest review of our one of our books/eBooks/audio books on Amazon, Itunes and GoodReads.

Please feel free to check out more
TRUE CRIME books by our friends at
www.RJPARKERPUBLISHING.com

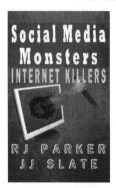

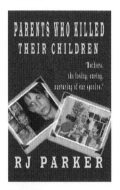